PAGODA TOEFL Actual Test

2026 Edition

파고다교육그룹 언어교육연구소 I 저

PAGODA Books

2026 Edition
PAGODA
TOEFL
Actual Test

초 판	1쇄 인쇄	2025년 11월 25일
초 판	1쇄 발행	2025년 12월 1일

지 은 이 | 파고다교육그룹 언어교육연구소
펴 낸 이 | 박서진
펴 낸 곳 | PAGODA Books 파고다북스
출판등록 | 2005년 5월 27일 제 300-2005-90호
주 소 | 06614 서울특별시 서초구 강남대로 419, 19층(서초동, 파고다타워)
전 화 | (02) 6940-4070
팩 스 | (02) 536-0660
홈페이지 | www.pagodabook.com

저작권자 | ⓒ 2025 파고다아카데미

이 책의 저작권은 저자와 출판사에 있습니다. 서면에 의한 저작권자와 출판사의 허락 없이
내용의 일부 혹은 전부를 인용 및 복제하거나 발췌하는 것을 금합니다.

Copyright ⓒ 2025 by PAGODA Academy

All rights reserved. No part of this publication may be reproduced, stored
in a retrieval system, or transmitted, in any form, or by any means, electronic,
mechanical, photocopying, recording or otherwise, without the prior written
permission of the copyright holder and the publisher.

ISBN 978-89-6281-020-2 (13740)

파고다북스	www.pagodabook.com
파고다 어학원	www.pagoda21.com
파고다 인강	www.pagodastar.com
테스트 클리닉	www.testclinic.com

Ⅰ 낙장 및 파본은 구매처에서 교환해 드립니다.

NEW TOEFL iBT®의 시작!

2026년 1월 21일부터 TOEFL iBT® 시험이 완전히 바뀐다.
- 문화적으로 편향되지 않은 보편적인 주제와 실생활 중심의 현대적인 소재를 다룬다.
- 매거진, 이메일, 온라인 콘텐츠, 가상 인터뷰 등 실제 생활과 밀접한 유형을 포함한다.
- 준비부터 접수, 응시까지의 절차가 빠르고 간소화되며, 최종 점수는 72시간 이내에 제공된다.
- 새로운 1~6 점수 척도를 도입해 국제 기준인 CEFR 레벨과 직관적으로 연계된다.
- 총 시험 시간이 2시간 미만 소요되며, 예상 시간에는 볼륨 조정이나 디렉션 시간이 포함되지 않는다.
- Reading과 Listening 영역에는 단계별 적응형 구조가 적용되어, 응시자의 실력에 따라 난이도가 조정된다. 모든 응시자는 Reading과 Listening의 Module 1에서 사전 테스트 항목(Dummy Questions)을 받게 된다.

영역	2026년 1월 21일 이전	2026년 1월 21일 이후
Reading (multistage)	총 20문항 ｜ 시험 시간 36분 지문 2개, 각 10문항	총 35~48문항 ｜ 시험 시간 약 27분 Module 1 1) Complete the Words 지문 1개, 10문항 2) Read in Daily Life 지문 2개, 각 2~3문항 3) Read an Academic Passage 지문 1개, 5문항 Module 2는 Module 1 시험 결과에 따라 달라짐
Listening (multistage)	총 28문항 ｜ 시험 시간 36분 대화 2개, 각 5문항 강의 3개, 각 6문항	총 35~45문항 ｜ 시험 시간 약 27분 Module 1 1) Listen and Choose a Response, 8문항 2) Listen to a Conversation 대화 2개, 각 2문항 3) Listen to an Announcement 1개, 2문항 4) Listen to an Academic Talk 1개, 4문항 Module 2는 Module 1 시험 결과에 따라 달라짐
Writing	총 2문항 ｜ 시험 시간 30분 통합형 과제 1문항 수업 토론형 과제 1문항	총 12문항 ｜ 시험 시간 약 23분 1) Build a Sentence, 10문항 2) Write an Email, 1문항 3) Write for an Academic Discussion, 1문항
Speaking	총 4문항 ｜ 시험 시간 17분 독립형 과제 1문항 통합형 과제 3문항	총 11문항 ｜ 시험 시간 약 8분 1) Listen and Repeat, 7문항 2) Take an Interview, 4문항

목차

이 책의 구성과 특징   5

iBT TOEFL® 개요   6

Actual Tests

Actual Test 1   16

Actual Test 2   56

Actual Test 3   96

해설서

이 책의 구성과 특징

▶▶ New TOEFL 변경 사항 및 최신 출제 유형 완벽 반영!
2026년 1월부터 변경되는 새로운 토플 시험을 반영, iBT TOEFL®의 출제 경향을 완벽하게 반영한 문제와 주제를 골고루 다루고 있습니다.

▶▶ 3회분의 Actual Test로 실전 완벽 대비!
실제 시험과 동일하게 구성된 3회분의 Actual Test를 수록해 실전에 철저하게 대비할 수 있도록 구성했습니다.

▶▶ 온라인 모의고사 체험 인증번호 제공!
PC에서 실제 시험과 유사한 형태로 모의 테스트를 볼 수 있는 시험 구현 시스템을 제공합니다. 본 교재에 수록되어 있는 Actual Test 3회분과 동일한 내용을 실제 iBT TOEFL® 시험을 보듯 온라인상에서 풀어 보실 수 있습니다.

▶ 온라인 모의고사 체험 인증번호는 앞표지 안쪽에서 확인하세요.

▶▶ 그룹 스터디와 독학에 유용한 단어 시험지 생성기 제공!
자동 단어 시험지 생성기를 통해 교재를 학습하면서 외운 단어 실력을 테스트해 볼 수 있습니다.

▶ 사용 방법: 파고다북스 홈페이지(www.pagodabook.com)에 로그인한 후 상단 메뉴의 [모의테스트] 클릭 > 모의테스트 메뉴에서 [단어 시험] 클릭 > TOEFL - PAGODA TOEFL Actual Test를 고른 후 원하는 문제 수를 입력하고 문제 유형 선택 > '단어 시험지 생성'을 누르고 별도의 브라우저 창으로 뜬 단어 시험지를 PDF로 내려 받거나 인쇄

▶▶ 무료 MP3 다운로드 제공
파고다북스 홈페이지(www.pagodabook.com)에서 교재 MP3 다운로드 가능합니다.

▶ 이용 방법: 파고다북스 홈페이지(www. pagodabook.com)에서 해당 도서 검색 > 도서 상세 페이지의 '도서 자료실' 코너에 등록된 MP3 자료 다운로드(로그인 필요)

iBT TOEFL® 개요 by ETS

Reading과 Listening 영역에 '단계별 적응형 구조' 도입

Reading과 Listening은 두 개의 단계를 거쳐 시험이 진행되는데, 기본으로 세팅된 첫 번째 단계 Module 1의 문제를 풀면 응시자의 응답에 따라 가장 적합한 난이도로 시험이 조정되어 두 번째 단계 Module 2의 문제가 제공되는 단계별 적응형 구조(multi-stage adaptive testing) 방식이 적용된다. 해당 구조는 Reading과 Listening에 한정하여 도입된다.

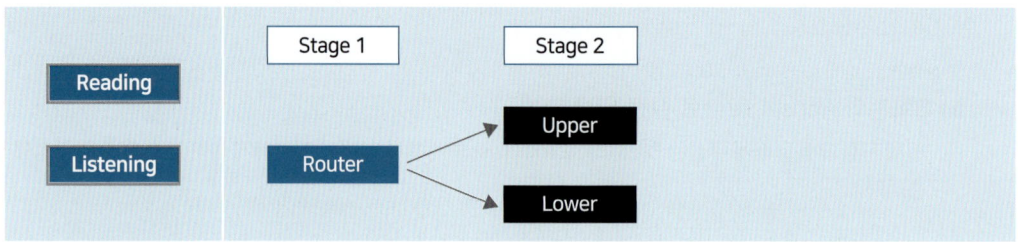

더 이해하기 쉽고, 신뢰감 있게 바뀌는 점수 체계

토플은 앞으로 1-6점(0.5점 단위)으로 구성된 새로운 점수 체계를 도입한다. 이는 국제 기준인 CEFR(Common European Framework of Reference)과 직관적으로 연계되어, 전 세계 학습자와 교육기관이 더 일관성 있게 점수를 활용할 수 있게 되었다. 적응을 돕기 위해 향후 2년간 기존의 0-120점 점수도 성적표에 병기된다.

CEFR	새로운 토플 점수	기존 토플 점수
C2	6	114+
C1	5.5	107+
C1	5	95+
B2	4.5	86+
B2	4	72+
B1	3.5	58+
B1	3	44+
A2	2.5	34+
A2	2	24+
A1	1.5	12+
A1	1	0

1. Reading 섹션의 과제 유형

Reading 섹션의 문항은 수험자가 다양한 영어권 맥락의 학술·비학술 텍스트를 이해하는 능력을 평가하기 위한 것으로, Reading 스킬은 다음 세 개의 과제 유형으로 측정된다.

1) Complete the Words (단어 완성하기)

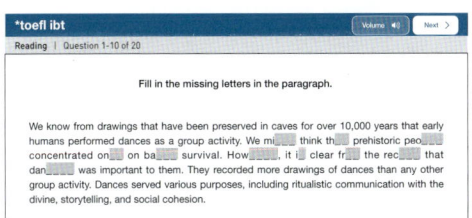

Complete the Words 과제에서는 약 70~100단어 길이의 학술 지문이 제시된다. 지문의 첫 번째 문장은 온전히 제시되며, 그다음부터는 두 단어마다 한 번(예: 2번째, 4번째, 6번째 … 단어) 해당 단어의 뒤 절반이 삭제되어 있다. 수험자는 빠진 글자를 채워 넣어야 하며, 각 지문에는 글자가 빠진 단어가 10개 포함된다.

2) Read in Daily Life (일상 생활 속 글 읽기)

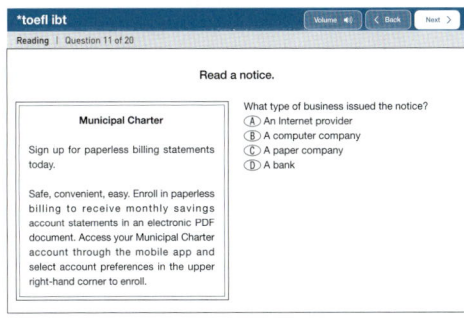

Read in Daily Life 과제는 전 세계의 일상 생활에서 흔히 접하는 비학술 지문을 다룬다. 텍스트 예시는 다음과 같다.

• 포스터, 표지판, 공지	• 문자메시지 대화
• 메뉴판	• 광고
• 소셜미디어 게시물, 웹페이지	• 뉴스 기사
• 일정표/시간표	• 양식
• 이메일	• 송장, 영수증

지문의 길이는 약 15~150 단어이며, 객관식 2~3문항이 제시된다. 질문은 응시자에게 다음을 요구한다.

- 일반적 비선형 텍스트 형식(예: 표, 목록, 표지판)에서 정보를 이해하기
- 글이 전달하려는 주된 목적을 파악하기
- 비격식적 표현(널리 쓰이는 관용구 포함)을 이해하기
- 글에 근거하여 추론하기
- 이메일, 문자메시지, 웹페이지 등의 전보체나 축약체 이해하기
- 필요한 정보를 훑어보고(skimming) 찾아내기(scanning)

3) Read an Academic Passage (학술 지문 읽기)

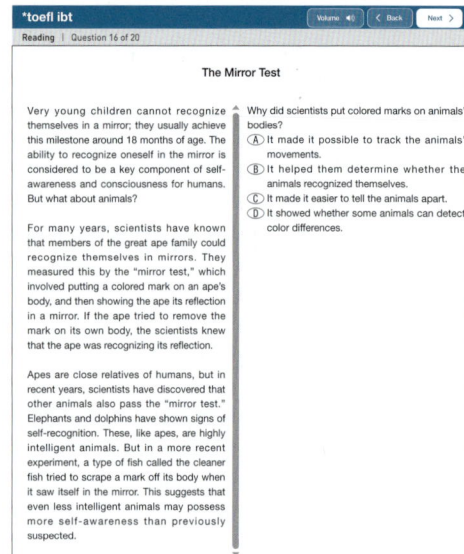

Read an Academic Passage 과제는 중등·고등교육에서 흔히 접하는 설명문 형태의 짧은 글을 다룬다. 지문 주제는 역사, 미술·음악, 경영·경제, 생명과학, 물리과학, 사회과학 등 다양한 분야에서 가져온다. 글의 길이는 약 200단어이며, 5개의 문항이 제시된다. 문항은 사실 정보, 문맥 속 어휘, 추론, 생각들 간의 관계, 그리고 글 전체 또는 일부의 목적을 물을 수 있다. 문항은 수험자에게 다음을 요구한다.

- '짧고 순차적으로 전개되는 글(선형 텍스트)'의 중심 생각과 기본 맥락을 파악하기
- 짧은 글의 핵심 세부사항을 이해하기
- 명시되지 않은 정보로부터 의미를 추론하기
- 폭넓은 학술 어휘를 이해하기
- 다양한 비유적·관용적 표현을 이해하기

2. Listening 섹션의 과제 유형

Listening 섹션의 문항은 학업 및 캠퍼스 생활 맥락에서 이루어지는 대화와 강연을 이해하는 수험자의 능력을 평가한다. 과제의 화자들은 북미, 영국, 호주, 뉴질랜드 등 세계 4개 지역의 억양을 사용한다. Listening 스킬은 다음 네 개의 과제 유형으로 측정된다.

1) Listen and Choose a Response (듣고 응답 선택하기)

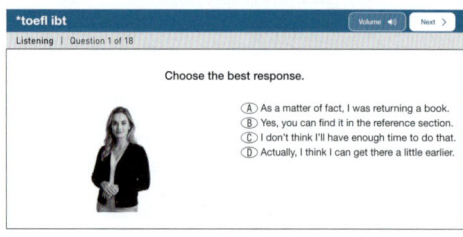

Listen and Choose a Response 과제는 짧은 구어 질문 또는 진술을 이해하고, 캠퍼스 생활과 관련된 짧은 대화에서 적절한 응답을 판별하는 능력을 측정하도록 고안되었다. 수험자는 짧은 상호작용의 첫 부분을 이루는 질문 또는 진술을 듣는다. 이 질문/진술은 화면에 글로 표시되지 않는다. 이어서 수험자는 그 질문 또는 진술에 대한 네 가지 응답 선택지를 읽고, 화자의 말에 가장 적절한 응답을 선택해야 한다. 문항은 수험자에게 다음을 요구한다.

- 흔히 쓰이는 어휘와 정형화된 표현을 이해하기
- 의문문 패턴을 포함한 기본 문법 구조를 이해하기
- 영어의 개별 발음 소리를 구별하고, 말할 때의 억양과 강세가 문장의 뜻을 어떻게 바꾸는지 이해하기
- 짧은 대화의 상호작용에서 함축 의미, 화자의 역할, 또는 맥락을 추론하기

2) **Listen to a Conversation (대화문 듣기)**

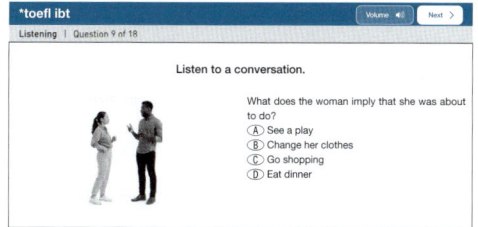

Listen to a Conversation 과제는 현대의 학업 상황에서 이루어지는 대화 내용을 이해하는 능력을 측정하도록 설계되었다. 수험자는 두 화자 사이의 짧은 대화를 듣고 그 대화에 대해 2개의 문항에 답한다. 대화 주제는 식사, 사회 활동, 교육, 오락, 각종 서비스, 건강, 취미, 가정, 쇼핑, 의사소통, 여행 등 사회 일반에서 흔한 주제가 될 수 있다. 문항은 수험자가 다음을 수행할 것을 요구한다.

- 대화의 핵심 생각과 기본 맥락 파악하기
- 대화의 중요한 세부정보 이해하기
- 관용적·구어적 표현을 포함한 폭넓은 어휘 이해하기
- 명시되지 않은 정보로부터 의미 추론하기
- 화자의 발화 목적 알아차리기
- 화자들이 앞으로 취할 간단한 행동을 예측하기

3) **Listen to an Announcement (안내문 듣기)**

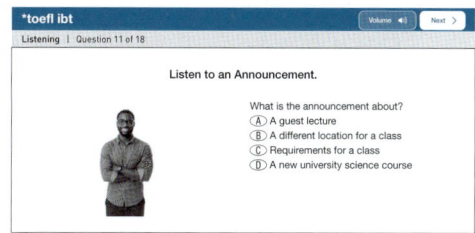

Listen to an Announcement 과제는 교실이나 학교 관련 행사처럼 학업 맥락에서, 대면 안내나 방송으로 전달되는 공지를 들을 때의 상황을 재현하도록 설계되었다. 수험자는 학업 관련 짧은 안내(약 40-85단어)를 듣고 그에 관한 문항에 답한다. 공지 내용에는 일정, 이동·방향 안내, 규칙·규정, 학생 성취 등에 대한 정보가 포함될 수 있다. 문항은 수험자가 다음을 수행하기를 요구한다.

- 짧은 메시지의 주요 내용과 기본 맥락 파악하기
- 짧은 메시지의 중요한 세부사항 이해하기
- 관용적·구어적 표현을 포함한 폭넓은 어휘 이해하기
- 명시되지 않은 정보로부터 의미 추론하기
- 화자의 말에 근거해 앞으로의 행동을 예측하기
- 화자의 메시지의 의도/목적을 식별하기

4) **Listen to an Academic Talk (학술 강의 듣기)**

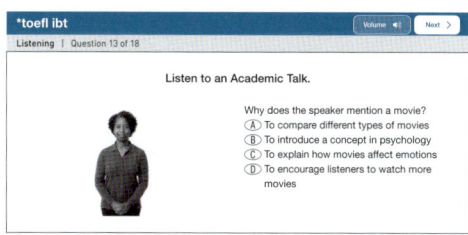

Listen to an Academic Talk 과제는 교수자들이 진행하는 학술 강연을 모의로 재현하도록 설계되었다. 수험자는 약 100-250단어 분량의 학업 관련 짧은 강연을 듣고 이에 관한 4개 문항에 답한다. 주제는 역사, 예술과 음악, 생명과학, 물리과학, 경영·경제, 사회과학 등 여러 분야에서 선정된다. 문항은 수험자에게 다음을 요구한다.

- 짧은 학술 강연의 주요 내용과 뒷받침하는 생각을 이해하기
- 다양한 문법 구조를 이해하기
- 발화된 내용을 근거로 추론하기
- 평소 자주 쓰이지 않거나, 일상 대화에 등장하는 표현과 관용구를 이해하기

3. Writing 섹션의 과제 유형

Writing 스킬은 다음 세 개의 과제 유형으로 측정된다.

1) Build a Sentence (문장 만들기)

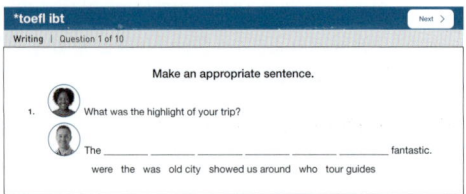

Build a Sentence 과제에서 응시자는 먼저 완전한 문장을 보고, 그 뒤에 단어나 구가 잘못된 순서로 제시된 또 다른 문장을 보게 된다. 이 두 문장은 화자들 간의 대화를 형성한 것으로, 응시자는 단어나 구를 올바르게 배열하여 문맥상 적절한, 문법적으로 맞는 문장을 만들어야 한다. 이 과제는 응시자가 문장 구조를 얼마나 잘 구사하는지를 측정한다.

2) Write an Email (이메일 쓰기)

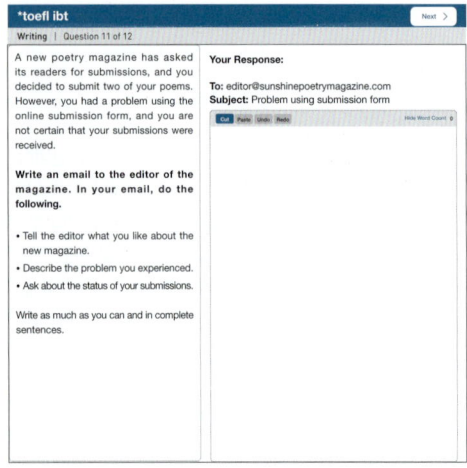

Write an Email 과제에서는 학문적 또는 사회적 상황과 관련된 시나리오를 제시한다. 응시자는 특정한 의사소통 목적을 위해 글을 작성해야 한다. 예를 들어, 추천을 하거나, 초대를 하거나, 문제에 대한 해결책을 제안하는 것 등이 해당된다. 응시자는 이 과제를 완료하는 데 7분의 시간이 주어진다. 이 쓰기 과제는 응시자가 여러 문장으로 구성된 글을 작성할 수 있는 능력을 평가한다. 이 글은 다음 조건을 충족해야 한다.

- 주어진 의사소통 목적을 달성할 것
- 충분히 구체적이고, 명확하며, 응집력 있게 작성할 것
- 다양한 문법 구조와 어휘를 정확하고 적절하게 사용할 것
- 영어의 규칙(철자, 구두점, 대문자 사용)을 따를 것

* Write an Email 채점 기준

점수	설명
5	응답이 효과적이며 명확하게 표현되어 있고, 언어 사용 능력이 일관되게 뛰어나다. • 의사소통 목적을 효과적으로 뒷받침하는 충분한 전개 • 문장 구조의 다양한 활용과 정확하며 자연스러운(관용적인) 어휘 선택 • 적절한 사회적 관습의 일관된 사용(예: 공손 표현, 화체/격식, 정보 조직 방식, 요청·거절·비판 등 행위의 구성) • 시간 제한 하에서 능숙한 필자가 범할 법한 수준을 제외하면 어휘·문법 오류가 거의 없음(예: 흔한 오타나 there/their 같은 일반적 철자 혼동)
4	응답이 대부분 효과적이고 이해하기 쉽다. 과제를 수행하기에 언어 능력이 충분하다. • 의사소통 목적을 뒷받침하기에 충분한 전개 • 문장 구조의 다양성과 적절한 어휘 선택 • 대체로 적절한 사회적 관습 사용 • 어휘 또는 문법 오류가 소수에 그침
3	응답이 전반적으로 과제를 수행하지만, 언어 능력의 한계로 인해 메시지의 일부가 충분히 명확하거나 효과적이지 않을 수 있다. • 의사소통 목적을 부분적으로만 뒷받침하는 전개 • 중간 수준의 문장 구조와 어휘 범위 • 구조, 단어 형태, 관용적 표현 사용 또는 사회적 관습에서 눈에 띄는 오류 일부
2	과제를 처리하려는 시도가 보이지만 대체로 효과적이지 않다. 메시지가 제한적이거나 해석하기 어려울 수 있다. • 제한적이거나 관련성이 낮은 전개 • 문장 수준의 연결은 있으나 문장 구조·어휘 범위가 제한적임 • 문장 구조 또는 언어 사용에서 오류가 누적됨
1	과제를 처리하려는 시도가 비효과적이다. 메시지가 이해하기 어려울 정도로 제한될 수 있다. 전개가 거의 없거나 전혀 없다. • 어휘 범위가 매우 제한된 전보체(짧거나 단절된 구·문장) • 언어 사용에서 심각하고 잦은 오류 • 독자적 표현이 거의 없고, 이해 가능한 언어가 있다면 제시문에서 그대로 차용한 수준
0	응답이 비어 있거나, 주제를 거부하거나, 영어가 아니거나, 과제문을 그대로 복사했거나, 과제와 전혀 관련이 없거나, 무작위 키 입력으로만 구성됨

3) Write for an Academic Discussion (학문적 토론 글쓰기)

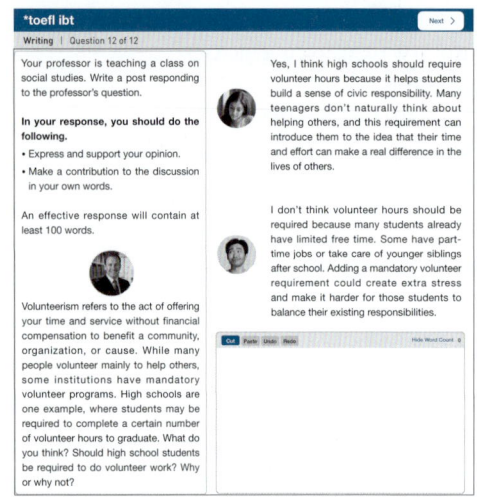

Write for an Academic Discussion 과제에서는 온라인 수업의 토론 포럼 맥락에서 자신의 의견을 제시하고 근거로 뒷받침하도록 요구한다. 교수의 게시글이 먼저 주제를 간략히 제시하고, 학급이 논의할 의견형 질문을 던진다. 이어서 두 명의 학생이 짧은 글로 그 쟁점에 대해 서로 다른 입장을 제시한다. 응시자는 그 질문에 대해 자신의 입장을 글로 올리되, 자신의 추론·경험·지식을 근거로 의견을 뒷받침해야 한다. 이 과제를 완성할 수 있는 시간은 10분이다. 이 과제는 응시자가 여러 문장으로 이루어진 글을 작성하는 능력을 측정하는데, 그 글은 다음을 충족해야 한다.

- 제시된 짧은 글의 정보를 활용하거나 반대 논거에 응답하면서, 자신의 입장을 뒷받침하는 주장을 분명하게 전개한다.
- 근거가 충분하고, 명확하며, 응집력이 있다.
- 다양한 문법 구조와 어휘를 정확하고 적절하게 사용한다.
- 영어의 형식적 규칙(철자, 구두점, 대문자 사용)을 준수한다.

* Write for an Academic Discussion 채점 기준

점수	설명
5	응답이 온라인 토론에 적절하며, 언어 사용 능력이 일관되게 뛰어나다. 주제와 관련성이 높은 설명·예시·세부 사항을 제시한다. • 다양한 문장 구조의 효과적 사용과 정확하고 관용적인 어휘 선택 • 시간 제한 하의 능숙한 필자에게서 기대되는 수준을 제외하면 어휘·문법 오류가 거의 없음 (예: 흔한 오타, 일반적 철자 오류 또는 there/their 같은 대치 실수)
4	응답이 온라인 토론에 적절하게 기여하며, 언어 사용 능력이 있어 필자의 생각이 쉽게 이해된다. • 관련성 있고 충분히 전개된 설명·예시·세부사항 • 여러 문장 구조의 사용과 적절한 어휘 선택 • 소수의 어휘 또는 문법 오류
3	응답이 온라인 토론에 대체로 관련 있고 대부분 이해 가능하며, 언어 사용에 일부 능숙함이 보인다. • 전개가 있으나 설명·예시·세부의 일부가 누락되었거나 불분명·비관련할 수 있음 • 어느 정도의 문장 구조 다양성과 어휘 범위 • 문장 구조·어형·관용적 표현 사용 등에서 눈에 띄는 어휘·문법 오류 일부
2	온라인 토론에 기여하려는 시도는 보이나, 언어 사용의 한계 때문에 아이디어를 따라가기 어렵게 만들 수 있다. • 전개가 부족하거나 부분적으로만 관련된 아이디어 • 제한된 문장 구조와 어휘 범위 • 문장 구조·어형·사용에서 오류가 누적
1	온라인 토론에 기여하려는 시도가 비효과적이며, 언어 사용의 한계로 아이디어 표현 자체가 어려워질 수 있다. • 과제를 수행하려는 흔적은 있으나 일관된 아이디어가 거의 없거나 없음 • 매우 제한된 문장 구조와 어휘 범위 • 언어 사용에서 심각하고 잦은 오류 • 원문 생산이 거의 없고, 이해 가능한 언어가 있다면 대부분 제시문에서 차용
0	응답이 비어있거나, 주제를 거부하거나, 영어가 아니거나, 지문을 그대로 복사했거나, 지문과 전혀 무관하거나, 무작위 키 입력으로만 이루어져 있음

4. Speaking 섹션의 과제 유형

Speaking 섹션의 과제들은 기초 언어 능력과 의사소통 능력을 모두 측정한다.

- 기초 능력은 언어를 처리하고, 유창하고 이해 가능한 발화를 산출하는 능력을 말하며, 이는 응시자가 주어진 입력을 듣고 그대로 발화할 수 있는지를 통해 측정된다.
- 의사소통 능력은 모의 대화 상황에서 응시자가 자신의 의견과 경험을 말하는 것을 통해 측정된다.

Speaking 스킬은 다음 두 가지 과제 유형을 통해 평가된다.

1) Listen and Repeat (듣고 따라 말하기)

Listen and Repeat 과제는 응시자가 들은 문장을 처리하고, 그것을 정확하고 명확하게 다시 말할 수 있는 능력을 측정한다.

- 듣고 따라 말하기 과제에서 응시자는 다양한 상황에서의 7개의 문장을 듣는다. 시나리오는 문장을 듣고 반복할 수 있도록 의사소통적 맥락을 제공한다.
- 각 문장 세트는 해당 상황을 시각적으로 보여주는 이미지와 연결되어 있으며, 문장이 진행됨에 따라 화면 속 그림도 단계적으로 움직이거나 변화한다.
- 각 문장이 끝나면 잠시 '일시 정지'가 되고, 응시자는 방금 들은 문장을 그대로 반복한다.
- 문장들은 시나리오가 진행될수록 점점 길어지고 복잡해진다.
- 각 문장에 대해 응시자에게는 8~12초의 응답 시간이 주어지며, 그 안에 문장을 녹음해야 한다.

* Listen and Repeat 채점 기준

점수	설명
5	응답이 지문을 정확히 반복한다. • 응답이 완전히 분명하게 들리며, 지문을 있는 그대로 정확히 반복함
4	응답이 지문의 의미를 정확히 담되 문자 그대로의 반복은 아니다. 즉, 단어 또는 문법의 작은 변화가 있으나, 지문의 핵심 의미는 달라지지 않는다. • 기능어 1~2개가 빠지거나 바뀜 • (긴 문장에서) 내용어 하나가 빠지거나 의미가 가까운 단어로 대체됨 • 시제/상/수 표지가 빠지거나 부정확함 • 단어 두 개의 위치가 맞바뀜 • 내용어 1~2개가 발음이 부정확해 모호하게 들림
3	응답이 대체로 전체를 포함하지만 원래 의미를 정확히 담지 못한다. • 지문의 대부분의 내용어/핵심 아이디어를 포함함 • 여러 기능어가 바뀌거나 누락될 수 있고, 하나 이상의 내용어가 누락되거나 의미가 상당히 변형될 수 있음 • 응답이 완전한 한 문장임 • 경우에 따라 명료성 문제로 의미 파악이 간헐적으로 어려울 수 있음 (특정 단어·구에서 더듬거나, 단어들을 붙여 말해 이해가능성이 떨어지는 경우)
2	지문의 상당 부분이 누락되거나 정확성이 크게 떨어진다. • 지문의 큰 부분이 빠져 원래의 중요한 의미가 빠져 있음 • 문장의 앞부분만 반복한 뒤 멈추거나, 부정확한 내용으로 채우고/혹은 마지막 몇 단어만 덧붙임 • 응답이 독립된 완전 문장이 아니며, 단편적 의미만 전달됨 • 명료성이 낮아, 지문을 모르는 청자에게는 이해가 어려운 수준임
1	지문을 거의 담지 못했거나 이해하기에 대체로 불명료한 응답이다. • 아주 짧은 몇 단어만 말하는 최소한의 응답으로, 지문의 대부분이 누락되어 있음 • 지문을 따라 말하려는 시도는 알아볼 수 있으나, 응답이 대세로 불명료함
0	무응답, 또는 응답이 완전히 불명료, 또는 영어가 전혀 없음, 또는 내용이 지문과 완전히 무관하다. (예: "I don't know" 같은 관용적 문구만으로 구성된 경우 포함)

2) Take an Interview (인터뷰하기)

Take an Interview 과제에서는 응시자가 사전 녹음된 면접관과의 모의 대화에 참여하게 된다. 이 인터뷰는 장학금 지원, 연구 조사 참여 등 다양한 상황 속에서 진행된다. 인터뷰 동안 응시자는 주어진 인터뷰 주제와 관련된 네 가지 질문에 답하며, 자신의 경험과 의견을 설명하게 된다. 각 질문에 대해 응시자에게는 45초의 답변 시간이 주어진다. 처음 몇 가지 질문은 '사실적 정보'와 '개인적 경험'에 초점을 맞추며, 이후 질문에서는 응시자가 더 넓은 주제에 대한 의견을 표현하고 뒷받침하도록 요구한다. 이 과제는 응시자가 일반적이고 학문적인 다양한 주제의 질문에 답할 수 있는 능력을 측정하며, 그 결과로 나오는 발화는 다음과 같은 특징을 지녀야 한다.

- 질문에 대해 적절하고 일관성 있게 확장된 답변을 한다.
- 자연스럽고 좋은 대화 속도를 유지한다.
- 명확하게 전달되며, 의미를 전달하기 위해 리듬과 억양을 효과적으로 사용한다.
- 다양한 어휘와 문법 구조를 정확하고 효과적으로 활용한다.

* Take an Interview 채점 기준

점수	설명
5	응답이 질문을 충분히 다루며, 명료하고 유창하다. - 주제에 정확히 부합하고 충분히 전개되어 있음 - 대화 상황에 알맞은 자연스러운 말하기 속도가 유지되고, "적절한 휴지(pause)"를 자연스럽게 사용함 - 발음이 쉽게 알아들을 수 있을 만큼 명료하며, 리듬과 억양이 의미 전달에 효과적임 - 정확한 문법과 어휘를 폭넓게 사용하여 구체적 의미를 분명하게 표현함
4	응답이 질문을 적절히 다루고, 전반적으로 명료하다. - 주제에 맞고 전개가 되어 있으나, 문장 수준 연결 표현이 다소 부족할 수 있음 - 대체로 안정적인 말하기 속도를 유지하며, 약간의 멈춤이 흐름에 큰 영향을 주지 않음 - 발음·리듬·억양 때문에 이해가 방해되지는 않지만, 가끔 단어/구에서 약간의 추가 해석 노력이 필요할 수 있음 - 문법과 어휘가 대체로 충분하여 대부분 상황에서 일반적 의미를 표현할 수 있음
3	응답이 질문을 다루기는 하나, 전개나 명료성이 제한적이다. - 전반적으로 주제에 부합하지만 전개가 비교적 제한적일 수 있음 - 잦거나 긴 멈춤으로 말하기가 덜 매끄럽고, 군더더기(filler) 사용이 잦음 - 단어 수준의 발음이나 강세/리듬의 부정확성으로 인해 명료성이 간헐적으로 저하됨 - 문법·어휘의 범위와 정확성이 제한되어 의미의 정확성·명료성이 눈에 띄게 제약됨
2	질문에 답하려는 시도는 보이나, 의미 있게 또는 명료하게 뒷받침되지는 않는다. - 면접관의 질문과의 연결성이 약간만 보이거나, 관련 전개가 거의/전혀 없고, 질문 문장의 표현이 주를 이룸 - 명료성이 낮아 화자의 의도한 의미 파악이 어려움 - 문법과 어휘의 범위가 매우 제한적임
1	질문을 최소한으로만 다루며, 언어 통제가 매우 제한적일 수 있다. - 면접관 질문의 언어와 희미하게만 관련됨 - 응답의 대부분이 불명료함 - 낱말 또는 짧은 구 위주로 구성됨
0	무응답, 또는 응답이 완전히 불명료, 또는 영어가 전혀 없음, 또는 내용이 지문과 전혀 무관하다. (예: "I don't know" 같은 관용적 문구만으로 구성된 경우 포함)

Actual Tests

Actual Test 1

Actual Test 1

*toefl ibt

Reading

Reading Section

In an actual test, you will answer 35—48 questions to demonstrate how well you understand academic and non-academic texts in English. There are three types of tasks.

Type of Task	Description
Complete the Words	Fill in the missing letters in a paragraph.
Read in Daily Life	Answer questions about everyday reading material.
Read an Academic Passage	Answer questions about academic passages.

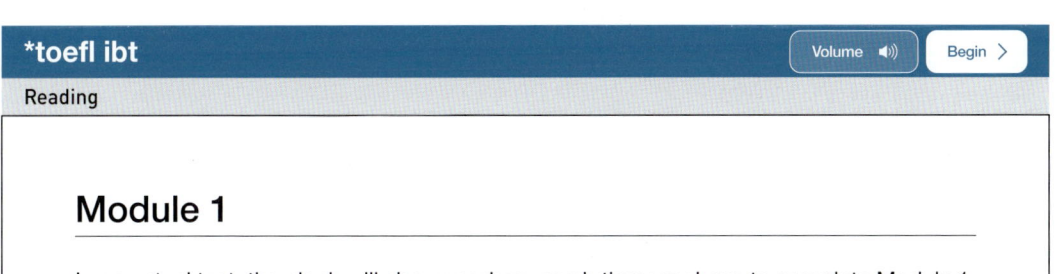

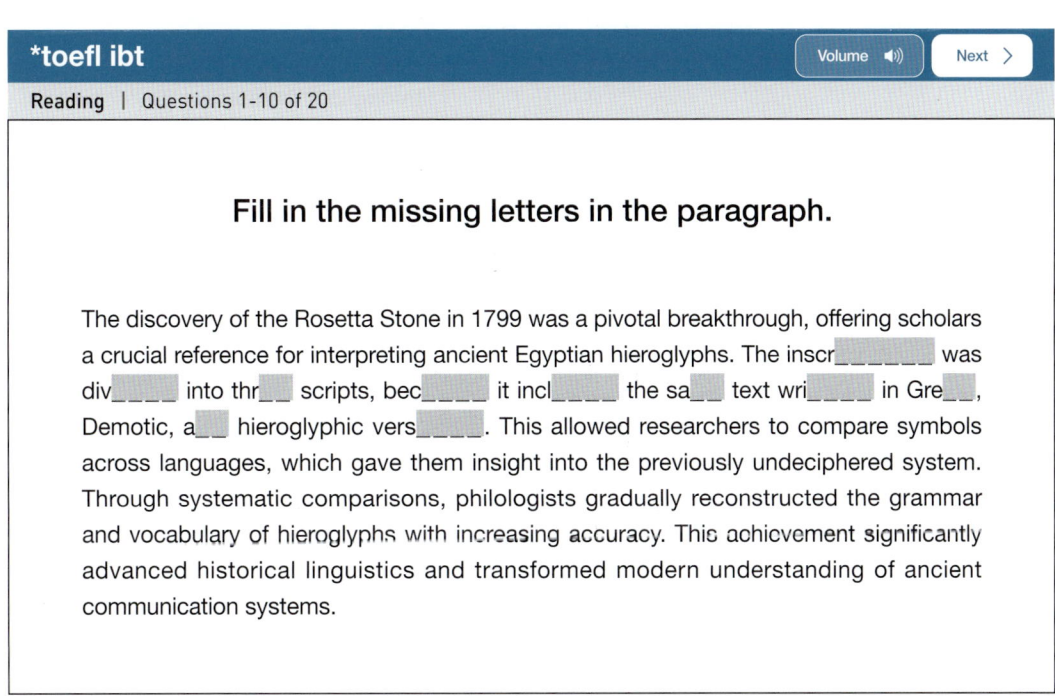

Read a text message.

From: City Transit Alerts

Due to scheduled roadwork on Main Avenue, bus routes 12 and 14 will follow a detour on Tuesday, April 14. Service will bypass Central Station between 8:00 A.M. and 2:00 P.M. Passengers traveling to Central Station should use shuttle buses available every 30 minutes from Riverside Plaza. Normal routes will resume after 2:00 P.M. Updates will be posted online.

11. What change will occur on April 14?
    - Ⓐ Shuttle service will be suspended.
    - Ⓑ Some routes will avoid Central Station.
    - Ⓒ Central Station will offer limited shuttle service.
    - Ⓓ Riverside Plaza will be closed for construction.

12. What can be inferred about the shuttle service?
    - Ⓐ It will end later on April 14.
    - Ⓑ It will be free for Riverside Plaza passengers.
    - Ⓒ It will depart every 30 minutes throughout the day.
    - Ⓓ It will continue after normal routes resume.

Read an e-mail.

To:	scholarship.applicants@hillside.edu
From:	finaid@hillside.edu
Date:	March 12
Subject:	Application Requirements – Hillside Merit Scholarship

Dear Students,

This message is to remind you that applications for the Hillside Merit Scholarship must be submitted no later than March 25. Applications must include the online form, faculty references, and an official transcript. Late submissions will not be reviewed.

Priority consideration will be given to students who demonstrate leadership in extracurricular activities. Applicants should also be prepared for a brief interview, which will be scheduled between March 28 and April 3. You will receive a separate e-mail confirming your interview time once your application has been processed.

Scholarship recipients will be announced on April 15 and will be invited to a recognition ceremony hosted by the university president. For more information, please visit the Financial Aid Office website or call extension 119.

Sincerely,
Financial Aid Office

---

13. What is the main purpose of the e-mail?
    - Ⓐ To invite alumni to contribute to a financial aid fund
    - Ⓑ To remind faculty members to submit letters of recommendation
    - Ⓒ To explain the university's new tuition assistance program
    - Ⓓ To inform students about the requirements for a scholarship application

14. Which document must be submitted by the application deadline?
    - Ⓐ A résumé describing extracurricular leadership activities
    - Ⓑ A set of letters of recommendation
    - Ⓒ A certificate showing volunteer service hours
    - Ⓓ A copy of the student's financial aid award letter

15. What can be inferred about the selection process?
    - Ⓐ Students who are active outside the classroom may be favored.
    - Ⓑ Applicants who submit materials on time are likely to be selected.
    - Ⓒ Graduate-level students are the primary group considered for this scholarship.
    - Ⓓ Recommendation letters are typically reviewed after the deadline has passed.

Bioluminescence in Nature

Bioluminescence, the ability of living organisms to produce light, is a remarkable phenomenon found in nature. This natural glow is caused by chemical reactions inside the organism's body, involving a substance called luciferin. Unlike sunlight or fire, bioluminescent light is produced without heat, making it highly efficient. Many deep-sea creatures rely on it for survival: fish use it to attract prey, communicate with one another, or confuse predators. For example, the anglerfish has a glowing lure that draws smaller fish close enough to be eaten. Other marine species, such as squid, release a burst of light to distract attackers while they escape.

Bioluminescence is not limited to the ocean. Fireflies are a well-known example on land, and their flashing lights serve as mating signals, allowing males and females to recognize each other. **(A)** In some regions, thousands of fireflies synchronize their flashes, creating a dazzling display that scientists are still trying to fully understand. **(B)**

Researchers are increasingly investigating practical applications of bioluminescence for humans. **(C)** Potential uses include medical imaging, environmental monitoring, and even sustainable lighting. **(D)** By studying how organisms create light so efficiently, scientists hope to develop technologies that reduce dependence on traditional energy sources. This ongoing research suggests that the glow of living organisms may ultimately contribute to innovations in fields beyond nature.

16. What is the passage mainly about?
    - Ⓐ The role of fireflies in land ecosystems and reproduction
    - Ⓑ The production and potential uses of light in living organisms
    - Ⓒ The dangers faced by deep-sea animals from natural predators
    - Ⓓ The chemical processes that create luciferin in certain organisms

17. Why does the author mention the anglerfish?
    - Ⓐ To illustrate how bioluminescence can be used to attract prey
    - Ⓑ To compare how land and sea creatures employ different signals
    - Ⓒ To explain how luciferin develops inside the bodies of fish
    - Ⓓ To describe the synchronized flashing behaviors of fireflies

18. The word "dazzling" in the passage is closest in meaning to
    - Ⓐ confusing
    - Ⓑ brief
    - Ⓒ ordinary
    - Ⓓ brilliant

Bioluminescence in Nature

Bioluminescence, the ability of living organisms to produce light, is a remarkable phenomenon found in nature. This natural glow is caused by chemical reactions inside the organism's body, involving a substance called luciferin. Unlike sunlight or fire, bioluminescent light is produced without heat, making it highly efficient. Many deep-sea creatures rely on it for survival: fish use it to attract prey, communicate with one another, or confuse predators. For example, the anglerfish has a glowing lure that draws smaller fish close enough to be eaten. Other marine species, such as squid, release a burst of light to distract attackers while they escape.

Bioluminescence is not limited to the ocean. Fireflies are a well-known example on land, and their flashing lights serve as mating signals, allowing males and females to recognize each other. **(A)** In some regions, thousands of fireflies synchronize their flashes, creating a dazzling display that scientists are still trying to fully understand. **(B)**

Researchers are increasingly investigating practical applications of bioluminescence for humans. **(C)** Potential uses include medical imaging, environmental monitoring, and even sustainable lighting. **(D)** By studying how organisms create light so efficiently, scientists hope to develop technologies that reduce dependence on traditional energy sources. This ongoing research suggests that the glow of living organisms may ultimately contribute to innovations in fields beyond nature.

19. What can be inferred about human interest in bioluminescence?
    - (A) It could inspire environmentally friendly technologies for the future.
    - (B) It will gradually replace sunlight as the main source of energy.
    - (C) It is already widely applied in modern medical procedures today.
    - (D) It primarily benefits scientists working on deep-sea exploration.

20. There are four locations in the passage that indicate where the following sentence could be added.

    These behaviors show that bioluminescence serves not only as a survival strategy but also as a means of communication and reproduction.

    Where would the sentence best fit? Select a location where the sentence could be added to the passage.
    - (A) Option (A)
    - (B) Option (B)
    - (C) Option (C)
    - (D) Option (D)

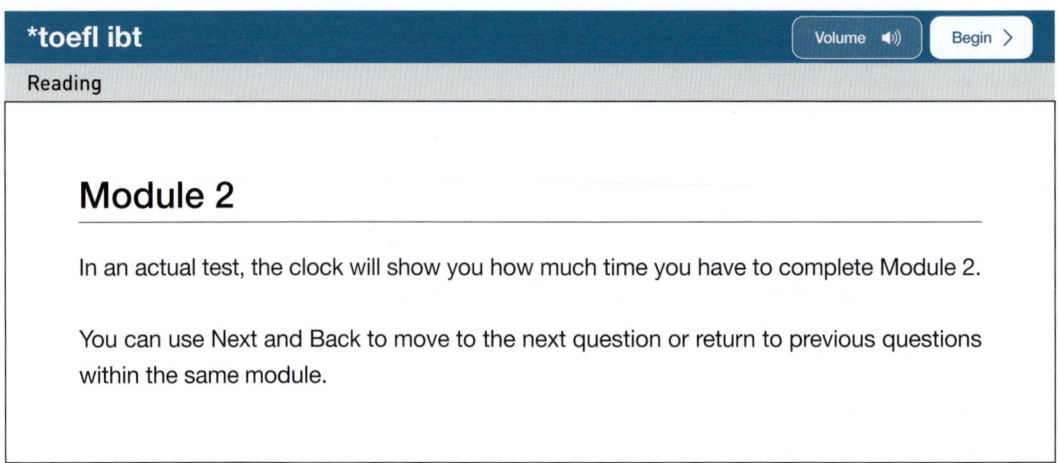

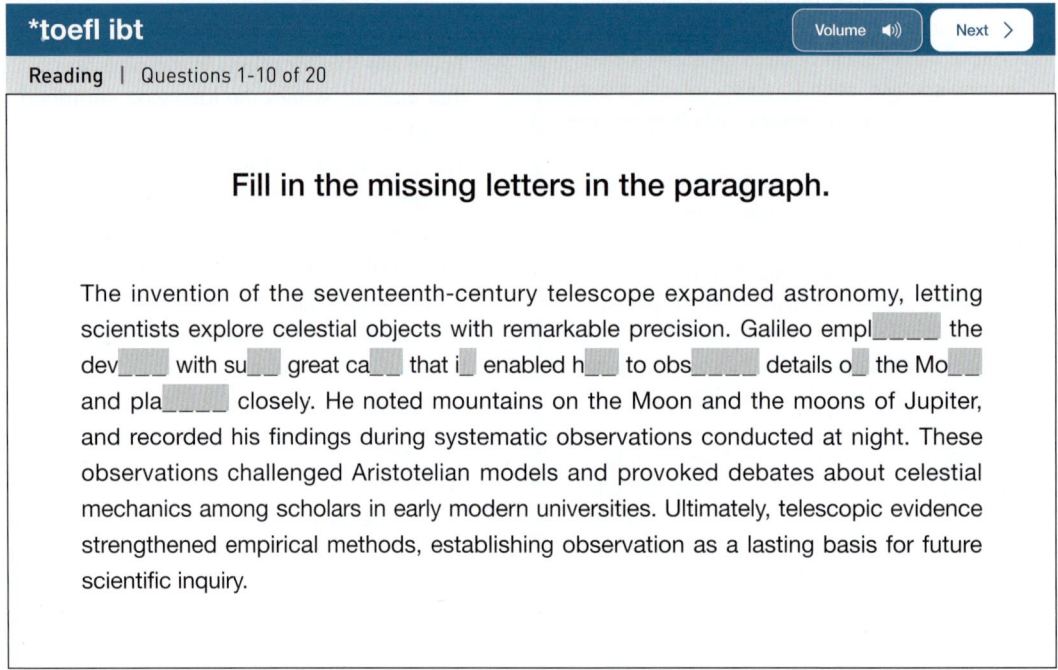

Read a notice.

> **City Art Museum – Free Admission Day**
>
> On Saturday, November 9, the City Art Museum will offer free admission to all visitors. The galleries will be open from 10:00 A.M. to 6:00 P.M., and guided tours will begin every hour. Family-friendly programs will take place in the education center throughout the afternoon.

11. What is the main purpose of the notice?
    - Ⓐ To announce the temporary opening of the galleries
    - Ⓑ To explain how to apply for museum membership
    - Ⓒ To promote a special day at the museum
    - Ⓓ To request volunteers for upcoming events

12. What is scheduled to happen later on November 9?
    - Ⓐ Free admission will end early.
    - Ⓑ Family activities will be held.
    - Ⓒ Guided tours will take place every hour.
    - Ⓓ The education center will not be available.

Read an e-mail.

To:	conference.participants@umail.com
From:	registrar@intltechforum.org
Date:	May 6
Subject:	Updated Procedures for International Tech Forum

Dear Participants,

We are writing to confirm your registration for the International Tech Forum, which will take place on May 22–23 at the Harborview Convention Center. In preparation for the event, please note that check-in counters will operate from 7:30 A.M. until 9:00 A.M. on the first day, and all attendees must present both a photo ID and the confirmation code issued at the time of registration. Without these documents, admission will not be guaranteed.

In addition, entry to the keynote lecture is restricted to registered participants and their invited guests only. Seating in the main hall is limited, so participants are encouraged to arrive early. Breakout sessions in the afternoon will focus on digital security, renewable energy, and cross-border e-commerce. As some sessions will run concurrently, please select your preferences in advance on the conference website.

Finally, a closing reception will be held on May 23 at 6:30 P.M. in the Riverside Ballroom. This event is intended for all participants, regardless of their session choices, and will feature a keynote panel and networking opportunities. Further details, including transportation options, are available on our website.

Sincerely,
Registration Office

---

13. What is the main purpose of the e-mail?
    - Ⓐ To request payment of a registration fee
    - Ⓑ To ask attendees to submit presentation proposals
    - Ⓒ To advertise future technology conferences
    - Ⓓ To provide participants with details about procedures

14. What can be inferred about admission to the keynote lecture?
    - Ⓐ It is accessible without any restrictions.
    - Ⓑ It is not open to the general public.
    - Ⓒ It depends only on arriving before 7:30 A.M.
    - Ⓓ It is available only to conference staff members.

15. What is indicated about the event taking place in the Riverside Ballroom?
    - Ⓐ It is intended for those who selected preferences on the website.
    - Ⓑ It will consist of several sessions occurring at the same time in the afternoon.
    - Ⓒ It gives participants opportunities to interact with one another.
    - Ⓓ It will provide complimentary transportation services.

How Sleep Shapes Memory

Sleep is not merely a period of rest but rather a fundamental process through which the brain consolidates memory. During sleep, neural activity selectively strengthens recently acquired information while filtering out less relevant details. This selective retention allows individuals to function more efficiently when awake, preserving cognitive resources for essential tasks.

Among the stages of sleep, rapid eye movement (REM) sleep appears to be especially integral to higher-order thinking. In this stage, brain activity resembles wakefulness, and research suggests that REM sleep enhances creativity and complex problem-solving. Experiments have shown, for instance, that students who review academic material before sleeping are more likely to recall it accurately compared to those who remain awake for the same period.

When sleep is disrupted, however, these benefits diminish. Sleep-deprived individuals often struggle with sustained attention and experience lapses in memory. Moreover, chronic deprivation has been linked to anxiety and depression. Studying how sleep stages affect memory not only informs educational strategies but also provides insight into potential treatments for conditions such as Alzheimer's disease.

16. Which of the following best states a main idea of the passage?
    - Ⓐ The connection between REM sleep and emotional stability
    - Ⓑ The critical role of sleep in strengthening memory and learning
    - Ⓒ The scientific methods used to measure neural activity during rest
    - Ⓓ The health problems that result from long-term sleep deprivation

17. The word "integral" in the passage is closest in meaning to
    - Ⓐ essential
    - Ⓑ harmful
    - Ⓒ limited
    - Ⓓ temporary

18. Why does the author mention students who review academic material before sleeping?
    - Ⓐ To show how different study habits produce the same results
    - Ⓑ To argue that staying awake can be equally effective for recall
    - Ⓒ To demonstrate that memory improves when rest follows learning
    - Ⓓ To explain why REM sleep is unrelated to long-term retention

How Sleep Shapes Memory

Sleep is not merely a period of rest but rather a fundamental process through which the brain consolidates memory. During sleep, neural activity selectively strengthens recently acquired information while filtering out less relevant details. This selective retention allows individuals to function more efficiently when awake, preserving cognitive resources for essential tasks.

Among the stages of sleep, rapid eye movement (REM) sleep appears to be especially integral to higher-order thinking. In this stage, brain activity resembles wakefulness, and research suggests that REM sleep enhances creativity and complex problem-solving. Experiments have shown, for instance, that students who review academic material before sleeping are more likely to recall it accurately compared to those who remain awake for the same period.

When sleep is disrupted, however, these benefits diminish. Sleep-deprived individuals often struggle with sustained attention and experience lapses in memory. Moreover, chronic deprivation has been linked to anxiety and depression. Studying how sleep stages affect memory not only informs educational strategies but also provides insight into potential treatments for conditions such as Alzheimer's disease.

19. What is the relationship between paragraphs 2 and 3?
    - Ⓐ Paragraph 3 provides evidence contradicting the claims in paragraph 2.
    - Ⓑ Paragraph 3 offers an example of the ideas introduced in paragraph 2.
    - Ⓒ Paragraph 3 describes the negative effects that result from paragraph 2.
    - Ⓓ Paragraph 3 introduces alternative theories unrelated to paragraph 2.

20. What does the passage suggest about future applications of sleep research?
    - Ⓐ It may contribute to educational practices and medical treatments.
    - Ⓑ It is unlikely to reveal further details about how memory works.
    - Ⓒ It will focus mainly on reducing the need for nightly sleep.
    - Ⓓ It is expected to concentrate on improving creativity in adults.

Listening Section

In the listening section, you will answer 30–40 questions to demonstrate how well you understand spoken English. There are three types of tasks.

Type of Task	Description
Listen and Choose a Response	Select the best response to the question or statement.
Conversations	Answer questions about short conversations.
Announcement and Academic Talks	Answer questions about announcements and academic talks.

You WILL NOT be able to return to previous questions.

Module 1

In an actual test, the clock will show you how much time you have to complete each question.

You can use Next to move to the next question.

You WILL NOT be able to return to previous questions.

Choose the best response.

1.
- Ⓐ The accounting unit.
- Ⓑ Next Thursday.
- Ⓒ The chair was out sick.
- Ⓓ Yes, it was.

2.
- Ⓐ Actually, it's in Room 204.
- Ⓑ Let's attend the seminar online!
- Ⓒ No, it's a virtual session.
- Ⓓ Who's presenting?

3.
- Ⓐ See you then.
- Ⓑ Join the noon one.
- Ⓒ Room A.
- Ⓓ So am I.

4.
- Ⓐ At the registrar's office window.
- Ⓑ I'll process your papers this afternoon.
- Ⓒ It's for late entries only.
- Ⓓ It won't exceed forty dollars.

Choose the best response.

5.
- Ⓐ In your inbox.
- Ⓑ It's already in the queue.
- Ⓒ It was signed last year.
- Ⓓ I'll squeeze it in before three.

6.
- Ⓐ No, it doesn't.
- Ⓑ On the events page.
- Ⓒ Before Friday at noon.
- Ⓓ The admissions office.

7.
- Ⓐ Is it even free tonight?
- Ⓑ It's near the main entrance.
- Ⓒ I scheduled tomorrow's event already.
- Ⓓ I'll check tomorrow morning.

8.
- Ⓐ By Friday, if possible.
- Ⓑ Upload them to the Finance portal.
- Ⓒ Label the receipts clearly.
- Ⓓ Have your supervisor sign them.

*toefl ibt
Listening

Conversation, Announcement, and Academic Talk

You will listen only one time and then answer questions.

In an actual test, the clock will indicate how much time you have to answer.

Listen to a conversation.

Listening | Questions 9-10 of 18

Listen to a conversation.

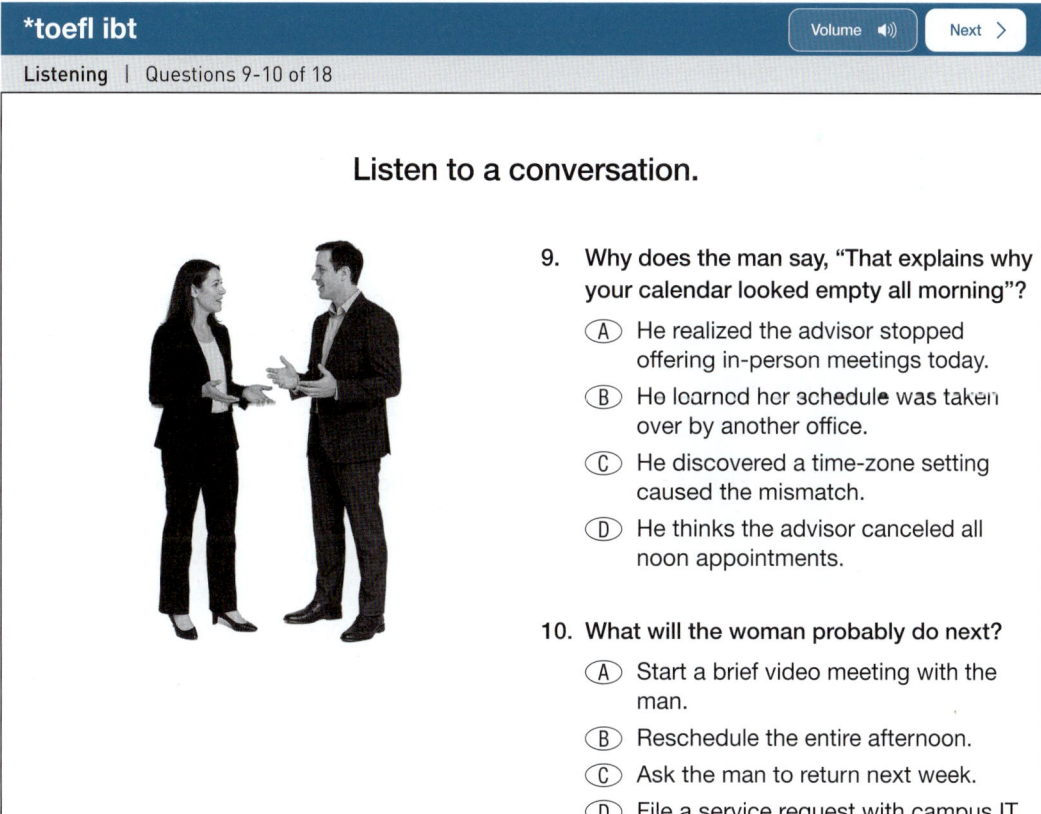

9. Why does the man say, "That explains why your calendar looked empty all morning"?
   - Ⓐ He realized the advisor stopped offering in-person meetings today.
   - Ⓑ He learned her schedule was taken over by another office.
   - Ⓒ He discovered a time-zone setting caused the mismatch.
   - Ⓓ He thinks the advisor canceled all noon appointments.

10. What will the woman probably do next?
    - Ⓐ Start a brief video meeting with the man.
    - Ⓑ Reschedule the entire afternoon.
    - Ⓒ Ask the man to return next week.
    - Ⓓ File a service request with campus IT.

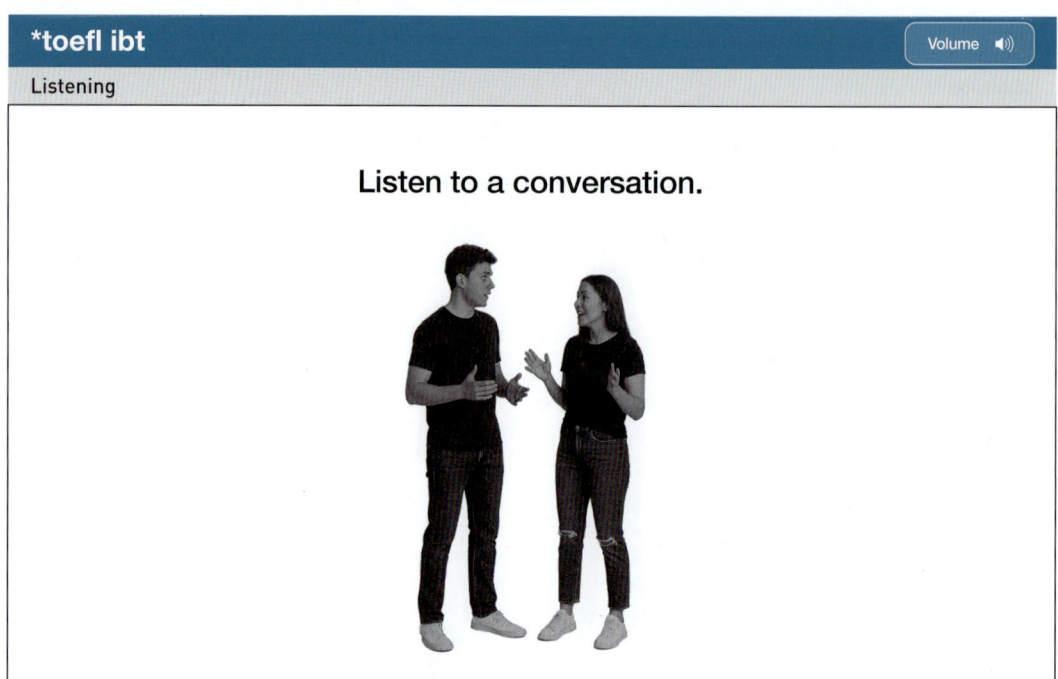

Listen to a conversation.

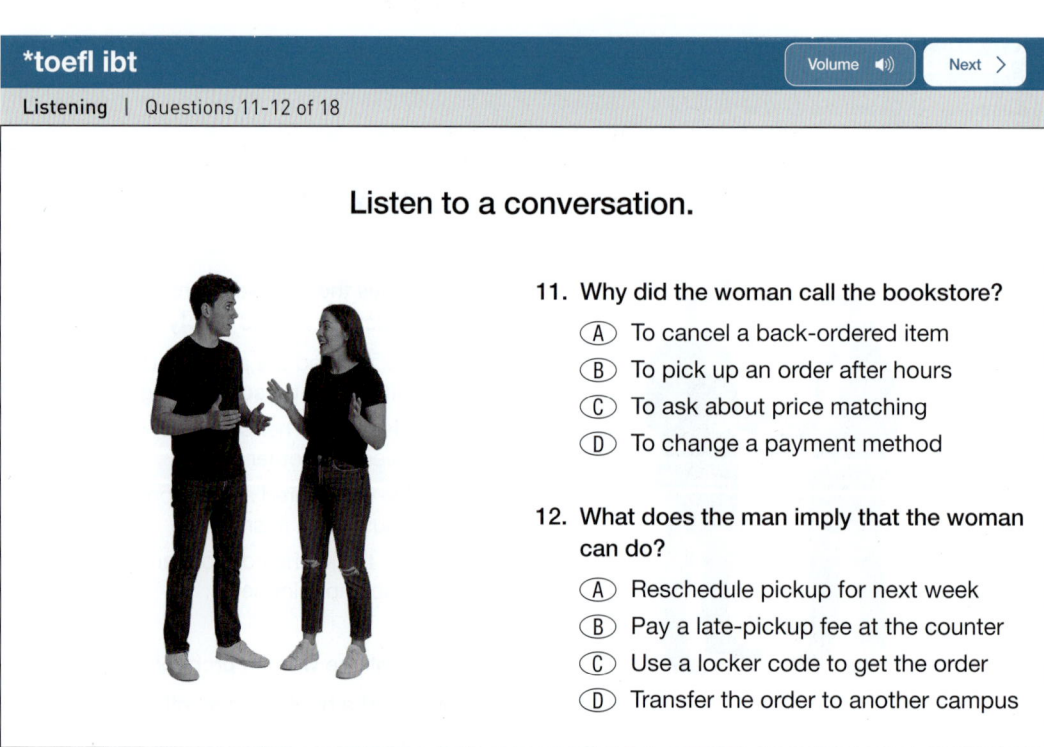

Listen to a conversation.

11. Why did the woman call the bookstore?
    - Ⓐ To cancel a back-ordered item
    - Ⓑ To pick up an order after hours
    - Ⓒ To ask about price matching
    - Ⓓ To change a payment method

12. What does the man imply that the woman can do?
    - Ⓐ Reschedule pickup for next week
    - Ⓑ Pay a late-pickup fee at the counter
    - Ⓒ Use a locker code to get the order
    - Ⓓ Transfer the order to another campus

Listen to an announcement in a university library.

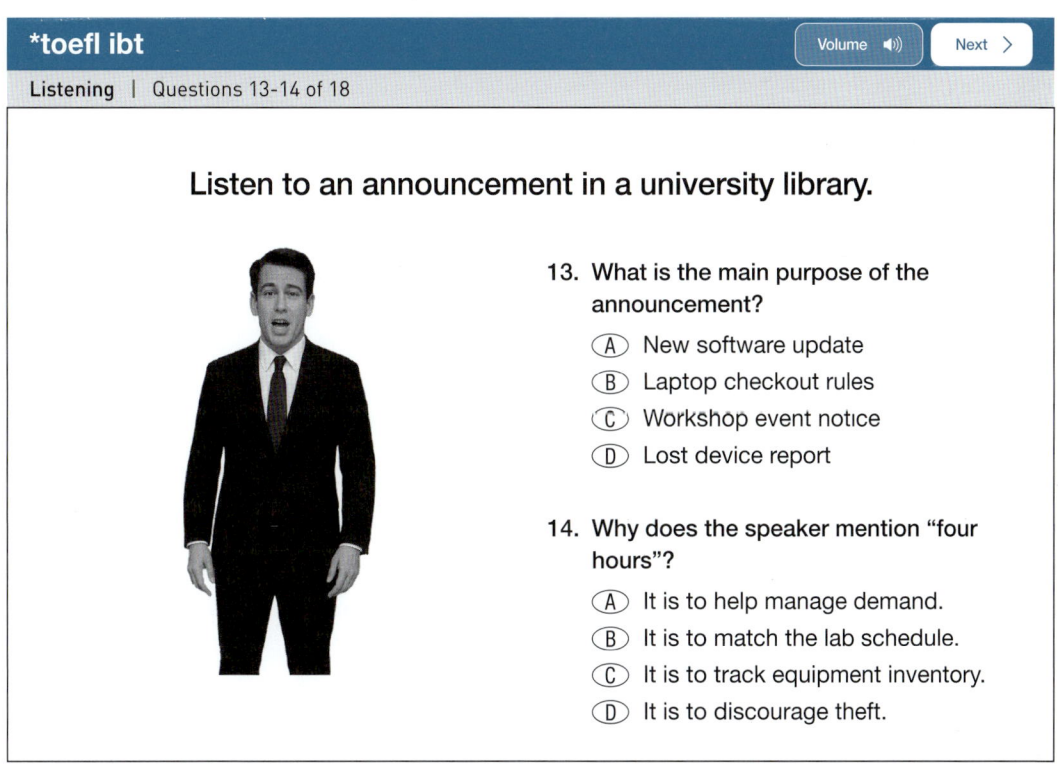

Listen to an announcement in a university library.

13. What is the main purpose of the announcement?
    - Ⓐ New software update
    - Ⓑ Laptop checkout rules
    - Ⓒ Workshop event notice
    - Ⓓ Lost device report

14. Why does the speaker mention "four hours"?
    - Ⓐ It is to help manage demand.
    - Ⓑ It is to match the lab schedule.
    - Ⓒ It is to track equipment inventory.
    - Ⓓ It is to discourage theft.

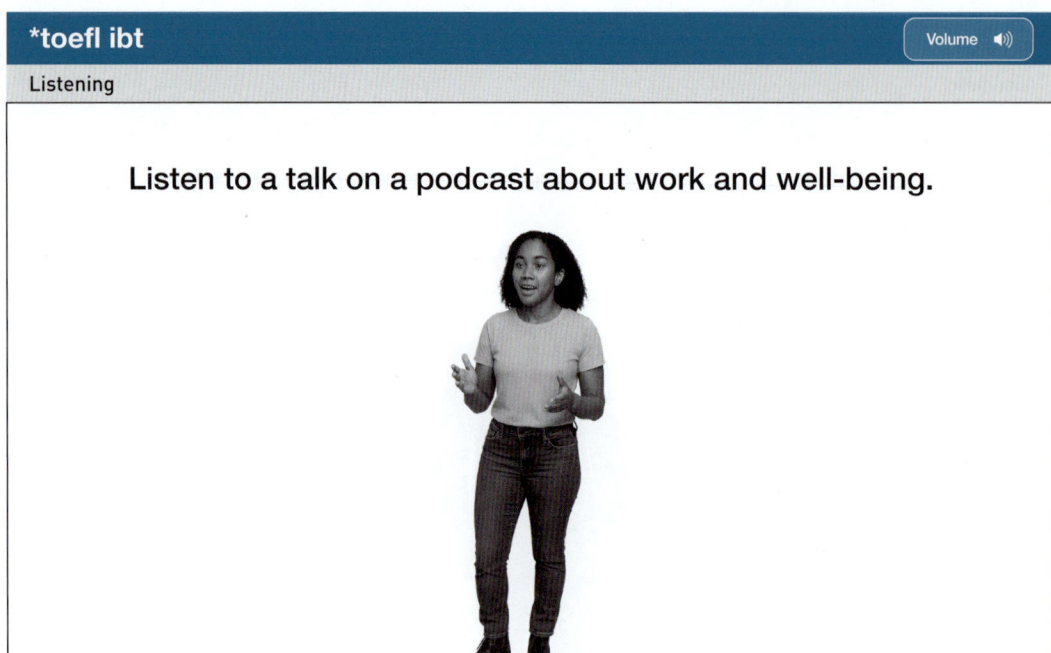

Listen to a talk on a podcast about work and well-being.

15. What is the talk mainly about?
    - Ⓐ Longer vacations as the main cure for burnout
    - Ⓑ How short pauses can restore focus and creativity
    - Ⓒ Whether removing screens increases office productivity
    - Ⓓ Training personality traits to raise workplace innovation

16. Why does the host mention "checking a news feed"?
    - Ⓐ To suggest regular news checks during the workday
    - Ⓑ To claim digital tools always improve efficiency
    - Ⓒ To show a pause that fails to restore attention
    - Ⓓ To argue for stricter rules on social media

17. What does the host imply about managers' concerns?
    - Ⓐ Strict time limits can reduce skepticism.
    - Ⓑ Their worries are baseless and should be ignored.
    - Ⓒ Only top leaders may approve micro-break policies.
    - Ⓓ Persistent doubts mean the idea should be abandoned.

18. What will the host most likely discuss next?
    - Ⓐ A history of corporate health promotion programs
    - Ⓑ Calculating costs of well-being initiatives at work
    - Ⓒ Brain research on memory with lab experiments
    - Ⓓ How to adapt micro-break schedules by job type

Module 2

In an actual test, the clock will show you how much time you have to complete each question.

You can use Next to move to the next question.

You WILL NOT be able to return to previous questions.

Choose the best response.

1.
- Ⓐ In the main lab.
- Ⓑ The administration office is.
- Ⓒ I do.
- Ⓓ By next Monday, please.

2.
- Ⓐ No, a lot of students get lost.
- Ⓑ Ask the registrar if your enrollment went through.
- Ⓒ Check the assignment board by Hall C.
- Ⓓ Rooms change after check-in.

3.
- Ⓐ Outside Hall 2 at Registration Desk B.
- Ⓑ After the opening ceremony ends.
- Ⓒ No, it's already been mailed to you.
- Ⓓ In the hotel gym on the basement floor.

4.
- Ⓐ I thought you were going to submit the form in person.
- Ⓑ You probably mean the fire-safety record.
- Ⓒ Yes, the training is mandatory.
- Ⓓ That's right–isn't it showing up?

Choose the best response.

5.
- (A) I moved last week's session already.
- (B) It's scheduled in the atrium lobby.
- (C) Only if facilities can set up stands.
- (D) Let's run the display outside tonight!

6.
- (A) I do—I'll send it now.
- (B) It's printed in the course reader.
- (C) Yes, I don't have it.
- (D) After the add/drop period ends.

7.
- (A) It begins right after the 6 p.m. orientation.
- (B) Court B is booked during the evening slot.
- (C) Check-ins for that class close at five-thirty.
- (D) The posted schedule shows Tuesdays only.

8.
- (A) Room 214 near the stairs.
- (B) Actually, it was shifted to one-thirty.
- (C) Yes, all four of them are here.
- (D) I booked tomorrow afternoon.

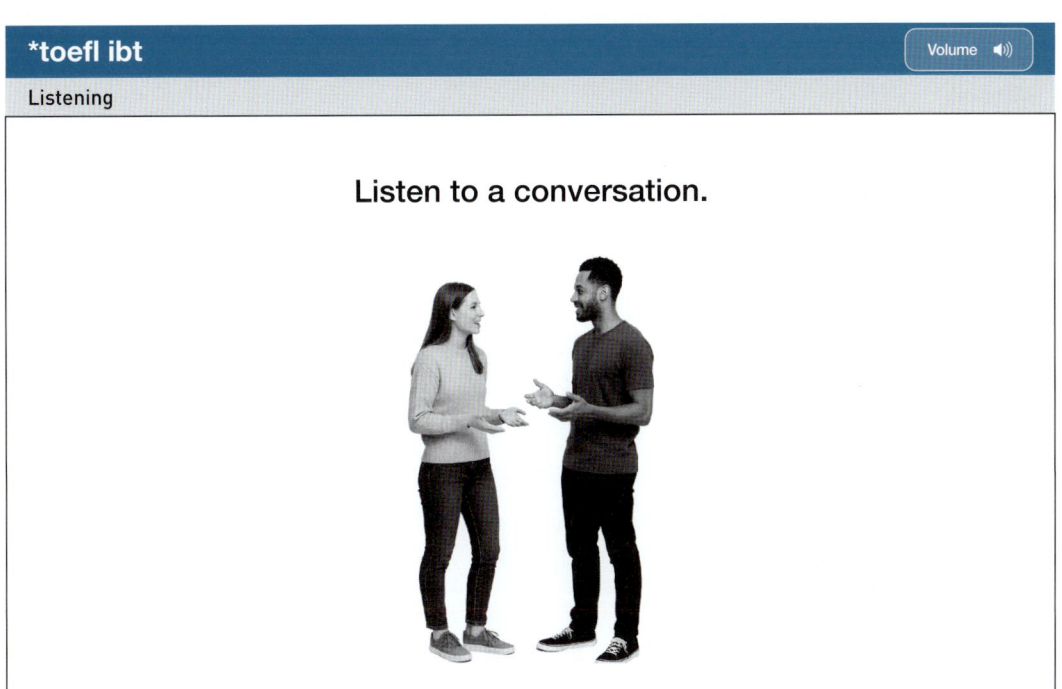

Listen to a conversation.

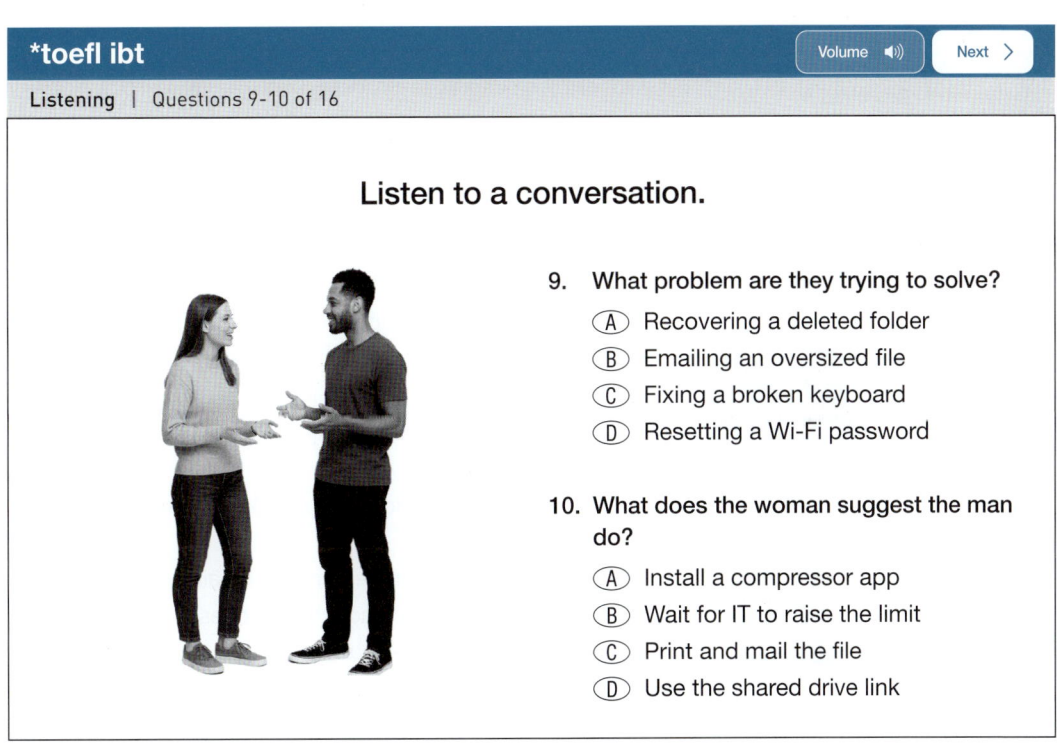

Listen to a conversation.

9. What problem are they trying to solve?
   Ⓐ Recovering a deleted folder
   Ⓑ Emailing an oversized file
   Ⓒ Fixing a broken keyboard
   Ⓓ Resetting a Wi-Fi password

10. What does the woman suggest the man do?
    Ⓐ Install a compressor app
    Ⓑ Wait for IT to raise the limit
    Ⓒ Print and mail the file
    Ⓓ Use the shared drive link

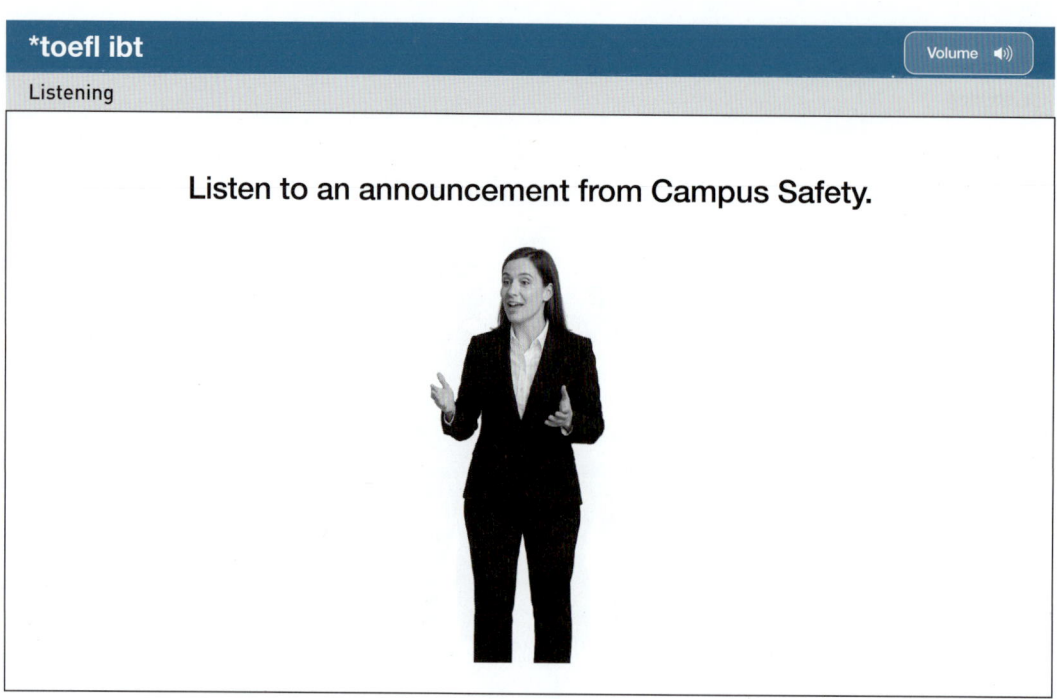

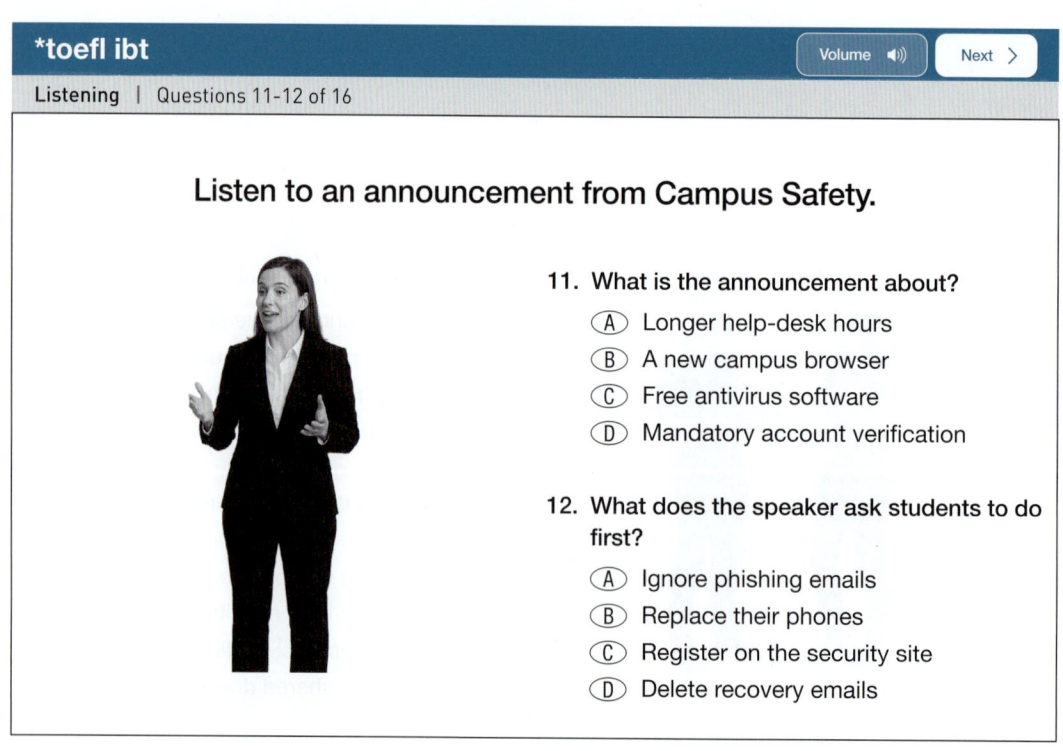

11. What is the announcement about?
    A) Longer help-desk hours
    B) A new campus browser
    C) Free antivirus software
    D) Mandatory account verification

12. What does the speaker ask students to do first?
    A) Ignore phishing emails
    B) Replace their phones
    C) Register on the security site
    D) Delete recovery emails

Listen to a talk in a biology class.

13. What topic does the professor mainly talk about?
    - Ⓐ Factors that guide long-distance bird migration
    - Ⓑ How urban lighting affects building safety
    - Ⓒ Why predators follow seasonal changes
    - Ⓓ Procedures for conditioning captive flocks

14. What does the professor discuss after traditional explanations?
    - Ⓐ Student opinions on research priorities
    - Ⓑ Recent discoveries about navigation mechanisms
    - Ⓒ Conservation campaigns before basic concepts
    - Ⓓ Field reports prior to experimental results

15. According to the professor, how does Earth's magnetic field assist migrants?
    - Ⓐ Heat storage enables slow release after sunset.
    - Ⓑ Nighttime winds increase between buildings.
    - Ⓒ It provides an internal compass for orientation.
    - Ⓓ Moisture uptake promotes longer rest during travel.

16. What does the professor imply about migration risks?
    - Ⓐ They show migration is no longer necessary.
    - Ⓑ They are minor compared with other issues.
    - Ⓒ They are mostly solved by current tools.
    - Ⓓ They highlight urgent need for conservation action.

Writing Section

In the writing section, you will answer 12 questions to demonstrate how well you can write in English. There are three types of tasks.

Type of Task	Description
Build a Sentence	Create a grammatical sentence.
Write an Email	Write an email using information provided.
Write for an Academic Discussion	Participate in an online discussion.

Build a Sentence

Move the words in the boxes to create grammatical sentences.

A clock will show you how much time you have to complete this task.

Make an appropriate sentence.

1. Why was the event postponed?

   It _____ _____ _____ _____ _____ _____.

   that   to delay it   forced   was   the severe weather   the organizers

2. I'm updating the calendar now.

   _____ _____ _____ whether _____ _____ _____?

   could   let me know   has been   rescheduled   the meeting   you

3. We're preparing for the conference.

   _____ _____ _____ _____ _____?

   the guest speakers   in charge of   is   who   coordinating

4. The professor mentioned an alternative assignment.

   _____ _____ _____ _____ _____ _____?

   when   you   posted   the new guidelines   know   do   will be

5. I couldn't access the dataset last night.

   _____ that _____ _____ _____ _____ _____.

   you   sent   me   no longer   works   the link

Make an appropriate sentence.

6. I need to improve my writing.

   ___ ___ ___ the ___ ___ ___.

   before   main points   how   helps   to outline   drafting   it

7. My laptop keeps freezing during tutorials.

   ___ ___ ___ ___ ___ ___ ___?

   updating   tried   the graphics   you   driver   have

8. We arrived late to the station.

   ___ ___ ___, ___ ___.

   by the time   had left   we   the last train   got there

9. What did the advisor recommend?

   She ___ ___ ___ ___ ___ ___.

   take   that   suggested   course load   a lighter   I

10. How did you handle the complaint?

    ___ ___ ___ ___ ___ ___.

    and   the damaged item   I   them   offered   apologized   to replace

Write an Email

You will read some information and use the information to write an email.

You will have 7 minutes to write the email.

Yesterday afternoon, the campus lab was closed without prior notice for maintenance. You had scheduled time to collect data for an assignment due later this week, but you could not finish the required trials. The equipment you need is only available in that lab, and your schedule limits rescheduling.

Write an email to your instructor. In your email, do the following.

- Explain the lab closure and missed trials.
- Request a short extension with a new date.
- Ask about acceptable alternatives for submission.

Write as much as you can and in complete sentences.

Your Response:

To: Prof. Nguyen
Subject: Lab Closure and Assignment Timeline

*toefl ibt
Writing

Write for an Academic Discussion

A professor has posted a question about a topic and students have responded with their thoughts and ideas. Make a contribution to the discussion.

You will have 10 minutes to write.

---

*toefl ibt
Writing | Question 12 of 12

Your professor is teaching a class on educational technology. Write a post responding to the professor's question.

In your response, you should do the following.

- Express and support your opinion.
- Make a contribution to the discussion in your own words.

An effective response will contain at least 100 words.

Professor:

Many courses now intersect with generative AI tools. Some universities are considering strict limits to protect academic integrity and skill development, while others argue that guided use reflects real-world practice. In your view, should universities ban generative AI in coursework or teach responsible use? Explain your position.

Student A: I think universities should teach responsible use of AI. These tools are already part of workplaces, so students need to learn how to cite outputs, check accuracy, and distinguish their own ideas. Clear guidelines can prevent misuse, while outright bans may simply push students to use AI secretly.

Student B: I support limited use, especially in early writing courses. Beginners need to develop basic skills like planning and revising without shortcuts. Later, instructors could allow AI under strict policies, requiring drafts and disclosure of prompts. A phased approach ensures assessment fairness while still preparing students for real-world practice.

Speaking Section

In the speaking section, you will answer 11 questions to demonstrate how well you can speak English. There are two types of tasks.

Type of Task	Description
Listen and Repeat	Listen and repeat what you heard
Take an Interview	Answer questions from the interviewer

Listen and Repeat

You will listen as someone speaks to you. Listen carefully and then repeat what you have heard. The clock will indicate how much time you have to speak.

No time for preparation will be provided.

You are learning how to greet visitors at a community library.
Listen to the staff trainer and repeat what she says.
Repeat only once.

*toefl ibt

Speaking | Questions 1-7 of 11

Listen and repeat only once.

1. RESPONSE TIME 🎤 00:00:08
2. RESPONSE TIME 🎤 00:00:08
3. RESPONSE TIME 🎤 00:00:10
4. RESPONSE TIME 🎤 00:00:10
5. RESPONSE TIME 🎤 00:00:10
6. RESPONSE TIME 🎤 00:00:12
7. RESPONSE TIME 🎤 00:00:12

Take an Interview

An interviewer will ask you questions. Answer the questions and be sure to say as much as you can in the time allowed.

No time for preparation will be provided.

You have agreed to take part in a research study about healthy eating. You will have a short online interview with a researcher. The researcher will ask you some questions.

*toefl ibt

Speaking | Questions 8-11 of 11

Please answer the interviewer's questions.

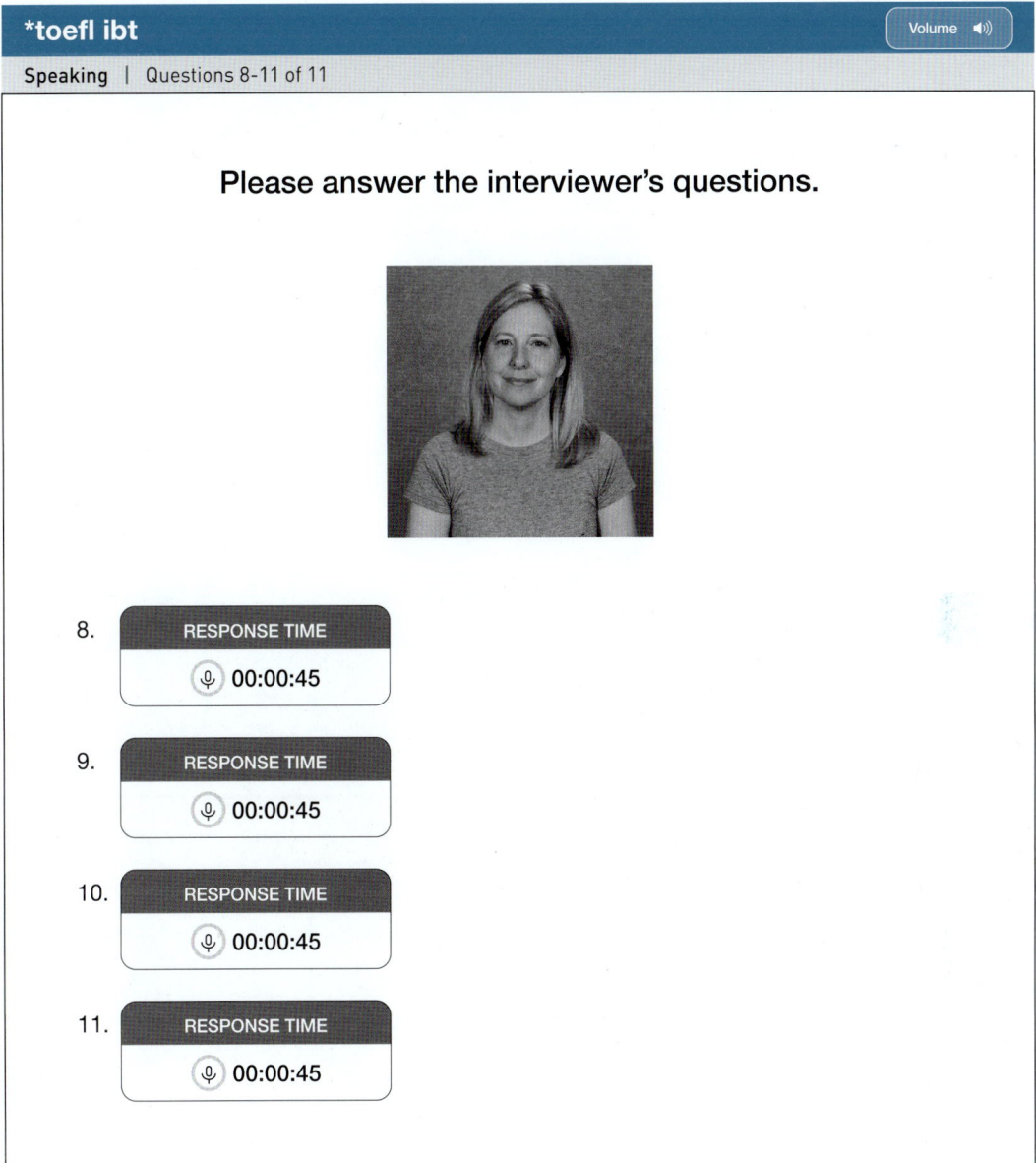

8. RESPONSE TIME 00:00:45

9. RESPONSE TIME 00:00:45

10. RESPONSE TIME 00:00:45

11. RESPONSE TIME 00:00:45

Actual Tests

Actual Test 2

Actual Test 2

---

*toefl ibt
Reading

Reading Section

In an actual test, you will answer 35—48 questions to demonstrate how well you understand academic and non-academic texts in English. There are three types of tasks.

Type of Task	Description
Complete the Words	Fill in the missing letters in a paragraph.
Read in Daily Life	Answer questions about everyday reading material.
Read an Academic Passage	Answer questions about academic passages.

Module 1

In an actual test, the clock will show you how much time you have to complete Module 1.

You can use Next and Back to move to the next question or return to previous questions within the same module.

In an actual test, you WILL NOT be able to return to Module 1 once you have begun Module 2.

Fill in the missing letters in the paragraph.

Whales use acoustic signals to interact across vast ocean spaces, demonstrating advanced biological adaptations for underwater communication. They prod____ low-frequency ca____ that tra____ long dist_____, allowing gro____ to st___ connected ev___ when wid____ separated. Su___ sounds gu____ migration, strengthen social bonds, and help whales coordinate cooperative behaviors in the deep sea. Marine biologists analyze these vocalizations to learn about population dynamics, environmental conditions, and marine ecological relationships. Continued research on whale sounds highlights the complexity of animal communication and the importance of preserving marine ecosystems.

Read a flyer.

**Community Theater –
Summer Film Festival**

Experience three evenings of international films at the Community Theater from July 10 to 12. Each screening commences at 7:00 P.M. Advance tickets cost $8, while admission at the door is $10. Students presenting valid identification will receive a $1 discount. Following every showing, a moderated session with local critics is scheduled in the lobby.

11. How much will a student without proper ID pay at the door?
    - Ⓐ $7
    - Ⓑ $8
    - Ⓒ $9
    - Ⓓ $10

12. What is scheduled to occur immediately after each screening?
    - Ⓐ A reception for visiting filmmakers
    - Ⓑ A talk led by local critics
    - Ⓒ A concert by the theater orchestra
    - Ⓓ A guided tour of backstage areas

Read an e-mail.

To:	allstudents@westfield.edu
From:	housingoffice@westfield.edu
Date:	August 12
Subject:	Oak Hall Renovation Notice

Dear Students,

Renovations in Oak Hall are scheduled to begin on September 1 and are expected to continue through October 15. During this period, the first-floor lounge and the laundry room will be closed to residents. To minimize inconvenience, several temporary laundry machines will be installed in the basement of Pine Hall, while additional seating has been arranged in the main cafeteria so that students still have a comfortable place to gather.

Construction activities will be concentrated between 9:00 A.M. and 5:00 P.M.; however, deliveries of equipment and minor adjustments may occasionally take place outside those hours. Because of the likelihood of disruptive noise, students who need quiet spaces for study are encouraged to use the library, which has extended its evening hours until 11:00 P.M., or the study rooms in Maple Hall. For further questions, please contact the Housing Office at extension 203.

Thank you for your cooperation.

Housing Office

---

13. What is the main purpose of the e-mail?
    - Ⓐ To announce the opening of new housing facilities
    - Ⓑ To inform students about upcoming renovations
    - Ⓒ To invite students to participate in construction projects
    - Ⓓ To provide details about changes to library operating hours

14. Which facility will continue to be available to students during the renovation?
    - Ⓐ The cafeteria
    - Ⓑ The first-floor lounge
    - Ⓒ The laundry room in Oak Hall
    - Ⓓ The Oak Hall lobby

15. What is indicated about the construction schedule?
    - Ⓐ It may occur less frequently than expected.
    - Ⓑ It may be completed before September 1.
    - Ⓒ It may not cause any significant noise problems.
    - Ⓓ It may continue outside regular daytime hours.

Papermaking along the Silk Road

Among the many cultural exchanges along the Silk Road, the transmission of papermaking from China to the West was one of the most influential. Developed during the Han Dynasty, Chinese papermaking relied on plant fibers that produced a durable writing surface. For centuries, this innovation remained largely confined to East Asia. However, as trade and travel expanded, knowledge of papermaking began to move westward, transforming communication in distant societies.

A turning point came in the eighth century, when papermaking techniques reached the Islamic world. Cities such as Samarkand and Baghdad became centers of production, adapting Chinese methods to local materials. Paper soon replaced parchment as the dominant medium for recording information. This shift supported advances in scholarship, bureaucracy, and literature. Libraries flourished, and texts could be copied and distributed with greater efficiency, spreading knowledge more widely than ever before.

From the Islamic world, papermaking eventually reached Europe by the twelfth century. The technology laid the foundation for later innovations such as the printing press, which revolutionized education and communication. Historians argue that the movement of papermaking through the Silk Road illustrates how a single technology, when transmitted across cultures, can reshape intellectual life on a global scale.

16. What is the passage mainly about?
    - Ⓐ The development of scholarship in medieval Islamic libraries
    - Ⓑ The spread of papermaking technology from China to other regions
    - Ⓒ The invention of the printing press in Europe during the twelfth century
    - Ⓓ The replacement of parchment with silk as a writing material

17. The word "confined" in the passage is closest in meaning to
    - Ⓐ shared
    - Ⓑ surrounded
    - Ⓒ recorded
    - Ⓓ restricted

18. Why did papermaking contribute to advances in scholarship in the Islamic world?
    - Ⓐ It made the production of written texts more efficient.
    - Ⓑ It encouraged the replacement of silk with parchment for writing.
    - Ⓒ It limited access to knowledge to government officials only.
    - Ⓓ It prevented the spread of literature beyond large cities.

Papermaking along the Silk Road

Among the many cultural exchanges along the Silk Road, the transmission of papermaking from China to the West was one of the most influential. Developed during the Han Dynasty, Chinese papermaking relied on plant fibers that produced a durable writing surface. For centuries, this innovation remained largely confined to East Asia. However, as trade and travel expanded, knowledge of papermaking began to move westward, transforming communication in distant societies.

A turning point came in the eighth century, when papermaking techniques reached the Islamic world. Cities such as Samarkand and Baghdad became centers of production, adapting Chinese methods to local materials. Paper soon replaced parchment as the dominant medium for recording information. This shift supported advances in scholarship, bureaucracy, and literature. Libraries flourished, and texts could be copied and distributed with greater efficiency, spreading knowledge more widely than ever before.

From the Islamic world, papermaking eventually reached Europe by the twelfth century. The technology laid the foundation for later innovations such as the printing press, which revolutionized education and communication. Historians argue that the movement of papermaking through the Silk Road illustrates how a single technology, when transmitted across cultures, can reshape intellectual life on a global scale.

19. According to the passage, all of the following are true about papermaking EXCEPT:
    - Ⓐ It was introduced to the Islamic world in the eighth century.
    - Ⓑ It replaced parchment as the primary writing material.
    - Ⓒ It was first developed in Europe during the twelfth century.
    - Ⓓ It supported the growth of libraries and scholarship.

20. What can be inferred about the historical impact of papermaking?
    - Ⓐ It played a pivotal role in expanding access to knowledge across cultures.
    - Ⓑ Its primary effect was to support administrative growth beyond its place of origin.
    - Ⓒ It contributed to later innovations but was not the main driving force.
    - Ⓓ It offered limited benefits and did not shape intellectual life broadly.

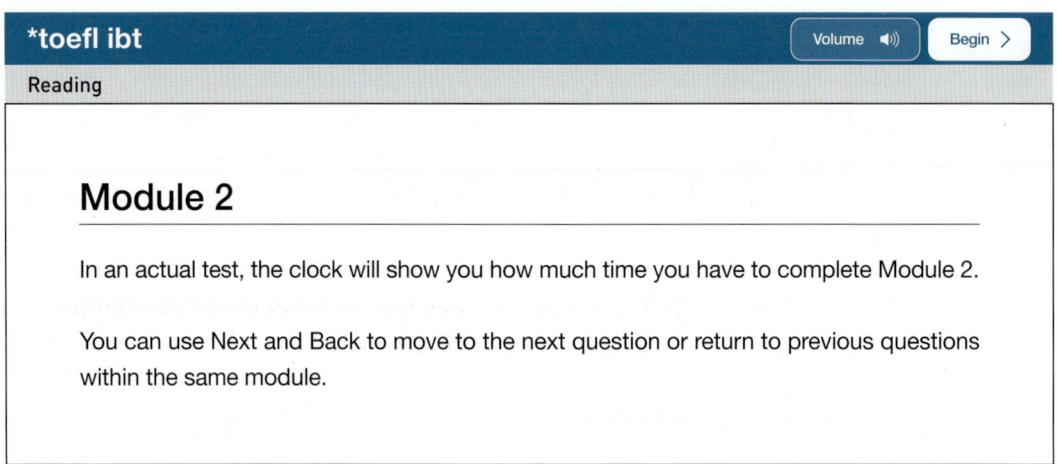

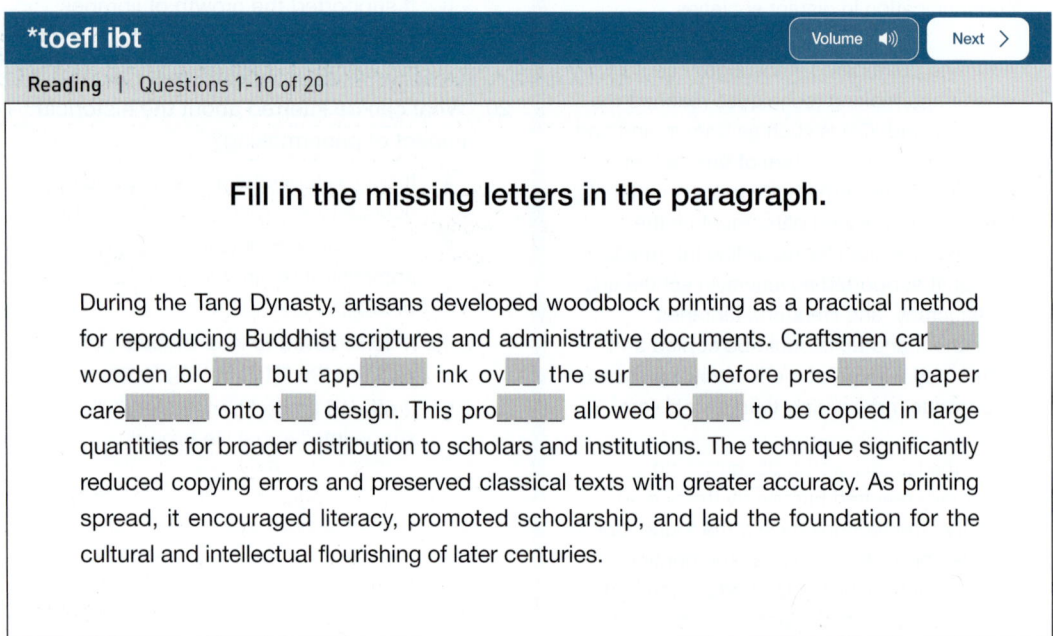

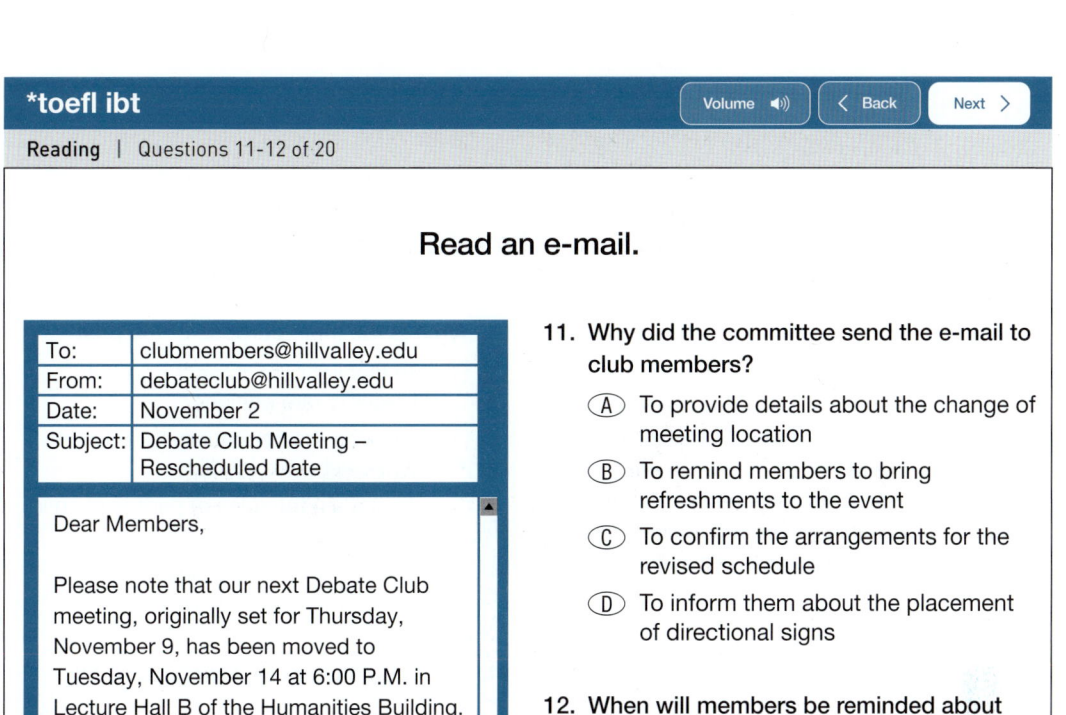

Read a social media post.

City Library

Looking for your next great read? Join us at the annual Autumn Book Fair, where shelves overflow with both timeless classics and exciting new releases. Independent publishers will showcase rare editions and debut works, offering chances to discover new authors.

Beyond books, the fair features lively storytelling sessions, craft corners for children, and a reading lounge where visitors can relax. Local cafés will provide complimentary samples of seasonal drinks, filling the air with the scent of spiced tea and roasted coffee.

This event has grown into a cherished community tradition, drawing readers of every age. More than just a marketplace, it celebrates imagination and shared stories. Don't miss the chance to explore, connect, and leave with inspiration for your next reading journey.

👍 Like   💬 Comment

13. What is the main purpose of the post?
    - Ⓐ To highlight the library's efforts to preserve rare editions
    - Ⓑ To invite the community to an event that celebrates reading
    - Ⓒ To explain the rules of participation in library programs
    - Ⓓ To encourage donations for the library's annual fundraiser

14. What unique feature distinguishes the fair?
    - Ⓐ Guests can listen to authors present their own debut works.
    - Ⓑ Visitors can sample seasonal drinks from nearby cafés.
    - Ⓒ Children are given complimentary books from the library.
    - Ⓓ Readers can participate in novel-writing contests.

15. What can be inferred about the Autumn Book Fair?
    - Ⓐ It is described as a specialized event for book collectors.
    - Ⓑ It is seen mainly as a commercial event for publishers.
    - Ⓒ It functions primarily as entertainment for children.
    - Ⓓ It serves as a cultural gathering, not merely a marketplace.

Social Bonds in Urban Life

Urbanization, the movement of populations from rural to urban areas, has been a defining feature of modern society. Cities often provide greater access to education, employment, and healthcare, which attracts people seeking opportunity. Yet rapid urban growth can also produce social challenges, such as overcrowding and weakened community ties. While villages typically maintain close-knit relationships, city life is often characterized by anonymity and reduced interaction among neighbors.

Nevertheless, urban areas also create new forms of connection. Public spaces such as parks, libraries, and marketplaces can foster interaction among diverse groups. Moreover, technological advances have allowed city residents to form digital communities that transcend physical boundaries. These social networks can strengthen solidarity, encourage cultural exchange, and provide platforms for civic engagement. However, the benefits of such connections are not equally distributed, as marginalized groups may still face barriers to participation.

Researchers studying urbanization argue that the relationship between population density and social bonds is complex. While cities may weaken traditional ties, they simultaneously generate opportunities for new affiliations. Understanding how urban environments shape human networks is critical for policymakers seeking to balance growth with social cohesion. By designing inclusive spaces and promoting equal access to resources, cities can cultivate both diversity and unity within their populations.

16. Which of the following best states a main idea of the passage?
    - Ⓐ The challenges of rural communities in maintaining social ties
    - Ⓑ The influence of urbanization on social networks
    - Ⓒ The role of digital technology in replacing face-to-face interaction
    - Ⓓ The economic benefits of living in large metropolitan areas

17. The word "solidarity" in paragraph 2 is closest in meaning to
    - Ⓐ independence
    - Ⓑ conflict
    - Ⓒ cooperation
    - Ⓓ autonomy

18. Why does the author mention public spaces such as parks and marketplaces?
    - Ⓐ To show how cities can create opportunities for interaction
    - Ⓑ To explain why rural areas maintain stronger family ties
    - Ⓒ To argue that physical environments discourage social participation
    - Ⓓ To provide evidence that urbanization reduces community engagement

Social Bonds in Urban Life

Urbanization, the movement of populations from rural to urban areas, has been a defining feature of modern society. Cities often provide greater access to education, employment, and healthcare, which attracts people seeking opportunity. Yet rapid urban growth can also produce social challenges, such as overcrowding and weakened community ties. While villages typically maintain close-knit relationships, city life is often characterized by anonymity and reduced interaction among neighbors.

Nevertheless, urban areas also create new forms of connection. Public spaces such as parks, libraries, and marketplaces can foster interaction among diverse groups. Moreover, technological advances have allowed city residents to form digital communities that transcend physical boundaries. These social networks can strengthen solidarity, encourage cultural exchange, and provide platforms for civic engagement. However, the benefits of such connections are not equally distributed, as marginalized groups may still face barriers to participation.

Researchers studying urbanization argue that the relationship between population density and social bonds is complex. While cities may weaken traditional ties, they simultaneously generate opportunities for new affiliations. Understanding how urban environments shape human networks is critical for policymakers seeking to balance growth with social cohesion. By designing inclusive spaces and promoting equal access to resources, cities can cultivate both diversity and unity within their populations.

19. What is the relationship between paragraphs 2 and 3?
    - Ⓐ Paragraph 3 provides additional examples supporting claims in paragraph 2.
    - Ⓑ Paragraph 3 introduces ideas that contradict the points made in paragraph 2.
    - Ⓒ Paragraph 3 explains the consequences of the issues introduced in paragraph 2.
    - Ⓓ Paragraph 3 suggests possible solutions to the problems described in paragraph 2.

20. What does the passage suggest about building stronger social networks in cities?
    - Ⓐ It requires creating inclusive spaces and equal access to resources.
    - Ⓑ It depends mainly on replacing public spaces with digital platforms.
    - Ⓒ It can be achieved by increasing population density in all areas.
    - Ⓓ It is only possible when traditional ties are completely preserved.

Listening Section

In the listening section, you will answer 30–40 questions to demonstrate how well you understand spoken English. There are three types of tasks.

Type of Task	Description
Listen and Choose a Response	Select the best response to the question or statement.
Conversations	Answer questions about short conversations.
Announcement and Academic Talks	Answer questions about announcements and academic talks.

You WILL NOT be able to return to previous questions.

Module 1

In an actual test, the clock will show you how much time you have to complete each question.

You can use Next to move to the next question.

You WILL NOT be able to return to previous questions.

Choose the best response.

1.
 Ⓐ I missed it.
 Ⓑ Yes, I would.
 Ⓒ After the lecture.
 Ⓓ It's a talk.

2.
 Ⓐ The library login desk.
 Ⓑ No, you don't.
 Ⓒ It's printed on the router.
 Ⓓ Tomorrow morning online.

3.
 Ⓐ At the main gate information desk.
 Ⓑ By next Monday, if possible.
 Ⓒ The International Programs Office does.
 Ⓓ I handle those requests.

4.
 Ⓐ As long as captions are enabled.
 Ⓑ The colloquium is at Hall C.
 Ⓒ I moved last month's session already.
 Ⓓ Why don't you check with the chair first?

Choose the best response.

5.
- Ⓐ I can sign right after lunch.
- Ⓑ The panel starts at three o'clock.
- Ⓒ Please send a printed final version.
- Ⓓ It's already in the queue.

6.
- Ⓐ They're on Building C's second floor.
- Ⓑ Do you mean the library or the dorms?
- Ⓒ Yes, they get cleaned regularly.
- Ⓓ After closing, around midnight.

7.
- Ⓐ By tomorrow afternoon would be better.
- Ⓑ The review guidelines are on the portal.
- Ⓒ Your outline might need more sources.
- Ⓓ I can carve out twenty minutes at ten.

8.
- Ⓐ Tours are exempt.
- Ⓑ In the main lab, Room 310.
- Ⓒ Eye protection is mandatory at all times.
- Ⓓ The stockroom sells lab-approved footwear.

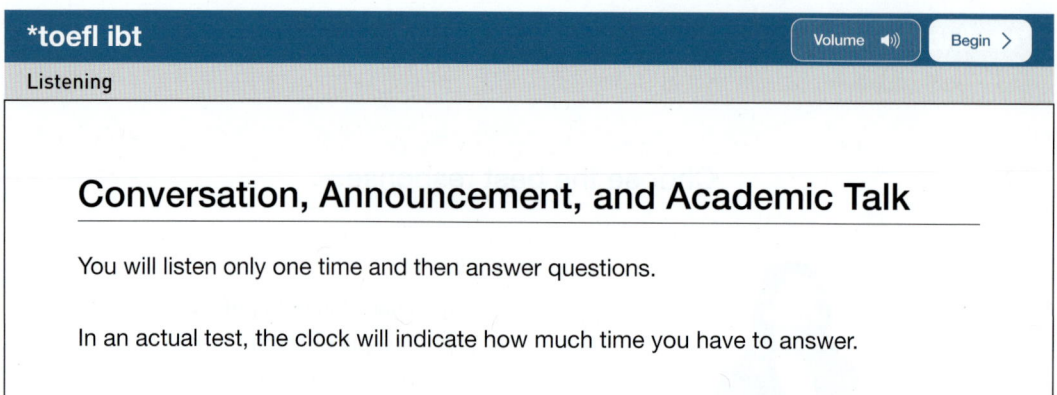

Conversation, Announcement, and Academic Talk

You will listen only one time and then answer questions.

In an actual test, the clock will indicate how much time you have to answer.

Listen to a conversation.

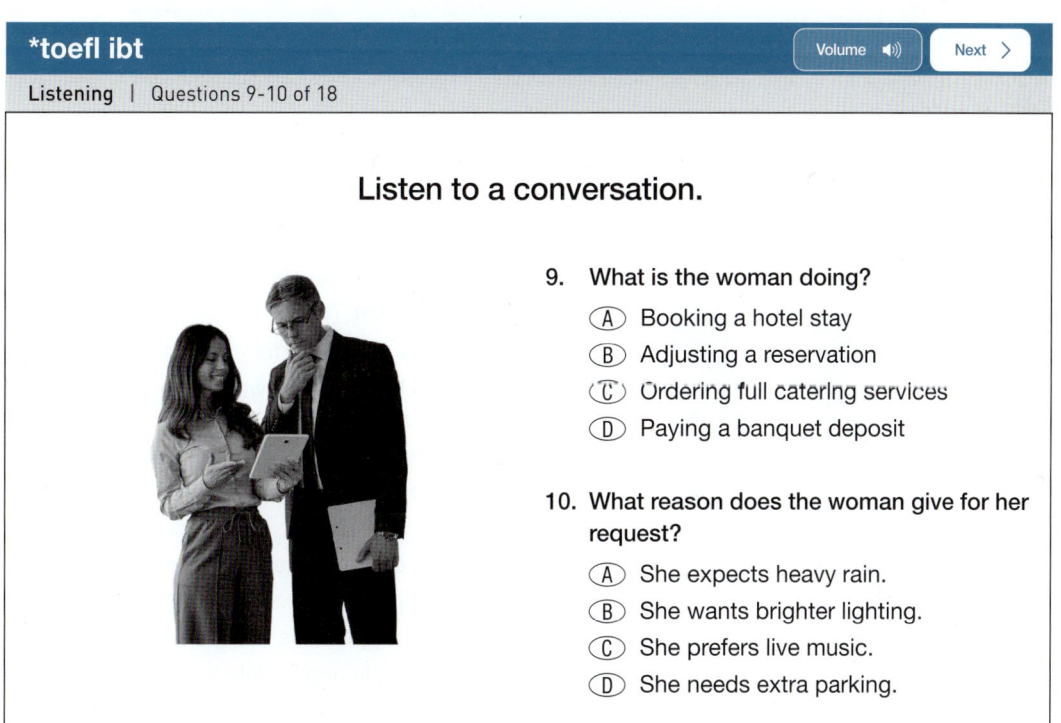

9. What is the woman doing?
   - Ⓐ Booking a hotel stay
   - Ⓑ Adjusting a reservation
   - Ⓒ Ordering full catering services
   - Ⓓ Paying a banquet deposit

10. What reason does the woman give for her request?
    - Ⓐ She expects heavy rain.
    - Ⓑ She wants brighter lighting.
    - Ⓒ She prefers live music.
    - Ⓓ She needs extra parking.

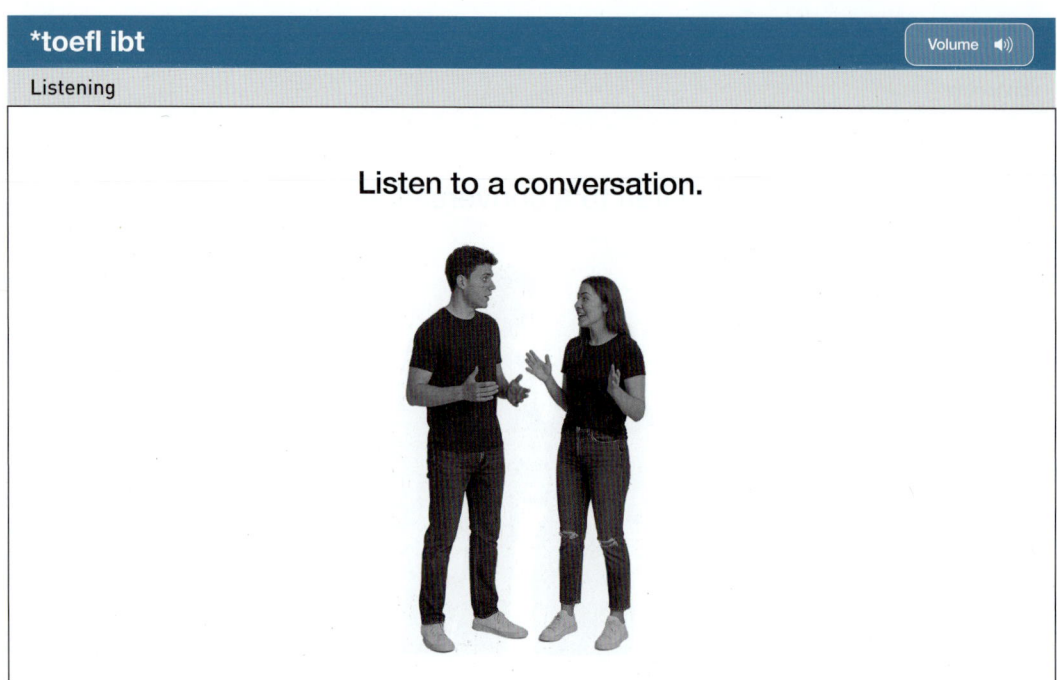

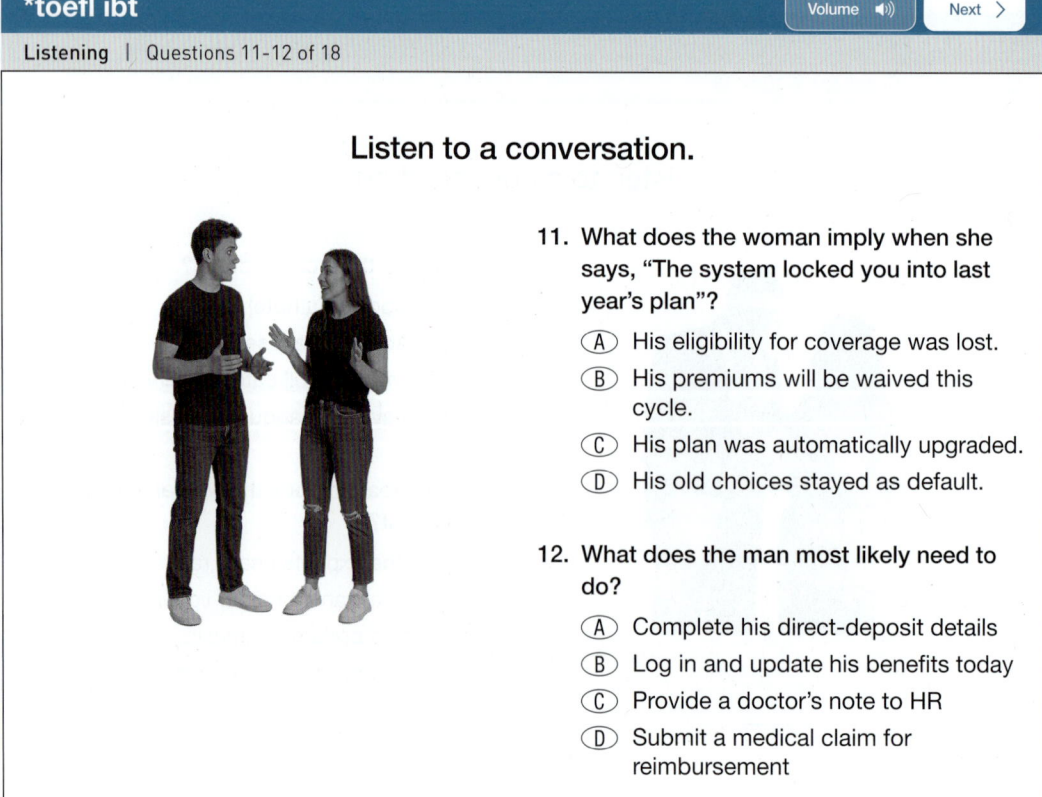

Listen to a conversation.

11. What does the woman imply when she says, "The system locked you into last year's plan"?
    - Ⓐ His eligibility for coverage was lost.
    - Ⓑ His premiums will be waived this cycle.
    - Ⓒ His plan was automatically upgraded.
    - Ⓓ His old choices stayed as default.

12. What does the man most likely need to do?
    - Ⓐ Complete his direct-deposit details
    - Ⓑ Log in and update his benefits today
    - Ⓒ Provide a doctor's note to HR
    - Ⓓ Submit a medical claim for reimbursement

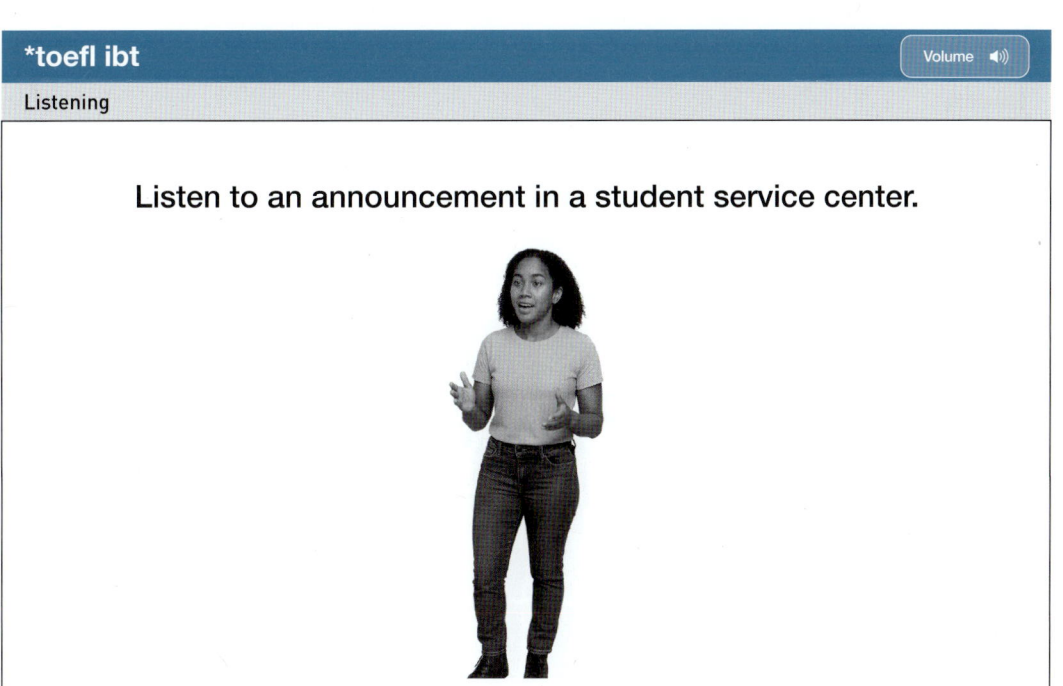

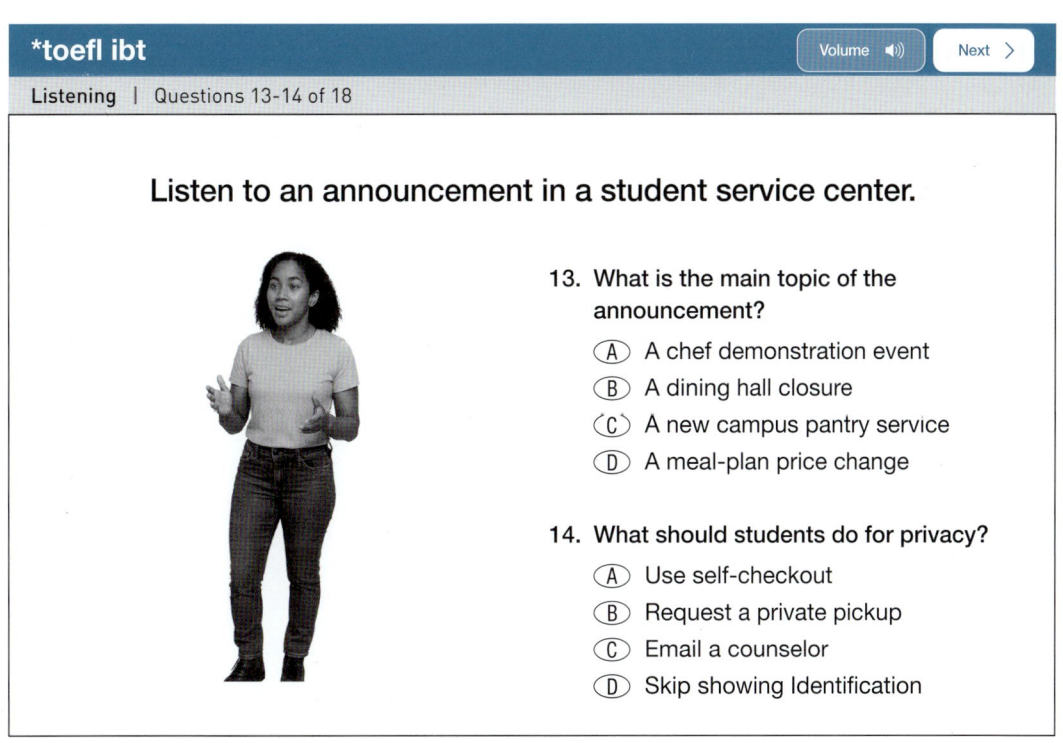

Listen to an announcement in a student service center.

13. What is the main topic of the announcement?
    - Ⓐ A chef demonstration event
    - Ⓑ A dining hall closure
    - Ⓒ A new campus pantry service
    - Ⓓ A meal-plan price change

14. What should students do for privacy?
    - Ⓐ Use self-checkout
    - Ⓑ Request a private pickup
    - Ⓒ Email a counselor
    - Ⓓ Skip showing Identification

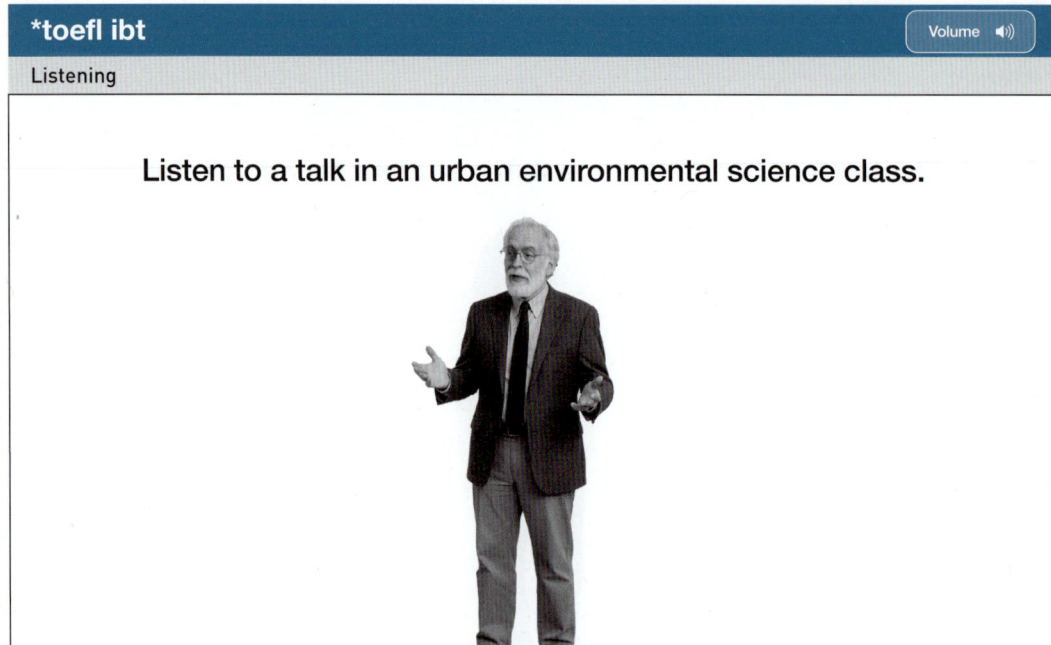

Listening | Questions 15-18 of 18

Listen to a talk in an urban environmental science class.

15. What is the lecture mainly about?
    - (A) Why urban areas heat up, with ways to cool them
    - (B) Government aid for household energy bills in large cities
    - (C) The chemistry of ozone during summer smog events
    - (D) Old methods for paving roads in the twentieth century

16. According to the lecture, how do high-albedo surfaces help?
    - (A) By storing heat for slow release after sunset
    - (B) By increasing nighttime wind between tall buildings
    - (C) By reflecting sunlight and lowering surface temperatures
    - (D) By absorbing moisture and promoting evaporation downtown

17. What does the professor imply about mitigation choices?
    - (A) One uniform solution works best for city budgets.
    - (B) Trade-offs require tailored mixes for each context.
    - (C) Reflective coatings are unsuitable due to glare.
    - (D) Trees are less effective than resurfacing projects.

18. What will the professor most likely discuss next?
    - (A) Rules for rooftop maintenance crews in cities
    - (B) Wildlife impacts of rural heat waves in drought
    - (C) Marketing strategies for reflective-coating companies
    - (D) How albedo compares with emissivity in case studies

Module 2

In an actual test, the clock will show you how much time you have to complete each question.

You can use Next to move to the next question.

You WILL NOT be able to return to previous questions.

Choose the best response.

1.
Ⓐ No, it's in Room 210.
Ⓑ Yes, they probably are.
Ⓒ Tomorrow.
Ⓓ The syllabus.

2.
Ⓐ The microphone is kept in the storage room.
Ⓑ It's near the podium in Hall A.
Ⓒ I'll ask IT to swap it before class.
Ⓓ Why don't you write the notes instead?

3.
Ⓐ Only if management agrees to it.
Ⓑ It's scheduled for the lobby anyway.
Ⓒ I moved last week's booth already.
Ⓓ That area gets crowded in the afternoon.

4.
Ⓐ The summary was uploaded last semester.
Ⓑ Which format do you need?
Ⓒ The charts are missing from it.
Ⓓ It's due by Friday.

Choose the best response.

5.
- Ⓐ The gym has brand-new treadmills.
- Ⓑ Membership cards were reissued last month.
- Ⓒ No, it reopens next Monday.
- Ⓓ The library hours changed recently.

6.
- Ⓐ Yes, but that's for the draft version.
- Ⓑ The registrar closes their office at five.
- Ⓒ Not unless you get an extension.
- Ⓓ The evaluation criteria are posted online.

7.
- Ⓐ In the main lab.
- Ⓑ Finance would know.
- Ⓒ Yes, I do.
- Ⓓ By next Monday, please.

8.
- Ⓐ It's usually held in Room 3 for practice.
- Ⓑ The syllabus only lists the lecture topics.
- Ⓒ The midterm for this course is scheduled next Monday.
- Ⓓ That's only required for Biology majors this year.

Listen to a conversation.

Listen to a conversation.

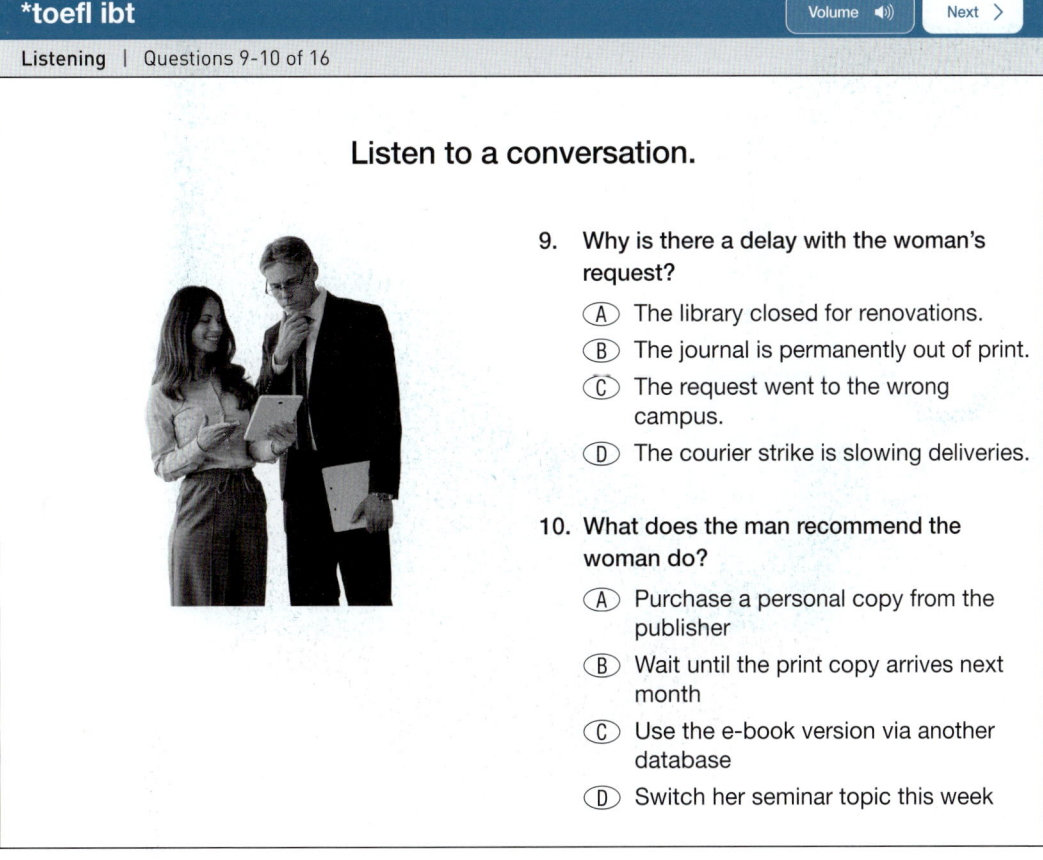

9. Why is there a delay with the woman's request?
   - Ⓐ The library closed for renovations.
   - Ⓑ The journal is permanently out of print.
   - Ⓒ The request went to the wrong campus.
   - Ⓓ The courier strike is slowing deliveries.

10. What does the man recommend the woman do?
    - Ⓐ Purchase a personal copy from the publisher
    - Ⓑ Wait until the print copy arrives next month
    - Ⓒ Use the e-book version via another database
    - Ⓓ Switch her seminar topic this week

Listen to an announcement in a computer lab.

Listen to an announcement in a computer lab.

11. What is the announcement about?
    A. A new photo course
    B. A mobile printing update
    C. A scanner replacement
    D. A fee increase notice

12. Why does the speaker mention "twenty-five megabytes"?
    A. He is warning that toner issues can corrupt large documents.
    B. He is claiming the uploader cannot accept PDFs.
    C. He is saying that students must use USB drives for big files.
    D. He is explaining that larger attachments may fail to send.

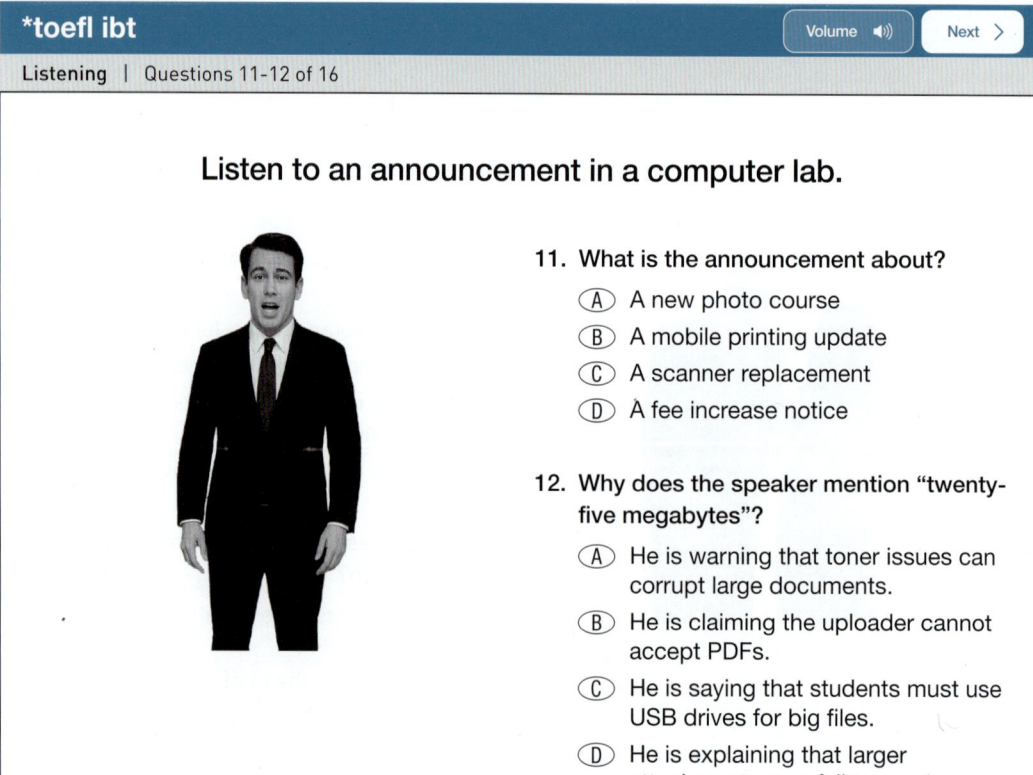

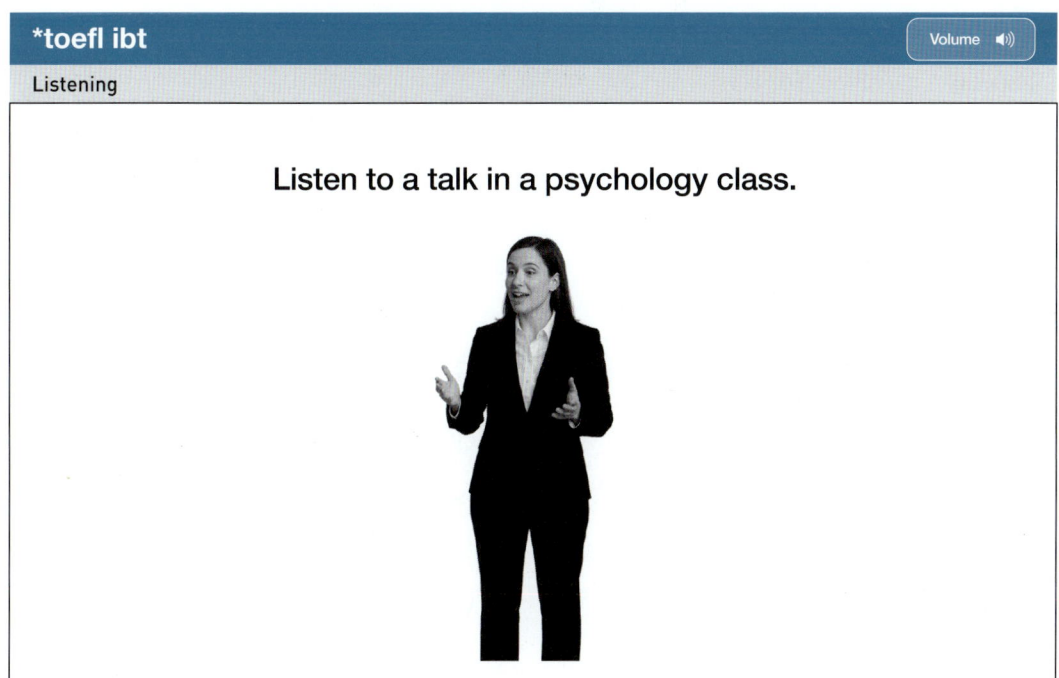

Listen to a talk in a psychology class.

13. What is the topic of the talk?
    - Ⓐ Effects of multitasking on efficiency and accuracy
    - Ⓑ The limited impact of study interruptions on performance
    - Ⓒ Negative effects of short breaks on long-term recall
    - Ⓓ The perceived ease of complex assignments in college courses

14. Why does the professor mention students who check messages while reading?
    - Ⓐ To claim that new brain scans are necessary for proof
    - Ⓑ To encourage students to text during planned study breaks
    - Ⓒ To exemplify how multitasking harms memory
    - Ⓓ To assert that learners enjoy juggling multiple tasks while studying

15. What does the professor imply about brief pauses?
    - Ⓐ Useful when kept separate from other tasks
    - Ⓑ Always damaging to concentration and recall
    - Ⓒ Preferable to single-task study sessions
    - Ⓓ Effective only with expensive equipment

16. What does the speaker say about the next class?
    - Ⓐ It will examine impacts of multitasking on industrial safety.
    - Ⓑ It will cover methods for strengthening attention control.
    - Ⓒ It will explain how laboratory memory tests are designed.
    - Ⓓ It will propose policies to remove digital devices from classrooms.

Writing Section

In the writing section, you will answer 12 questions to demonstrate how well you can write in English. There are three types of tasks.

Type of Task	Description
Build a Sentence	Create a grammatical sentence.
Write an Email	Write an email using information provided.
Write for an Academic Discussion	Participate in an online discussion.

Build a Sentence

Move the words in the boxes to create grammatical sentences.

A clock will show you how much time you have to complete this task.

Make an appropriate sentence.

1. What was most helpful during your research?

   I _____ _____ _____ _____ _____ _____.

   because   quickly   guided me   the librarian   learned

2. Students need to see the final exam schedule.

   _____ _____ _____ _____ _____ _____ _____.

   they log   when   can check   in   they   why   it

3. I'm applying for an internship next month.

   _____ _____ _____ _____ _____ _____ _____.

   need   if   reference letter   tell me   a   you

4. Please find out about the workshop.

   _____ _____ _____ _____ _____.

   once   the details   are posted   I'll   register

5. Why did the team postpone the presentation?

   _____ _____ _____ _____ _____.

   the projector   delayed it   broke   they   because

Make an appropriate sentence.

6.  I missed the deadline by one day.

    _____ _____ _____ _____ _____.

   submit it   though   you can   it's late   still

7. We're booking rooms for the conference.

   _____ _____ _____ _____ _____.

   since   our   Cedar Hall   it has   choose   more space

8. How will the lab handle late samples?

   _____ _____ _____ _____ _____ _____.

   until   processing   tomorrow   begins   store them   they'll

9. The coordinator had a question about the form.

   _____ _____ _____ _____ _____ _____?

   was unclear   she   because   something   ask   did

10. I was unsure about the application steps.

    _____ _____ _____ _____ _____ _____.

    the checklist   if   you   succeed   follow   you'll

*toefl ibt
Writing

Write an Email

You will read some information and use the information to write an email.

You will have 7 minutes to write the email.

---

*toefl ibt
Writing | Question 11 of 12

This morning, you emailed a report to your client and then discovered the attachment was the wrong version. The file they received does not include revisions discussed with their team, and a review meeting is scheduled soon. You need to correct the mistake quickly and keep the timeline on track.

Write an email to the client. In your email, do the following.

- Apologize for sending the wrong attachment.
- Provide the correct file with key updates.
- Ask for receipt confirmation and next steps.

Write as much as you can and in complete sentences.

Your Response:

To: client@northbridgeconsulting.com
Subject: Corrected Report Attachment

Write for an Academic Discussion

A professor has posted a question about a topic and students have responded with their thoughts and ideas. Make a contribution to the discussion.

You will have 10 minutes to write.

Writing | Question 12 of 12

Your professor is teaching a class on environmental studies. Write a post responding to the professor's question.

In your response, you should do the following.

- Express and support your opinion.
- Make a contribution to the discussion in your own words.

An effective response will contain at least 100 words.

Professor:

Many cities are facing serious air pollution problems caused by traffic, industry, and population growth. Some governments propose stricter regulations on car emissions and factory operations, while others prefer encouraging individuals to change their habits, such as using public transportation or reducing energy use at home. In your opinion, which approach is more effective in improving air quality: government regulation or individual action? Why?

Student A:

I believe government regulation is more effective. Without strong laws, companies and individuals often choose convenience over responsibility. Strict emission standards and enforcement can bring large-scale improvements that personal choices alone cannot achieve.

Student B:

I think individual action is more powerful. People can decide to walk, bike, or take buses immediately, while waiting for government rules takes time. If enough people change their habits, the community can see real progress quickly.

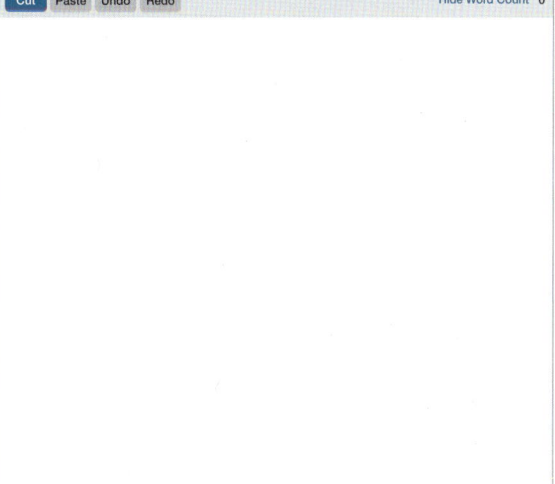

Speaking Section

In the speaking section, you will answer 11 questions to demonstrate how well you can speak English. There are two types of tasks.

Type of Task	Description
Listen and Repeat	Listen and repeat what you heard
Take an Interview	Answer questions from the interviewer

Listen and Repeat

You will listen as someone speaks to you. Listen carefully and then repeat what you have heard. The clock will indicate how much time you have to speak.

No time for preparation will be provided.

*toefl ibt
Speaking

You are training to guide visitors at a city aquarium.
Listen to the guide and repeat what she says.
Repeat only once.

*toefl ibt

Speaking | Questions 1-7 of 11

Listen and repeat only once.

1. RESPONSE TIME 00:00:08
2. RESPONSE TIME 00:00:08
3. RESPONSE TIME 00:00:10
4. RESPONSE TIME 00:00:10
5. RESPONSE TIME 00:00:10
6. RESPONSE TIME 00:00:12
7. RESPONSE TIME 00:00:12

Take an Interview

An interviewer will ask you questions. Answer the questions and be sure to say as much as you can in the time allowed.

No time for preparation will be provided.

You have volunteered for a research study about online learning. You will have a short online interview with a researcher. The researcher will ask you some questions.

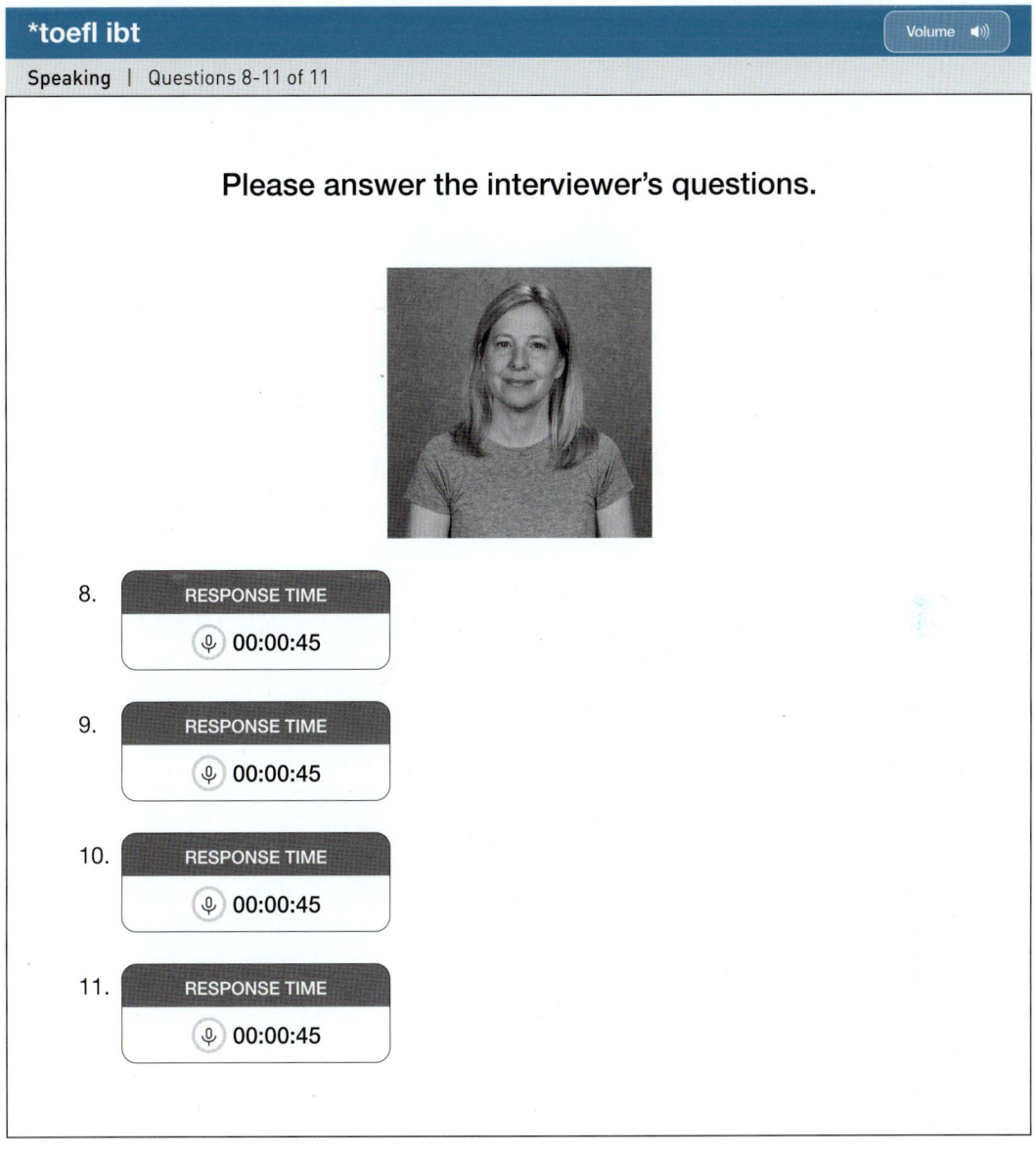

Actual Tests

Actual Test 3

Actual Test 3

Reading Section

In an actual test, you will answer 35—48 questions to demonstrate how well you understand academic and non-academic texts in English. There are three types of tasks.

Type of Task	Description
Complete the Words	Fill in the missing letters in a paragraph.
Read in Daily Life	Answer questions about everyday reading material.
Read an Academic Passage	Answer questions about academic passages.

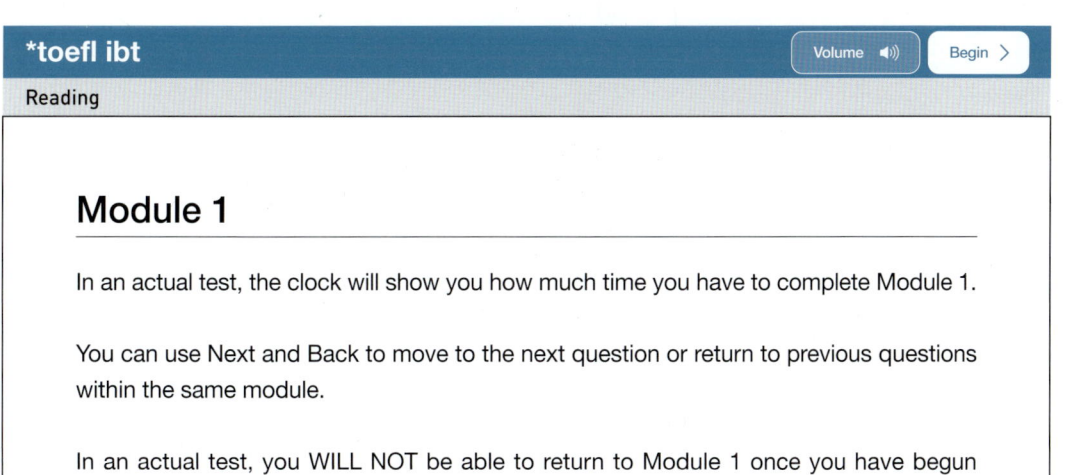

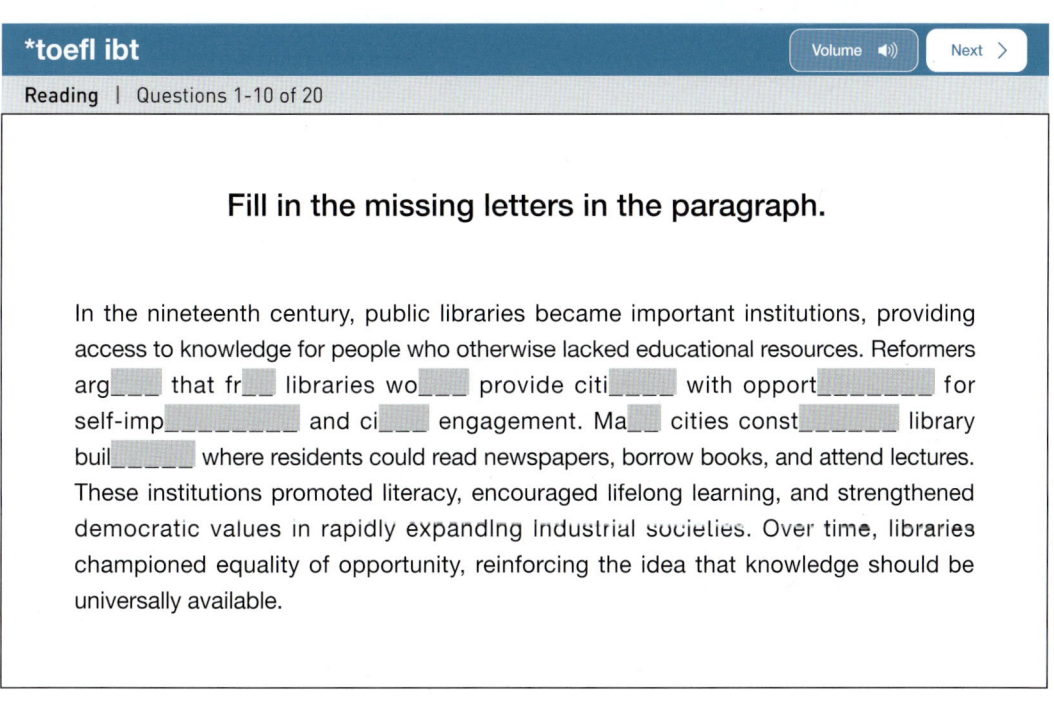

Fill in the missing letters in the paragraph.

In the nineteenth century, public libraries became important institutions, providing access to knowledge for people who otherwise lacked educational resources. Reformers arg____ that fr__ libraries wo____ provide citi____ with opport_____ for self-imp_____ and ci____ engagement. Ma__ cities const_____ library buil_____ where residents could read newspapers, borrow books, and attend lectures. These institutions promoted literacy, encouraged lifelong learning, and strengthened democratic values in rapidly expanding industrial societies. Over time, libraries championed equality of opportunity, reinforcing the idea that knowledge should be universally available.

Read a text message.

Riverside College Library

Effective immediately, we have revised our lending regulations. Overdue materials will now accrue a daily fine of $1, which will be charged directly to each borrower's account until the item is returned. In cases where an item is declared lost, both the replacement cost and an administrative fee will be imposed. Library access rights will be suspended automatically once unpaid fines exceed $10. Those with outstanding accounts are urged to monitor them closely to prevent service interruptions.

11. Who is the message primarily intended for?
    - Ⓐ Alumni with limited library access
    - Ⓑ Library staff responsible for enforcing fines
    - Ⓒ Students who borrow library materials
    - Ⓓ Community residents with guest borrowing cards

12. What will happen when fines remain unpaid beyond a certain amount?
    - Ⓐ Borrowing privileges will be revoked.
    - Ⓑ Fines will be automatically deducted from the account.
    - Ⓒ A final return deadline will be imposed on the account.
    - Ⓓ A decrease in borrowing limits will be recorded.

Read a social media post.

👤 Campus Sustainability Council

Did you know that over 40 percent of our campus waste could be recycled but often ends up in landfills? To address this, the Sustainability Council is launching a "Sort It Right" campaign. Specially marked bins for paper, plastics, and metals are now placed across the main academic buildings. Clear signage explains which items belong where, and volunteers are available during peak hours to guide proper disposal.

This effort reduces waste and fosters shared responsibility. Improper sorting increases costs for the university and undermines local recycling initiatives. By participating, students help conserve resources and demonstrate commitment to environmental stewardship. Join us in making small actions count toward a more sustainable campus community.

👍 Like   💬 Comment

13. What is the main purpose of the post?
   - Ⓐ To describe the university's budget for waste disposal
   - Ⓑ To encourage students to follow new recycling guidelines
   - Ⓒ To advertise volunteer opportunities in the student council
   - Ⓓ To compare landfill usage at different universities

14. What feature has been added to support the recycling campaign?
   - Ⓐ Additional storage rooms for discarded items
   - Ⓑ Trucks that collect waste every evening
   - Ⓒ A new office within the Sustainability Council
   - Ⓓ Clearly labeled bins located in campus buildings

15. What can be inferred about improper waste sorting?
   - Ⓐ It raises expenses for the institution.
   - Ⓑ It provides more jobs for student volunteers.
   - Ⓒ It eliminates the need for landfill space.
   - Ⓓ It strengthens recycling programs in the region.

The Invention of the Telegraph

Before the nineteenth century, long-distance communication was limited to the speed of messengers, ships, or postal services. This changed dramatically with the invention of the telegraph, a device that used electrical signals transmitted along wires to convey information almost instantly. In 1837, Samuel Morse developed a system that converted messages into a series of dots and dashes, later known as Morse code. The telegraph transformed communication from a slow, uncertain process into a rapid and reliable exchange of information.

The telegraph quickly found applications in commerce, journalism, and government. Businesses used it to coordinate shipments and prices across great distances. Newspapers could receive reports from distant locations within hours rather than weeks, and governments relied on it to send urgent military commands. In this way, the telegraph not only accelerated communication but also reshaped the flow of information, binding distant regions together in unprecedented ways.

Although the telegraph was eventually replaced by the telephone and later by wireless technologies, its influence remained profound. It established the first global communication networks, laying the foundation for later innovations. Historians argue that the telegraph's true legacy lies less in the device itself than in the idea it introduced: that information could travel faster than physical movement, forever altering human expectations about speed and connectivity.

16. Why does the author mention newspapers in the passage?
    - Ⓐ To compare the telegraph with the telephone and radio
    - Ⓑ To explain why military commands were often delayed
    - Ⓒ To emphasize the decline of postal services in the nineteenth century
    - Ⓓ To show how journalism was transformed by rapid communication

17. According to the passage, in which area was the telegraph especially important?
    - Ⓐ Religious rituals and ceremonies
    - Ⓑ Military coordination and decision-making
    - Ⓒ Agricultural techniques and farming tools
    - Ⓓ Artistic movements and cultural traditions

18. The word "profound" in the passage is closest in meaning to
    - Ⓐ deep
    - Ⓑ rare
    - Ⓒ careful
    - Ⓓ unusual

The Invention of the Telegraph

Before the nineteenth century, long-distance communication was limited to the speed of messengers, ships, or postal services. This changed dramatically with the invention of the telegraph, a device that used electrical signals transmitted along wires to convey information almost instantly. In 1837, Samuel Morse developed a system that converted messages into a series of dots and dashes, later known as Morse code. The telegraph transformed communication from a slow, uncertain process into a rapid and reliable exchange of information.

The telegraph quickly found applications in commerce, journalism, and government. Businesses used it to coordinate shipments and prices across great distances. Newspapers could receive reports from distant locations within hours rather than weeks, and governments relied on it to send urgent military commands. In this way, the telegraph not only accelerated communication but also reshaped the flow of information, binding distant regions together in unprecedented ways.

Although the telegraph was eventually replaced by the telephone and later by wireless technologies, its influence remained profound. It established the first global communication networks, laying the foundation for later innovations. Historians argue that the telegraph's true legacy lies less in the device itself than in the idea it introduced: that information could travel faster than physical movement, forever altering human expectations about speed and connectivity.

19. What is the relationship between paragraphs 2 and 3?
    - Ⓐ Paragraph 3 raises limitations of the uses described in paragraph 2.
    - Ⓑ Paragraph 3 discusses the long-term impact of the developments described in paragraph 2.
    - Ⓒ Paragraph 3 shifts the focus from practical uses to historical significance, extending ideas in paragraph 2.
    - Ⓓ Paragraph 3 presents additional areas of application beyond those mentioned in paragraph 2.

20. What does the passage suggest about the legacy of the telegraph?
    - Ⓐ It lies in creating faster physical transport routes for messages.
    - Ⓑ It was important mainly for its decorative and mechanical design.
    - Ⓒ It introduced the concept of instantaneous information transfer.
    - Ⓓ It ended the need for later communication technologies.

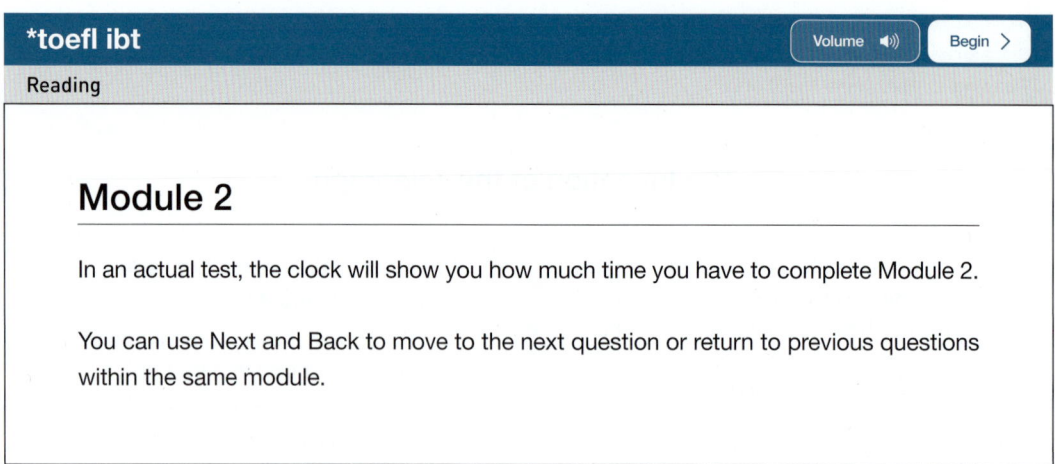

Module 2

In an actual test, the clock will show you how much time you have to complete Module 2.

You can use Next and Back to move to the next question or return to previous questions within the same module.

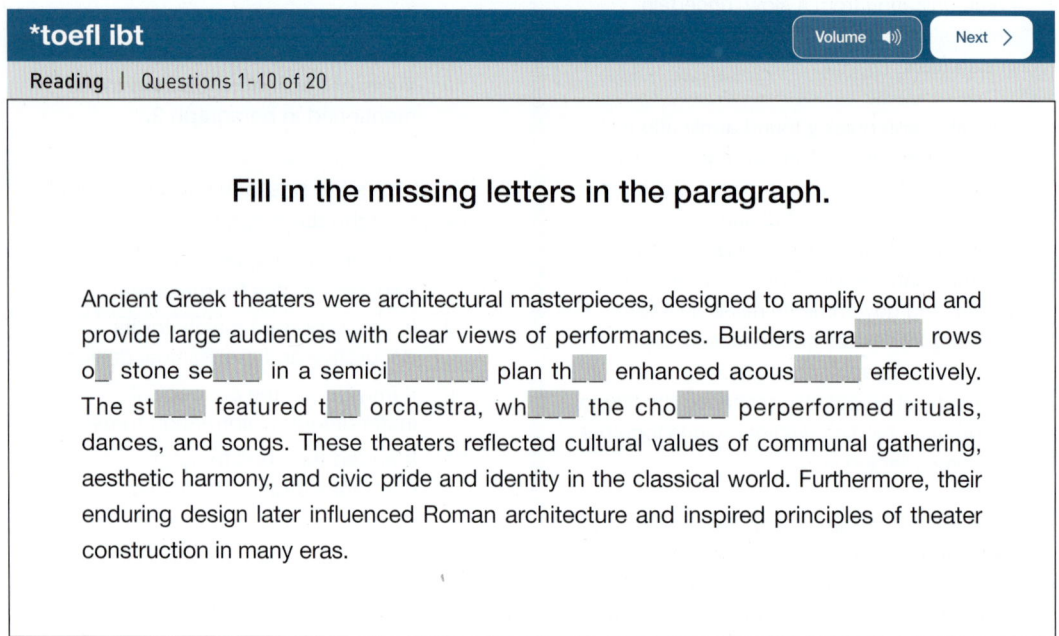

Fill in the missing letters in the paragraph.

Ancient Greek theaters were architectural masterpieces, designed to amplify sound and provide large audiences with clear views of performances. Builders arra_____ rows o_ stone se____ in a semici_____ plan th___ enhanced acous_____ effectively. The st____ featured t___ orchestra, wh_____ the cho____ perperformed rituals, dances, and songs. These theaters reflected cultural values of communal gathering, aesthetic harmony, and civic pride and identity in the classical world. Furthermore, their enduring design later influenced Roman architecture and inspired principles of theater construction in many eras.

Read a flyer.

Student Art Exhibition

Discover creativity on campus!
The Fine Arts Department invites you to view the annual Student Art Exhibition, now open in the Horizon Gallery on the second floor of the Arts Building. Works range from traditional oil paintings to experimental digital media, all produced by current undergraduates. Admission is free, and exhibition guides provide brief commentaries on selected pieces. This showcase highlights the diversity of student talent and celebrates the role of the arts in academic life.

11. Who is most likely to have created the works in the exhibition?
    A. Traditional artists trained on campus
    B. Students currently enrolled at the university
    C. Faculty members in the Fine Arts Department
    D. Amateur painters from the community

12. What is offered to visitors at the exhibition?
    A. Instructions on traditional painting methods
    B. Commentaries on artworks
    C. Discounts on digital media supplies
    D. Demonstrations of studio techniques

Read an e-mail.

To:	All Registered Undergraduates
From:	Campus IT Services
Subject:	Printing Quota Policy Update

As part of the university's cost-containment efforts and commitment to sustainability, IT Services has instituted a revised quota framework for student printing. Beginning this semester, each undergraduate is allocated 200 nontransferable credits, valid only for the current term and redeemable at any campus printer. Once these credits are exhausted, additional pages must be purchased at a rate of 5 cents per sheet, payable directly to the bursar's account.

Students with outstanding balances will be unable to release new print jobs until the debt is cleared. Instructions for tracking account activity and making electronic payments are available on the IT Services portal.

This measure is intended not merely to reduce waste but also to foster a more deliberate and responsible use of shared campus resources.

13. What is the main purpose of the message?
    Ⓐ To notify students of mandatory sustainability workshops
    Ⓑ To highlight electronic submission procedures for coursework
    Ⓒ To introduce a revised policy on student printing quotas
    Ⓓ To outline equipment upgrades in the computer labs

14. How can students clear their overdue printing balances?
    Ⓐ By settling the charge online using a payment platform
    Ⓑ By requesting additional print credits from their academic department
    Ⓒ By submitting previously used printouts to the library for review
    Ⓓ By arranging an in-person consultation with the bursar's office

15. What is indicated about the printing credits?
    Ⓐ They cannot be carried over into the following term.
    Ⓑ They may be exchanged for other campus services.
    Ⓒ They increase automatically if students take more courses.
    Ⓓ They apply only to graduate-level research printing.

Streaming's Impact on the Film Industry

In recent years, streaming platforms such as Netflix, Disney+, and Amazon Prime have transformed the way audiences consume films. Instead of traveling to theaters, viewers can now access a vast library of movies and television shows at home, often for a modest monthly fee. This convenience has reshaped viewing habits, allowing people to watch content on demand and across multiple devices.

For filmmakers, streaming platforms present both opportunities and challenges. On one hand, independent directors have gained new outlets for distributing their work to international audiences without relying on traditional studios. On the other hand, some critics argue that the prevalence of streaming services reduces the visibility of smaller films, since recommendation algorithms often promote popular titles. This tension illustrates how digital platforms can both democratize and limit artistic expression.

The rise of streaming has also raised questions about the future of theaters. While blockbusters may still draw crowds, many viewers prefer the comfort and affordability of home viewing. Industry analysts suggest that theaters may increasingly focus on large-scale releases and special events, while streaming platforms dominate everyday entertainment. This shift reflects a broader cultural change in how audiences value convenience, choice, and accessibility in the arts.

---

16. Which of the following best states a main idea of the passage?
    - Ⓐ Streaming platforms have reshaped viewing habits while also challenging traditional theaters.
    - Ⓑ Streaming platforms have changed how films are distributed and viewed.
    - Ⓒ Streaming platforms have provided new opportunities but also limitations for filmmakers.
    - Ⓓ Streaming platforms have made convenience and accessibility central to cultural consumption.

17. The word "prevalence" in paragraph 2 is closest in meaning to
    - Ⓐ frequency
    - Ⓑ limitation
    - Ⓒ strength
    - Ⓓ occurrence

18. According to the passage, all of the following are true about streaming platforms EXCEPT:
    - Ⓐ They allow people to watch films without leaving home.
    - Ⓑ They help independent directors reach international audiences.
    - Ⓒ They guarantee equal visibility for smaller films.
    - Ⓓ They often use algorithms to promote popular titles.

Streaming's Impact on the Film Industry

In recent years, streaming platforms such as Netflix, Disney+, and Amazon Prime have transformed the way audiences consume films. Instead of traveling to theaters, viewers can now access a vast library of movies and television shows at home, often for a modest monthly fee. This convenience has reshaped viewing habits, allowing people to watch content on demand and across multiple devices.

For filmmakers, streaming platforms present both opportunities and challenges. On one hand, independent directors have gained new outlets for distributing their work to international audiences without relying on traditional studios. On the other hand, some critics argue that the prevalence of streaming services reduces the visibility of smaller films, since recommendation algorithms often promote popular titles. This tension illustrates how digital platforms can both democratize and limit artistic expression.

The rise of streaming has also raised questions about the future of theaters. While blockbusters may still draw crowds, many viewers prefer the comfort and affordability of home viewing. Industry analysts suggest that theaters may increasingly focus on large-scale releases and special events, while streaming platforms dominate everyday entertainment. This shift reflects a broader cultural change in how audiences value convenience, choice, and accessibility in the arts.

19. What is the relationship between paragraphs 2 and 3?
    - Ⓐ Paragraph 3 emphasizes limitations that contrast with the opportunities noted in paragraph 2.
    - Ⓑ Paragraph 3 introduces examples that appear to challenge the arguments in paragraph 2.
    - Ⓒ Paragraph 3 shifts from specific applications to the cultural implications introduced in paragraph 2.
    - Ⓓ Paragraph 3 discusses broader industry effects following the issues described in paragraph 2.

20. What does the passage suggest about the future of theaters?
    - Ⓐ They will specialize in blockbuster films and limited-run showings.
    - Ⓑ They will dominate everyday entertainment instead of streaming platforms.
    - Ⓒ They will disappear entirely within the next decade.
    - Ⓓ They will replace streaming services as the most affordable option.

Listening Section

In the listening section, you will answer 30–40 questions to demonstrate how well you understand spoken English. There are three types of tasks.

Type of Task	Description
Listen and Choose a Response	Select the best response to the question or statement.
Conversations	Answer questions about short conversations.
Announcement and Academic Talks	Answer questions about announcements and academic talks.

You WILL NOT be able to return to previous questions.

Module 1

In an actual test, the clock will show you how much time you have to complete each question.

You can use Next to move to the next question.

You WILL NOT be able to return to previous questions.

Choose the best response.

1.
- Ⓐ Yes, it does.
- Ⓑ That's where it was last year.
- Ⓒ It's on Friday afternoon.
- Ⓓ Great, parking's tight near there.

2.
- Ⓐ They raised the fare last month.
- Ⓑ At the stop by the library.
- Ⓒ The transit desk opens at nine.
- Ⓓ About every twenty minutes or so.

3.
- Ⓐ It's card-only now.
- Ⓑ Try the south garage.
- Ⓒ Yes, it won't.
- Ⓓ After peak hours.

4.
- Ⓐ The gear is in Room 110.
- Ⓑ Yes, all of this equipment is needed for the training.
- Ⓒ A quiz replaced training this term.
- Ⓓ Ask the cashier about equipment rentals.

Choose the best response.

5.
- Ⓐ Deadline's posted.
- Ⓑ On the course site.
- Ⓒ That's not a bad idea.
- Ⓓ That's unfortunate.

6.
- Ⓐ Doors open at seven tomorrow.
- Ⓑ Just a rehearsal tonight.
- Ⓒ At the Black Box.
- Ⓓ Auditions were this morning.

7.
- Ⓐ It wraps up just before noon.
- Ⓑ By the main gate entrance.
- Ⓒ Ten dollars with student ID.
- Ⓓ The tour guide wouldn't know.

8.
- Ⓐ Where can I edit the page?
- Ⓑ The website went live today.
- Ⓒ I'd rather not.
- Ⓓ No, it's up to you.

*toefl ibt
Listening

Conversation, Announcement, and Academic Talk

You will listen only one time and then answer questions.

In an actual test, the clock will indicate how much time you have to answer.

Listening

Listen to a conversation.

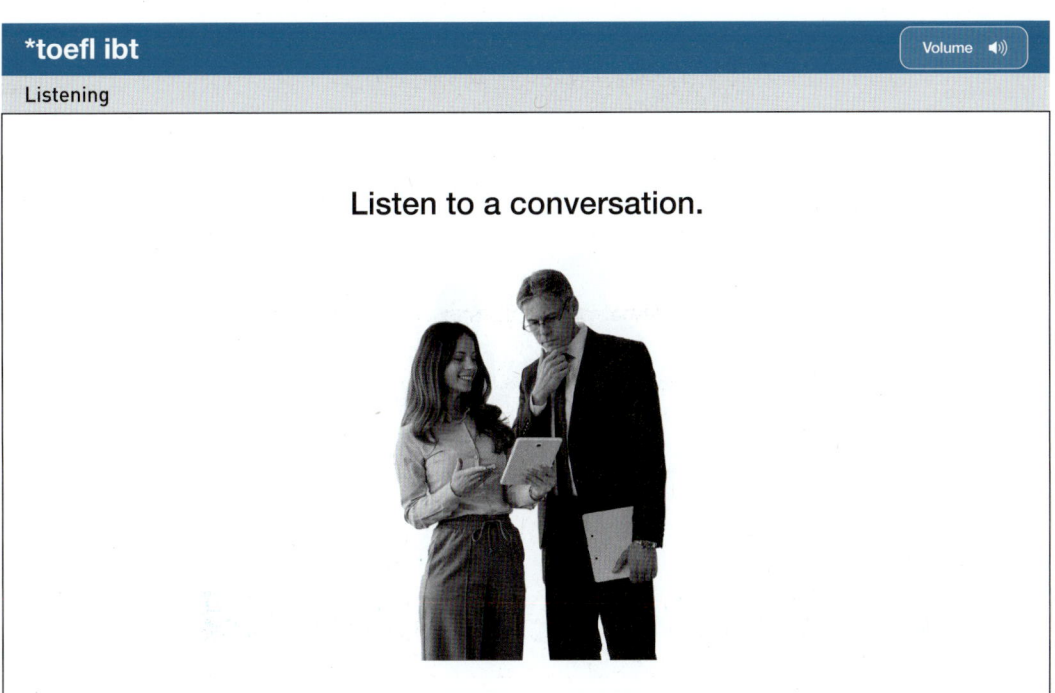

Listening | Questions 9-10 of 18

Listen to a conversation.

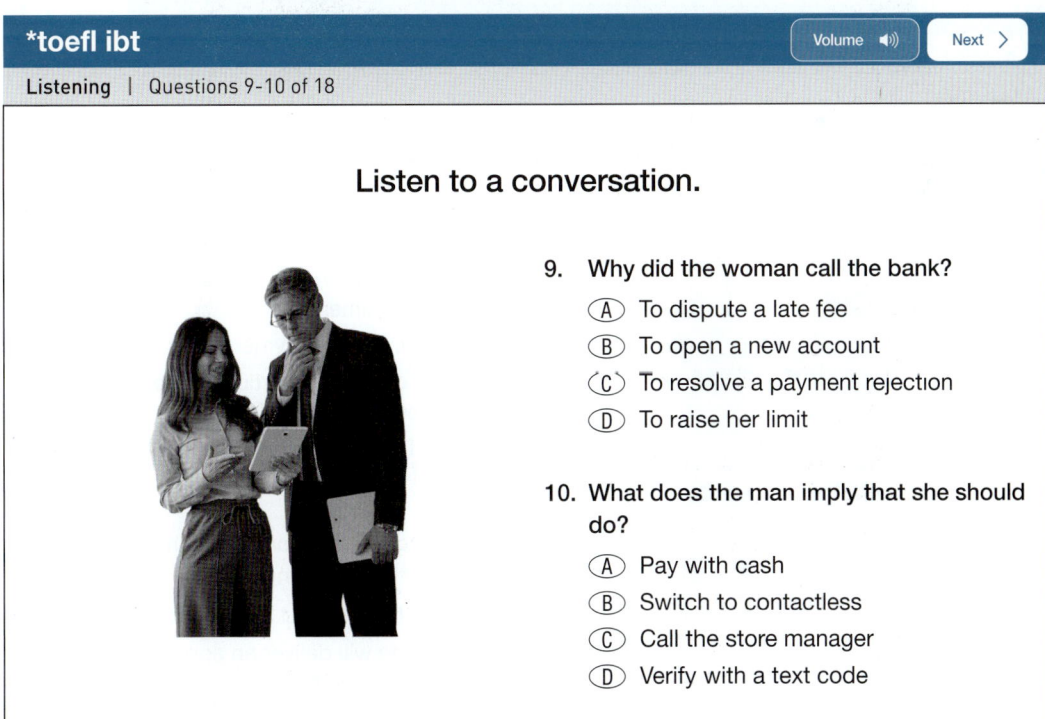

9. Why did the woman call the bank?
   - Ⓐ To dispute a late fee
   - Ⓑ To open a new account
   - Ⓒ To resolve a payment rejection
   - Ⓓ To raise her limit

10. What does the man imply that she should do?
    - Ⓐ Pay with cash
    - Ⓑ Switch to contactless
    - Ⓒ Call the store manager
    - Ⓓ Verify with a text code

Listen to a conversation.

Questions 11-12 of 18

Listen to a conversation.

11. What is the main purpose of the call?
    - Ⓐ To confirm the man's course enrollment
    - Ⓑ To collect payment for a workshop
    - Ⓒ To inform a participant about a session cancellation
    - Ⓓ To advertise an advanced certificate track

12. What does the woman mean when she says, "I'll push a notification tonight"?
    - Ⓐ She will send a paper notice by mail.
    - Ⓑ She will deliver an app alert to participants.
    - Ⓒ She will update the course syllabus automatically.
    - Ⓓ She will postpone the make-up until next week.

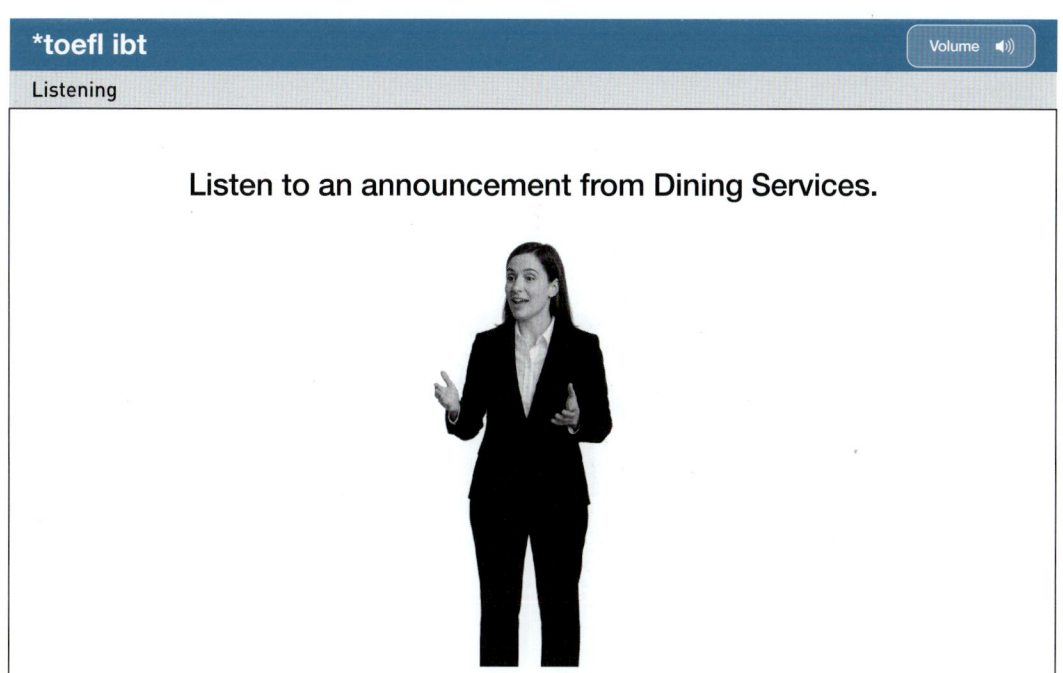

Listen to an announcement from Dining Services.

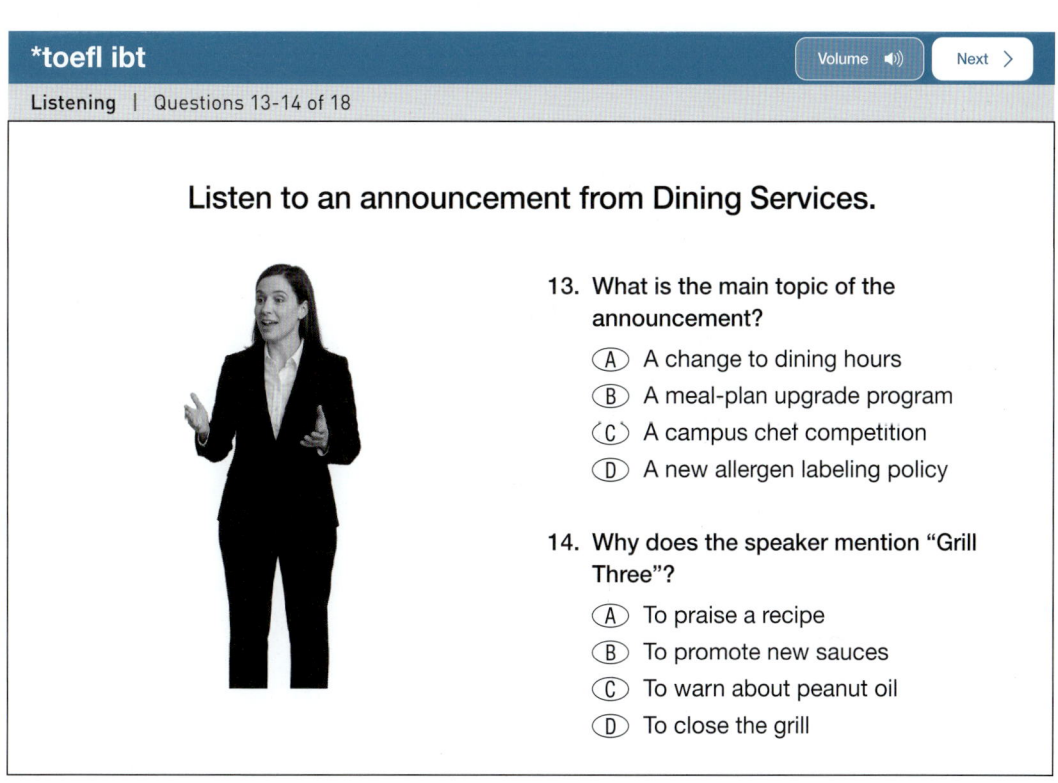

Listen to an announcement from Dining Services.

13. What is the main topic of the announcement?
    - A) A change to dining hours
    - B) A meal-plan upgrade program
    - C) A campus chef competition
    - D) A new allergen labeling policy

14. Why does the speaker mention "Grill Three"?
    - A) To praise a recipe
    - B) To promote new sauces
    - C) To warn about peanut oil
    - D) To close the grill

Listen to a talk in a history class.

15. What point does the professor mainly make?
    - Ⓐ Movable type disappeared soon after invention.
    - Ⓑ Hand copying was more accurate than machine typesetting.
    - Ⓒ Authorities largely prevented the spread of books.
    - Ⓓ The press transformed European society.

16. Why does the professor mention Martin Luther?
    - Ⓐ To prove that rulers opposed new media equally
    - Ⓑ To show how pamphlets carried religious ideas widely
    - Ⓒ To argue pamphlets were superior to bound volumes
    - Ⓓ To suggest Luther invented movable type

17. What does the professor imply about science in this period?
    - Ⓐ Data exchange stayed confined to monasteries.
    - Ⓑ Standardization declined after books spread.
    - Ⓒ Shared texts helped research communities grow.
    - Ⓓ Printed diagrams lost precision.

18. According to the professor, what will be discussed next?
    - Ⓐ Development of newspapers, then journals
    - Ⓑ Monastic methods for preserving manuscripts
    - Ⓒ Storage of ancient scrolls in libraries
    - Ⓓ Oral traditions replacing written media

Module 2

In an actual test, the clock will show you how much time you have to complete each question.

You can use Next to move to the next question.

You WILL NOT be able to return to previous questions.

Choose the best response.

1.

- Ⓐ By a narrow margin.
- Ⓑ Engineering did.
- Ⓒ The judges announced it.
- Ⓓ Today's winner.

2.

- Ⓐ Toggle airplane mode and reconnect.
- Ⓑ Building Services handles cleaning.
- Ⓒ Floor maps are posted by the elevator.
- Ⓓ Fire-drill notices go up on Mondays.

3.

- Ⓐ Four through six.
- Ⓑ Yes, but only chapter four.
- Ⓒ In the syllabus.
- Ⓓ The professor said it skips five.

4.

- Ⓐ That update was about the campus concert.
- Ⓑ The shuttle roster's posted at the union.
- Ⓒ It's been moved to Saturday instead.
- Ⓓ Registration remains open through tomorrow.

Choose the best response.

5.
- Ⓐ The room fits fifty.
- Ⓑ Advising does placement, not registration.
- Ⓒ The deadline is this Friday.
- Ⓓ The atrium kiosk shows maps.

6.
- Ⓐ The doors close at six–don't be late.
- Ⓑ Check-in opens at five-thirty, though.
- Ⓒ It's in the Grand Hall upstairs.
- Ⓓ They emailed the schedule this morning.

7.
- Ⓐ On weekdays only.
- Ⓑ Service still runs every ten minutes.
- Ⓒ Parking permit renewals.
- Ⓓ They're adding two new stops.

8.
- Ⓐ The bulletin covered last year's program.
- Ⓑ The sign-up link opens next month.
- Ⓒ That was for the orientation session.
- Ⓓ It was emailed to all students.

*toefl ibt
Listening

Listen to a conversation.

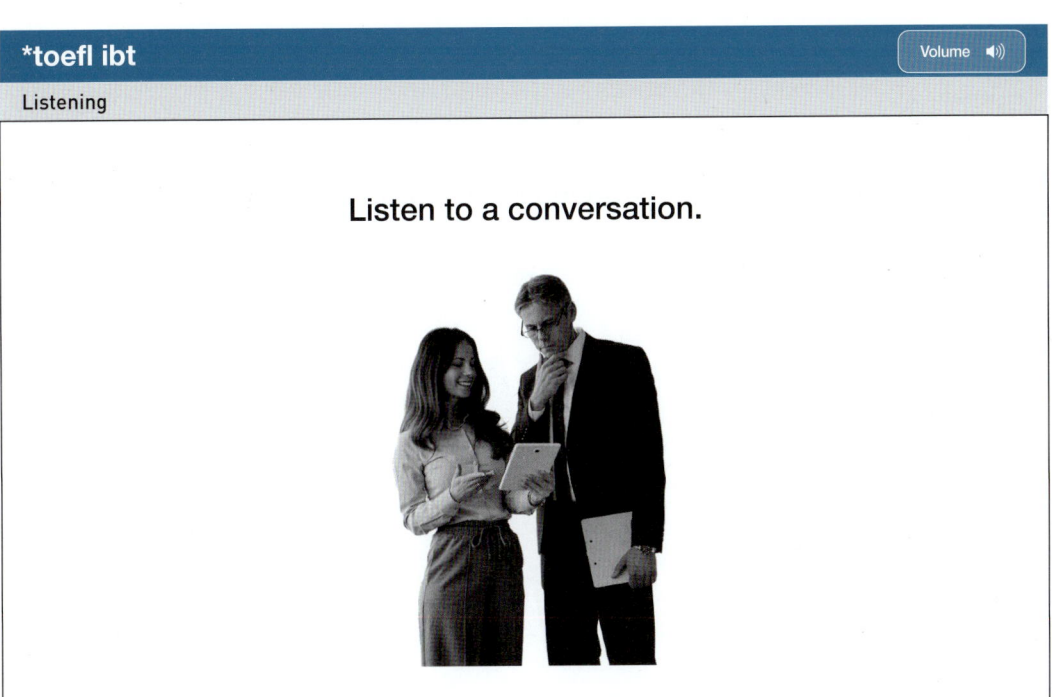

*toefl ibt
Listening | Questions 9-10 of 16

Listen to a conversation.

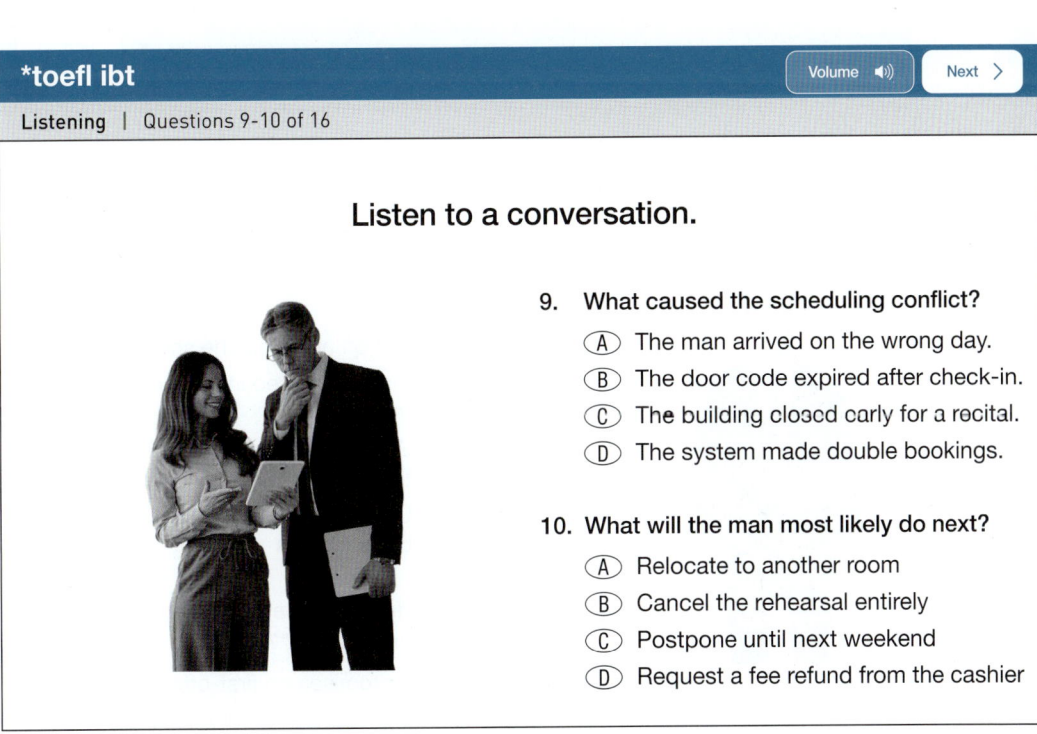

9. What caused the scheduling conflict?
   - (A) The man arrived on the wrong day.
   - (B) The door code expired after check-in.
   - (C) The building closed early for a recital.
   - (D) The system made double bookings.

10. What will the man most likely do next?
    - (A) Relocate to another room
    - (B) Cancel the rehearsal entirely
    - (C) Postpone until next weekend
    - (D) Request a fee refund from the cashier

Listen to an announcement from Campus Safety.

Listen to an announcement from Campus Safety.

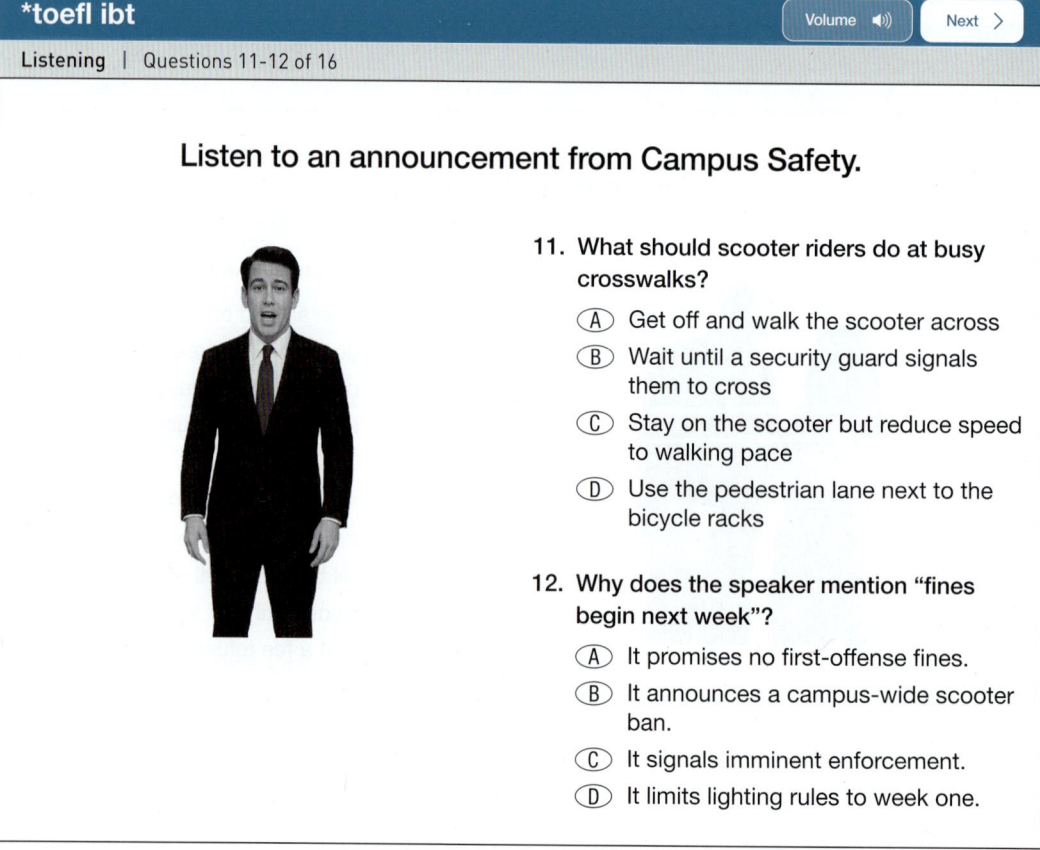

11. What should scooter riders do at busy crosswalks?
    - (A) Get off and walk the scooter across
    - (B) Wait until a security guard signals them to cross
    - (C) Stay on the scooter but reduce speed to walking pace
    - (D) Use the pedestrian lane next to the bicycle racks

12. Why does the speaker mention "fines begin next week"?
    - (A) It promises no first-offense fines.
    - (B) It announces a campus-wide scooter ban.
    - (C) It signals imminent enforcement.
    - (D) It limits lighting rules to week one.

*toefl ibt
Listening

Listen to a talk on a podcast about learning and study skills.

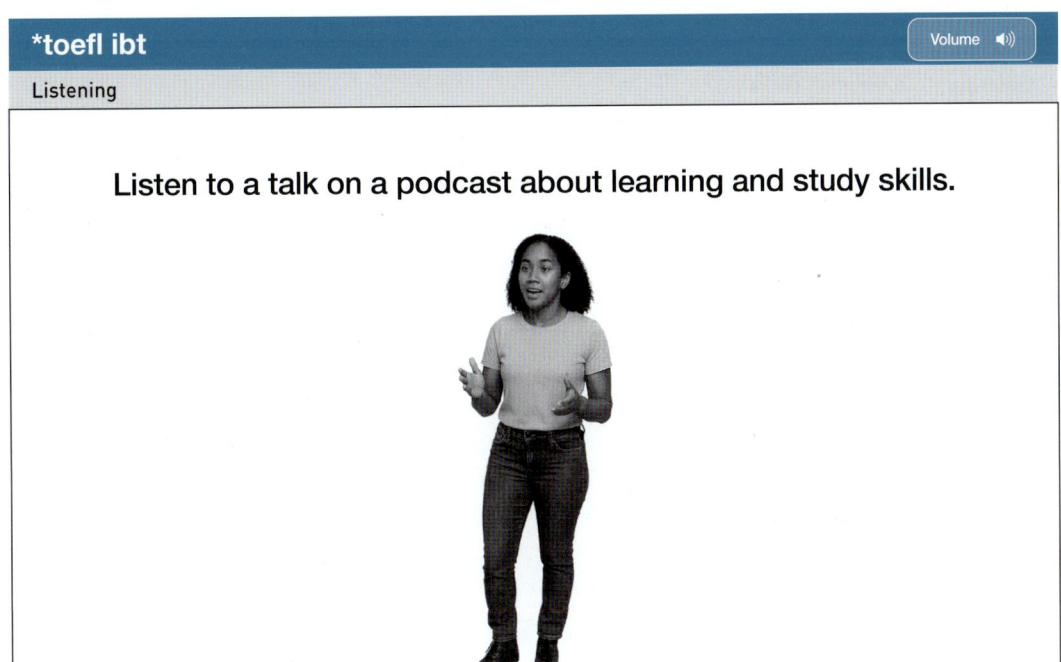

Listen to a talk on a podcast about learning and study skills.

13. What is the main topic of the talk?
    - Ⓐ Benefits of handwritten note-taking during college lectures
    - Ⓑ How note-taking methods shape understanding in college lectures
    - Ⓒ Whether laptop use influences the way notes are taken
    - Ⓓ Why students avoid writing by hand during lectures

14. What does the speaker say about typed notes?
    - Ⓐ Typed notes typically record more words, but prompt less thinking.
    - Ⓑ Typing reduces distraction for most students during long lectures.
    - Ⓒ Typing slows writing speed compared with paper notebooks.
    - Ⓓ Typed notes eliminate later review for exams in many cases.

15. Why does the speaker mention highlighting entire paragraphs?
    - Ⓐ To show a passive review habit that only feels productive
    - Ⓑ To encourage frequent highlighting for dense exam chapters
    - Ⓒ To contrast low-effort review with deeper generative processing
    - Ⓓ To argue that highlighters damage library books over time

16. According to the speaker, what can be inferred about laptop bans?
    - Ⓐ Blanket bans should replace device policies across all departments.
    - Ⓑ Such bans guarantee higher grades in nearly every course.
    - Ⓒ Bans are preferred by most students who take notes.
    - Ⓓ Blanket bans may be unnecessary with structured digital use.

Writing Section

In the writing section, you will answer 12 questions to demonstrate how well you can write in English. There are three types of tasks.

Type of Task	Description
Build a Sentence	Create a grammatical sentence.
Write an Email	Write an email using information provided.
Write for an Academic Discussion	Participate in an online discussion.

Build a Sentence

Move the words in the boxes to create grammatical sentences.

A clock will show you how much time you have to complete this task.

Make an appropriate sentence.

1. I missed the orientation yesterday.

   _____ _____ _____ the _____ _____.

   watch   can   next   session   you   recorded

2. Could you check the lab schedule?

   _____ _____ _____ _____ _____ _____ _____ ?

   need   for   the   do   this week   you   timetable

3. The library is closed on Sundays.

   I'll _____ _____ _____ _____ _____ _____ .

   the library   for   day   plan   another   visit

4. I'm applying for the internship.

   _____ _____ _____ _____ _____ _____ ?

   to   are   they   which   company   you   applying

5. I heard there's a guest lecture tomorrow.

   _____ _____ _____ _____ _____ 2 p.m.

   scheduled   the Science Museum   it's   at   in

Make an appropriate sentence.

6. The printer was jammed all morning.

   _____?

   manage   it   fix   did   maintenance   to

7. I'm choosing courses for next term.

   _____?

   you   prerequisites   have   checked   the

8. Can you share the photos from the event?

   I'll _____.

   them   the   this evening   shared   upload   drive   to

9. We booked a cabin for the retreat.

   _____, _____?

   near   located   or   the lake   where   is it   in the woods

10. The team is meeting on Friday.

    _____?

    the meeting   during   do you   begin   what   will   know   time

Write an Email

You will read some information and use the information to write an email.

You will have 7 minutes to write the email.

The course you need for your program filled during registration, and the online system lists it as closed with a waitlist. You have completed the prerequisites, the topic fits your plan of study, and the meeting time works. You hope to obtain permission to enroll if a space becomes available.

Write an email to the course instructor. In your email, do the following.

- State your interest and relevant background.
- Request permission to enroll in the course.
- Ask about waitlist process and enrollment steps.

Write as much as you can and in complete sentences.

Your Response:

To: Professor Chen
Subject: Enrollment Request for Cognitive Psychology

Write for an Academic Discussion

A professor has posted a question about a topic and students have responded with their thoughts and ideas. Make a contribution to the discussion.

You will have 10 minutes to write.

Your professor is teaching a class on economics and society. Write a post responding to the professor's question.

In your response, you should do the following.

- Express and support your opinion
- Make a contribution to the discussion in your own words.

An effective response will contain at least 100 words.

Professor:

Many countries are debating whether governments should raise the minimum wage to support workers. Supporters argue that a higher wage helps families escape poverty and increases consumer spending. Opponents say it could make businesses cut jobs or raise prices, which may harm the economy. What do you think? Should the minimum wage be increased? Why or why not?

Student A:

I believe the minimum wage should definitely be raised. Too many workers struggle to cover basic expenses like rent and groceries, and this creates long-term stress for families. A higher wage would not only improve living conditions but also give people more money to spend, which can support local businesses.

Student B:

I disagree with raising the minimum wage at this time. When labor costs increase, small businesses may reduce staff hours or stop hiring new workers, which can harm employees overall. Higher wages could also force companies to raise prices, and consumers may end up paying more for everyday goods and services.

Speaking Section

In the speaking section, you will answer 11 questions to demonstrate how well you can speak English. There are two types of tasks.

Type of Task	Description
Listen and Repeat	Listen and repeat what you heard
Take an Interview	Answer questions from the interviewer

Listen and Repeat

You will listen as someone speaks to you. Listen carefully and then repeat what you have heard. The clock will indicate how much time you have to speak.

No time for preparation will be provided.

Speaking

You are learning to assist visitors at a city train station.
Listen to the coordinator and repeat what he says.
Repeat only once.

toefl ibt

Speaking | Questions 1-7 of 11

Listen and repeat only once.

1. RESPONSE TIME 00:00:08
2. RESPONSE TIME 00:00:08
3. RESPONSE TIME 00:00:10
4. RESPONSE TIME 00:00:10
5. RESPONSE TIME 00:00:12
6. RESPONSE TIME 00:00:12
7. RESPONSE TIME 00:00:12

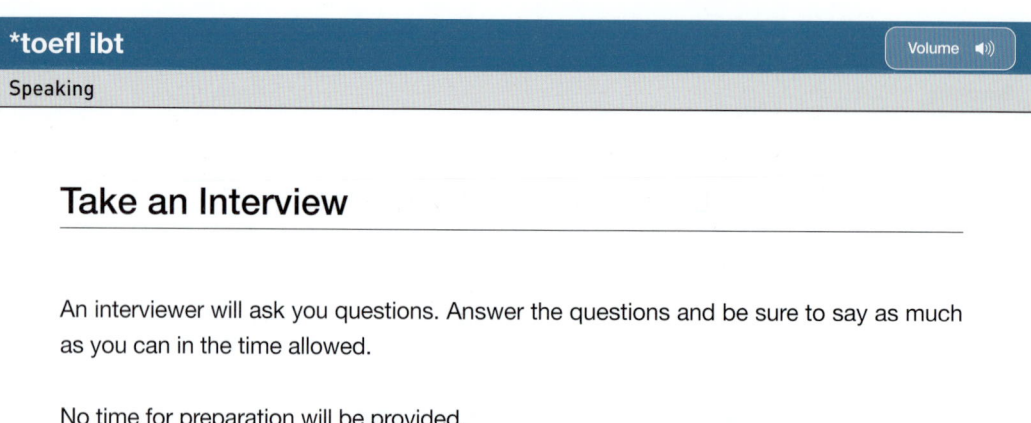

Take an Interview

An interviewer will ask you questions. Answer the questions and be sure to say as much as you can in the time allowed.

No time for preparation will be provided.

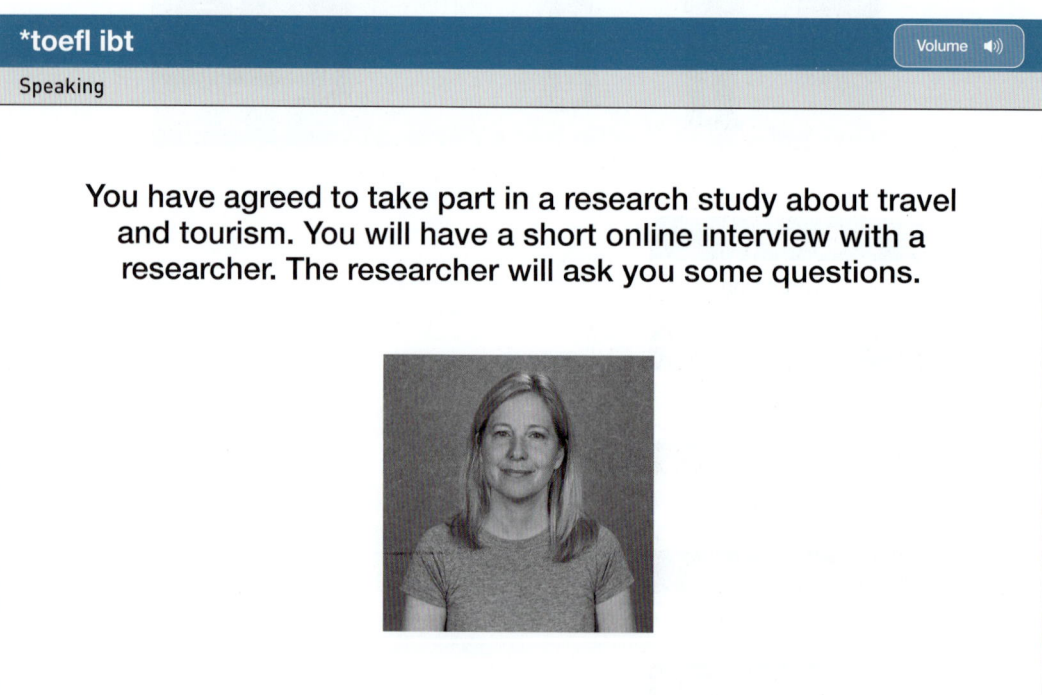

You have agreed to take part in a research study about travel and tourism. You will have a short online interview with a researcher. The researcher will ask you some questions.

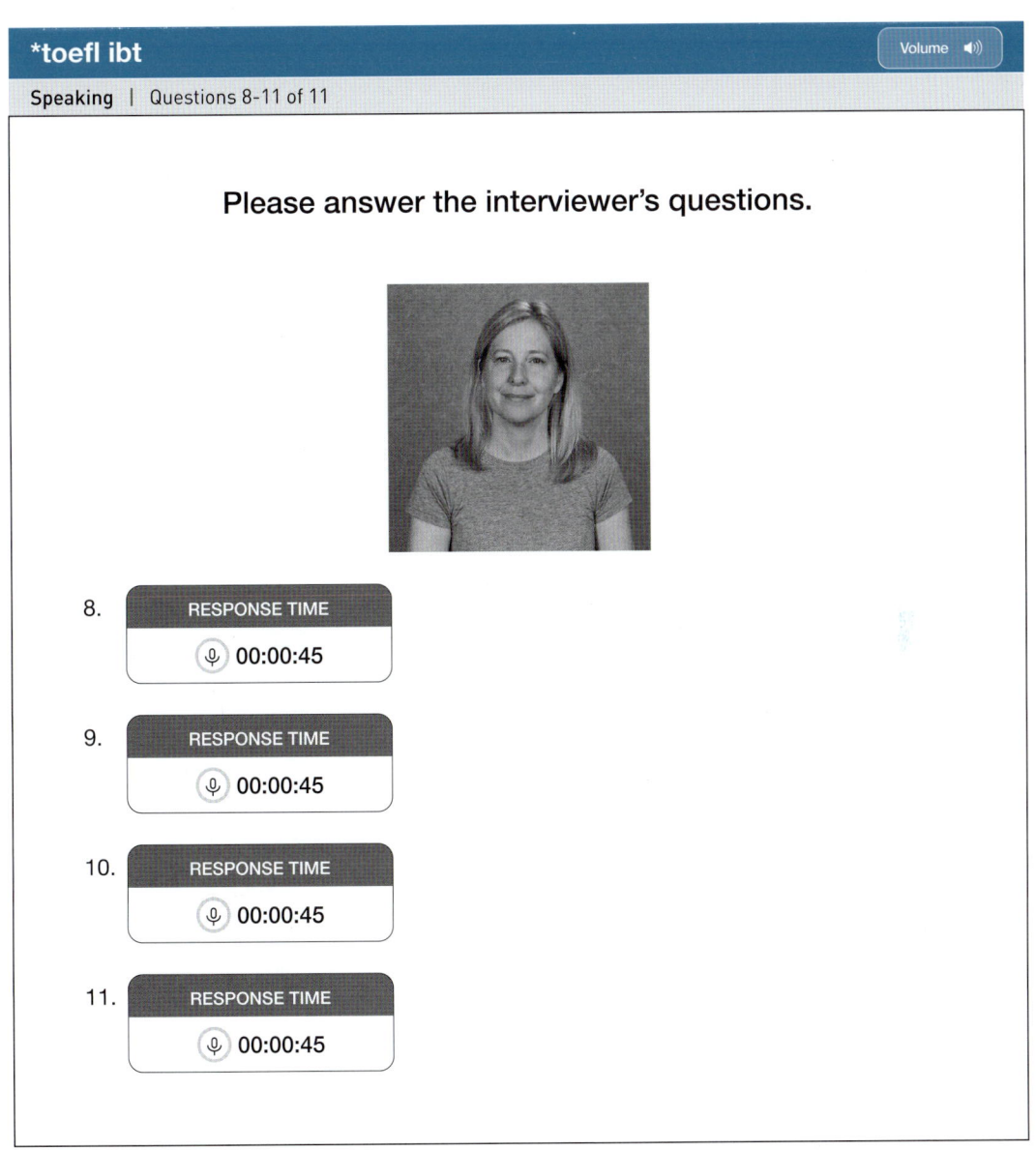

PAGODA TOEFL

Actual Test

PAGODA TOEFL Actual Test RW SW

2026 Edition

파고다교육그룹 언어교육연구소 저

해설서

TOEFL® is a registered trademark of Educational Testing Service (ETS).
This publication is not endorsed or approved by ETS.

PAGODA Books

2026 Edition

PAGODA TOEFL Actual Test

파고다교육그룹 언어교육연구소 | 저

해설서

PAGODA Books

Actual Test 1

Reading Module 1

01. inscri**ption**	02. div**ided**	03. three	04. bec**ause**	05. inc**luded**
06. same	07. wri**tten**	08. Greek	09. and	10. vers**ions**
11. Ⓑ	12. Ⓐ	13. Ⓓ	14. Ⓑ	15. Ⓐ
16. Ⓑ	17. Ⓐ	18. Ⓓ	19. Ⓐ	20. Ⓑ

[1-10] Fill in the missing letters in the paragraph.

[1-10] 문단에서 빠진 글자들을 채워 넣으세요.

The discovery of the Rosetta Stone in 1799 was a pivotal breakthrough, offering scholars a crucial reference for interpreting ancient Egyptian hieroglyphs. The inscri**ption** was div**ided** into three scripts, bec**ause** it inc**luded** the same text wri**tten** in Greek, Demotic, and hieroglyphic vers**ions**. This allowed researchers to compare symbols across languages, which gave them insight into the previously undeciphered system. Through systematic comparisons, philologists gradually reconstructed the grammar and vocabulary of hieroglyphs with increasing accuracy. This achievement significantly advanced historical linguistics and transformed modern understanding of ancient communication systems.

1799년에 로제타 스톤이 발견된 것은 중대한 돌파구였으며, 고대 이집트 상형문자를 해독하는 데 학자들에게 결정적인 기준점을 제공했다. 비문은 그리스어, 데모틱 문자, 상형문자로 같은 내용이 쓰여 있었기에 세 부분으로 나뉘어 있었다. 이를 통해 연구자들은 언어 간 기호를 비교할 수 있었다. 그 결과 이전까지 판독되지 않던 체계를 이해하는 데 통찰을 얻을 수 있었다. 체계적인 대조 작업을 통해 언어학자들은 상형문자의 문법과 어휘를 점차 더 정확하게 복원해 나갔다. 이 성취는 역사언어학을 크게 발전시켰고, 고대의 의사소통 체계에 대한 현대적 이해를 바꾸어 놓았다.

어휘

pivotal adj 핵심적인, 중추적인 | **breakthrough** n 획기적 발견, 돌파구 | **hieroglyphs** n 상형문자 | **inscription** n 명각, 비문(새겨진 글) | **Demotic** n 데모틱(고대 이집트) 문자(의) | **hieroglyphic** adj 상형문자의 n 상형문자 | **undeciphered** adj 해독되지 않은 | **philologist** n 문헌언어학자, 언어학자 | **reconstruct** v 재구성하다, 복원하다 | **linguistics** n 언어학

[11-12] Read a text message.

[11-12] 문자 메시지를 보세요.

From: City Transit Alerts

Due to scheduled roadwork on Main Avenue, ⑪ **bus routes 12 and 14 will follow a detour on Tuesday, April 14.** Service will bypass Central Station between 8:00 A.M. and 2:00 P.M. Passengers traveling to Central Station should use shuttle buses available every 30 minutes from Riverside Plaza. ⑫ **Normal routes will resume after 2:00 P.M.** Updates will be posted online.

발신: 시 교통국 알림

메인 애비뉴의 예정된 도로 공사로 인해, 4월 14일 화요일에는 12번·14번 버스가 우회 운행합니다. 오전 8시부터 오후 2시까지는 센트럴역을 경유하지 않습니다. 센트럴역으로 가는 승객은 리버사이드 플라자에서 30분 간격으로 운행하는 셔틀버스를 이용하시기 바랍니다. 오후 2시 이후 정상 노선으로 복귀합니다. 최신 공지는 온라인에 게시될 예정입니다.

어휘

scheduled adj 예정된 | roadwork n 도로 공사 | route n 노선, 경로 | detour n 우회로, 우회 | bypass v 우회하다, 피하다 | shuttle n 셔틀버스 | available adj 이용 가능한 | resume v 재개하다 | update n (공지) 업데이트, 최신 정보 | post v 게시하다, 올리다

11. What change will occur on April 14?
   (A) Shuttle service will be suspended.
   (B) Some routes will avoid Central Station.
   (C) Central Station will offer limited shuttle service.
   (D) Riverside Plaza will be closed for construction.

12. What can be inferred about the shuttle service?
   (A) It will end later on April 14.
   (B) It will be free for Riverside Plaza passengers.
   (C) It will depart every 30 minutes throughout the day.
   (D) It will continue after normal routes resume.

11. 4월 14일에 어떤 변화가 예정되어 있는가?
   (A) 셔틀 서비스가 중단될 것이다.
   (B) 일부 노선이 센트럴역에 정차하지 않을 것이다.
   (C) 센트럴역이 제한된 셔틀 서비스를 제공할 것이다.
   (D) 리버사이드 플라자가 공사로 폐쇄될 것이다.

12. 셔틀 운행에 대해 무엇을 추론할 수 있는가?
   (A) 4월 14일 오후에 종료된다.
   (B) 리버사이드 플라자 승객에게 무료로 제공된다.
   (C) 하루 종일 30분 간격으로 운행된다.
   (D) 정상 노선이 재개된 후에도 계속된다.

[13-15] Read an e-mail.

To: scholarship.applicants@hillside.edu
From: finaid@hillside.edu
Date: March 12
Subject: **13 Application Requirements – Hillside Merit Scholarship**

Dear Students,

13 This message is to remind you that applications for the Hillside Merit Scholarship must be submitted no later than March 25. **14 Applications must include the online form, faculty references, and an official transcript. Late submissions will not be reviewed.**

15 Priority consideration will be given to students who demonstrate leadership in extracurricular activities. Applicants should also be prepared for a brief interview, which will be scheduled between March 28 and April 3. You will receive a separate e-mail confirming your interview time once your application has been processed.

Scholarship recipients will be announced on April 15 and will be invited to a recognition ceremony hosted by the university president. For more information, please visit the Financial Aid Office website or call extension 119.

[13-15] 이메일을 보세요.

수신: scholarship.applicants@hillside.edu
발신: finaid@hillside.edu
날짜: 3월 12일
제목: 신청 요건 – 힐사이드 우수 장학금

학생 여러분께,

이 메일은 힐사이드 우수 장학금 신청 마감일이 3월 25일임을 상기시키기 위함입니다. 신청서에는 온라인 양식, 교수 추천서, 공식 성적표가 반드시 포함되어야 합니다. 마감일 이후 제출된 신청서는 검토되지 않습니다.

또한, 교외 활동에서 리더십을 보여준 학생들이 우선적으로 고려됩니다. 신청자는 3월 28일부터 4월 3일 사이에 예정된 짧은 면접을 준비해야 합니다. 신청서가 처리된 후 면접 시간을 확인하는 별도의 이메일을 받게 됩니다.

장학금 수혜자는 4월 15일에 발표되며, 총장 주최의 시상식에 초대될 예정입니다. 더 많은 정보를 원하시면 재정지원실 웹사이트를 방문하거나 내선번호 119로 전화하시기 바랍니다.

Sincerely,
Financial Aid Office

재정지원실 드림

어휘

remind ⓥ 상기시키다 | **submit** ⓥ 제출하다 | **transcript** ⓝ 성적표 | **review** ⓥ 검토하다 | **priority** ⓝ 우선권, 우선순위 | **consideration** ⓝ 고려, 심사 | **demonstrate** ⓥ 보여주다, 입증하다 | **extracurricular** ⓐⓓⓙ 교과 외의, 과외 활동의 | **recipient** ⓝ 수혜자, 받는 사람 | **recognition** ⓝ 인정, 표창

13. What is the main purpose of the e-mail?
    A To invite alumni to contribute to a financial aid fund
    B To remind faculty members to submit letters of recommendation
    C To explain the university's new tuition assistance program
    D To inform students about the requirements for a scholarship application

14. Which document must be submitted by the application deadline?
    A A résumé describing extracurricular leadership activities
    B A set of letters of recommendation
    C A certificate showing volunteer service hours
    D A copy of the student's financial aid award letter

15. What can be inferred about the selection process?
    A Students who are active outside the classroom may be favored.
    B Applicants who submit materials on time are likely to be selected.
    C Graduate-level students are the primary group considered for this scholarship.
    D Recommendation letters are typically reviewed after the deadline has passed.

13. 이 이메일의 주된 목적은 무엇인가?
    A 동문들에게 재정 지원 기금 기부를 요청하기 위해
    B 교수들에게 추천서 제출을 상기시키기 위해
    C 대학의 새로운 학자금 지원 프로그램을 설명하기 위해
    D 학생들에게 장학금 신청 요건을 알리기 위해

14. 신청 마감일까지 제출해야 하는 문서는 무엇인가?
    A 교외 활동 리더십을 설명하는 이력서
    B 추천서
    C 자원봉사 시간 증명서
    D 학생의 재정 보조 수혜 내역서 사본

15. 선발 과정에 대해 무엇을 추론할 수 있는가?
    A 교실 밖 활동에 적극적인 학생들이 우선적으로 고려될 수 있다.
    B 제시간에 서류를 제출한 지원자는 선정될 가능성이 크다.
    C 대학원생이 이 장학금의 주요 대상이다.
    D 추천서는 보통 마감일 이후에 검토된다.

[16-20] Bioluminescence in Nature

[16-20] 자연 속의 발광 현상

16 **Bioluminescence, the ability of living organisms to produce light, is a remarkable phenomenon found in nature.** This natural glow is caused by chemical reactions inside the organism's body, involving a substance called luciferin. Unlike sunlight or fire, bioluminescent light is produced

발광이란 살아 있는 생물이 빛을 만들어내는 능력으로, 자연에서 발견되는 놀라운 현상이다. 이러한 자연스러운 빛은 루시페린이라는 물질이 관여하는 화학 반응에 의해 생물의 몸속에서 발생한다. 햇빛이나 불과는 달리, 발광의 빛은 열을 내지 않고 만들어져 매우 효율적이다. 많은 심해 생물들은 생존을 위해 발광에 의존한

without heat, making it highly efficient. Many deep-sea creatures rely on it for survival: fish use it to attract prey, communicate with one another, or confuse predators. **17 For example, the anglerfish has a glowing lure that draws smaller fish close enough to be eaten.** Other marine species, such as squid, release a burst of light to distract attackers while they escape.

Bioluminescence is not limited to the ocean. **20 Fireflies are a well-known example on land, and their flashing lights serve as mating signals, allowing males and females to recognize each other. 18 (A) In some regions, thousands of fireflies synchronize their flashes, creating a dazzling display that scientists are still trying to fully understand. (B)**

16 Researchers are increasingly investigating practical applications of bioluminescence for humans. (C) Potential uses include medical imaging, environmental monitoring, and even sustainable lighting. **(D)** By studying how organisms create light so efficiently, **16 19 scientists hope to develop technologies that reduce dependence on traditional energy sources. This ongoing research suggests that the glow of living organisms may ultimately contribute to innovations in fields beyond nature.**

다. 물고기들은 이를 이용해 먹이를 유인하거나, 서로 의사소통하거나, 포식자를 혼란스럽게 한다. 예를 들어, 아귀는 작은 물고기를 유인할 수 있는 빛나는 미끼를 가지고 있어 가까이 다가오면 잡아먹는다. 다른 해양 생물들, 예컨대 오징어는 빛을 순간적으로 방출해 공격자를 혼란스럽게 한 다음 도망간다.

발광은 바다에만 국한되지 않는다. 반딧불이는 육지에서 잘 알려진 사례이며, 그들의 깜빡이는 빛은 짝짓기 신호로 사용되어 수컷과 암컷이 서로를 인식할 수 있게 한다. (A) 어떤 지역에서는 수천 마리의 반딧불이가 불빛을 동시에 반짝이며 과학자들이 아직 완전히 이해하지 못한 눈부신 장관을 만들어낸다. (B)

연구자들은 인간을 위한 발광의 실제 응용 가능성을 점점 더 많이 탐구하고 있다. (C) 잠재적인 활용 예로는 의료 영상, 환경 모니터링, 지속 가능한 조명 등이 있다. (D) 생물들이 어떻게 그렇게 효율적으로 빛을 만들어내는지를 연구함으로써, 과학자들은 기존의 에너지 자원 의존도를 줄일 수 있는 기술을 개발하기를 기대한다. 이러한 지속적인 연구는 살아 있는 생물들의 빛이 궁극적으로 자연을 넘어선 분야에서 혁신에 기여할 수 있음을 시사한다.

어휘

bioluminescence n 발광, 생물 발광 | **organism** n 생물, 유기체 | **phenomenon** n 현상 | **reaction** n 반응 | **luciferin** n 루시페린(발광 물질) | **efficient** adj 효율적인 | **creature** n 생물, 동물 | **prey** n 먹잇감 | **predator** n 포식자 | **lure** n 미끼, 유인 도구 | **species** n 종, 종류 | **burst** n (갑작스러운) 분출, 폭발 | **synchronize** v 동시에 맞추다, 동기화하다 | **dazzling** adj 눈부신, 현란한 | **strategy** n 전략 | **reproduction** n 번식, 생식 | **investigate** v 연구하다, 조사하다 | **monitoring** n 감시, 모니터링 | **sustainable** adj 지속 가능한 | **innovation** n 혁신

16. What is the passage mainly about?
    Ⓐ The role of fireflies in land ecosystems and reproduction
    Ⓑ **The production and potential uses of light in living organisms**
    Ⓒ The dangers faced by deep-sea animals from natural predators
    Ⓓ The chemical processes that create luciferin in certain organisms

16. 이 글의 주된 주제는 무엇인가?
    Ⓐ 육상 생태계와 번식에서 반딧불이의 역할
    Ⓑ 생물이 만들어내는 빛의 생성과 잠재적 활용
    Ⓒ 심해 동물이 자연 포식자에 의해 직면하는 위험
    Ⓓ 특정 생물에서 루시페린을 생성하는 화학적 과정

17. Why does the author mention the anglerfish?
    - (A) **To illustrate how bioluminescence can be used to attract prey**
    - (B) To compare how land and sea creatures employ different signals
    - (C) To explain how luciferin develops inside the bodies of fish
    - (D) To describe the synchronized flashing behaviors of fireflies

18. The word "dazzling" in the passage is closest in meaning to
    - (A) confusing
    - (B) brief
    - (C) ordinary
    - (D) **brilliant**

19. What can be inferred about human interest in bioluminescence?
    - (A) **It could inspire environmentally friendly technologies for the future.**
    - (B) It will gradually replace sunlight as the main source of energy.
    - (C) It is already widely applied in modern medical procedures today.
    - (D) It primarily benefits scientists working on deep-sea exploration.

20. There are four locations in the passage that indicate where the following sentence could be added.

    These behaviors show that bioluminescence serves not only as a survival strategy but also as a means of communication and reproduction.

    Where would the sentence best fit? Select a location where the sentence could be added to the passage.
    - (A) Option (A)
    - (B) **Option (B)**
    - (C) Option (C)
    - (D) Option (D)

17. 저자가 아귀를 언급한 이유는?
    - (A) 발광이 먹이를 유인하는 데 어떻게 쓰일 수 있는지를 보여주기 위해
    - (B) 육지와 바다 생물이 서로 다른 신호를 사용하는 방식을 비교하기 위해
    - (C) 루시페린이 물고기 몸속에서 어떻게 형성되는지 설명하기 위해
    - (D) 반딧불이의 동시 깜박임 행동을 묘사하기 위해

18. 본문에서 "dazzling"이라는 단어의 의미와 가장 가까운 것은?
    - (A) 혼란스러운
    - (B) 짧은
    - (C) 평범한
    - (D) 눈부신

19. 발광에 대한 인간의 관심에 대해 추론할 수 있는 것은?
    - (A) 미래에 환경 친화적인 기술을 고안하는 데 영감을 줄 수 있다.
    - (B) 점차 태양빛을 주요 에너지원으로 대체할 것이다.
    - (C) 이미 현대 의료 분야에 널리 적용되고 있다.
    - (D) 주로 심해 탐사 연구자들에게만 이익이 된다.

20. 지문에 다음 문장을 추가할 수 있는 네 개의 위치가 표시되어 있다.

    이러한 행동들은 발광이 단순히 생존 전략일 뿐만 아니라 의사소통과 번식 수단으로도 기능한다는 것을 보여준다.

    이 문장은 어디에 가장 잘 어울리는가? 이 문장이 추가될 수 있는 위치를 고르시오.
    - (A) (A) 위치
    - (B) (B) 위치
    - (C) (C) 위치
    - (D) (D) 위치

Reading Module 2

01. empl**oyed**	02. devi**ce**	03. **such**	04. **care**	05. **it**
06. **him**	07. obs**erve**	08. **of**	09. **Moon**	10. pl**anets**
11. ⓒ	12. ⓑ	13. ⓓ	14. ⓑ	15. ⓒ
16. ⓑ	17. ⓐ	18. ⓒ	19. ⓒ	20. ⓐ

[1-10] Fill in the missing letters in the paragraph.

[1-10] 문단에서 빠진 글자들을 채워 넣으세요.

The invention of the seventeenth-century telescope expanded astronomy, letting scientists explore celestial objects with remarkable precision. Galileo empl**oyed** the devi**ce** with s**uch** great c**are** that **it** enabled **him** to obs**erve** details **of** the M**oon** and pl**anets** closely. He noted mountains on the Moon and the moons of Jupiter, and recorded his findings during systematic observations conducted at night. These observations challenged Aristotelian models and provoked debates about celestial mechanics among scholars in early modern universities. Ultimately, telescopic evidence strengthened empirical methods, establishing observation as a lasting basis for future scientific inquiry.

17세기 망원경의 발명은 천문학을 확장시켜 과학자들이 놀라운 정밀함으로 천체를 탐구할 수 있게 했다. 갈릴레오는 그 장치를 매우 신중하게 사용하여 달과 행성의 세부 사항을 면밀히 관찰할 수 있었다. 그는 달의 산과 목성의 위성에 주목했고, 밤에 이루어진 체계적인 관측 동안 자신의 조사 결과들을 기록했다. 이러한 관측은 아리스토텔레스의 우주 모델 학설에 도전을 제기했으며, 초기 근대 대학의 학자들 사이에서 천체 역학에 관한 논쟁을 촉발했다. 궁극적으로 망원경 증거는 경험적 방법을 강화했고, 관찰을 미래 과학 탐구의 지속적인 기반으로 확립하였다.

어휘

telescope n 망원경 | **astronomy** n 천문학 | **celestial** adj 하늘의, 천체의 | **precision** n 정밀함 | **employ** v 사용하다, 활용하다 | **systematic** adj 체계적인 | **Aristotelian** adj 아리스토텔레스 학설의 | **mechanics** n 역학, 원리 | **empirical** adj 경험에 기반한, 실증적인 | **inquiry** n 탐구, 조사

[11-12] Read a notice.

[11-12] 공지를 보세요.

City Art Museum – Free Admission Day

On Saturday, November 9, **⑪ the City Art Museum will offer free admission to all visitors.** The galleries will be open from 10:00 A.M. to 6:00 P.M., and guided tours will begin every hour. **⑫ Family-friendly programs will take place in the education center throughout the afternoon.**

시립 미술관 – 무료 입장의 날

토요일, 11월 9일에 **시립 미술관은 모든 방문객에게 무료 입장을 제공합니다.** 전시는 오전 10시부터 오후 6시까지 운영되며, 가이드 투어는 매시간 시작됩니다. **가족 친화 프로그램은 오후 내내 교육 센터에서 진행됩니다.**

어휘

offer v 제공하다 | **admission** n 입장, 입장료 | **visitor** n 방문객 | **gallery** n 전시실, 갤러리 | **guided** adj 안내가 있는 | **tour** n 투어, 관람 | **family-friendly** adj 가족 친화적인 | **program** n 프로그램 | **education center** 교육 센터 | **throughout** prep ~내내 adv 내내

11. What is the main purpose of the notice?
   Ⓐ To announce the temporary opening of the galleries
   Ⓑ To explain how to apply for museum membership
   Ⓒ To promote a special day at the museum
   Ⓓ To request volunteers for upcoming events

12. What is scheduled to happen later on November 9?
   Ⓐ Free admission will end early.
   Ⓑ Family activities will be held.
   Ⓒ Guided tours will take place every hour.
   Ⓓ The education center will not be available.

[13-15] Read an e-mail.

To: conference.participants@umail.com
From: registrar@intltechforum.org
Date: May 6
Subject: Updated Procedures for International Tech Forum

Dear Participants,

We are writing to confirm your registration for the International Tech Forum, which will take place on May 22–23 at the Harborview Convention Center. In preparation for the event, please note that **⑬ check-in counters will operate from 7:30 A.M. until 9:00 A.M. on the first day, and all attendees must present both a photo ID and the confirmation code issued at the time of registration. Without these documents, admission will not be guaranteed.**

In addition, **⑭ entry to the keynote lecture is restricted to registered participants and their invited guests only.** Seating in the main hall is limited, so participants are encouraged to arrive early. Breakout sessions in the afternoon will focus on digital security, renewable energy, and cross-border e-commerce. As some sessions will run concurrently, please select your preferences in advance on the conference website.

Finally, **⑮ a closing reception will be held on May 23 at 6:30 P.M. in the Riverside Ballroom. This event is intended for all participants, regardless of their session choices, and will feature a keynote panel and networking opportunities. Further details, including transportation options, are available on our website.

Sincerely,
Registration Office

어휘

registration n 등록 | **attendee** n 참석자 | **confirmation** n 확인, 확증 | **guarantee** v 보장하다 | **restricted** adj 제한된 | **concurrently** adv 동시에 | **reception** n 리셉션, 환영 행사 | **regardless of** ~에 상관없이 | **networking** n 인맥 쌓기, 교류 | **transportation** n 교통, 수송

---

13. What is the main purpose of the e-mail?
    (A) To request payment of a registration fee
    (B) To ask attendees to submit presentation proposals
    (C) To advertise future technology conferences
    (D) **To provide participants with details about procedures**

14. What can be inferred about admission to the keynote lecture?
    (A) It is accessible without any restrictions.
    (B) **It is not open to the general public.**
    (C) It depends only on arriving before 7:30 A.M.
    (D) It is available only to conference staff members.

15. What is indicated about the event taking place in the Riverside Ballroom?
    (A) It is intended for those who selected preferences on the website.
    (B) It will consist of several sessions occurring at the same time in the afternoon.
    (C) **It gives participants opportunities to interact with one another.**
    (D) It will provide complimentary transportation services.

[16-20] How Sleep Shapes Memory

16 Sleep is not merely a period of rest but rather a fundamental process through which the brain consolidates memory. During sleep, neural activity selectively strengthens recently acquired information while filtering out less relevant details. This selective retention allows individuals to function more efficiently when awake, preserving cognitive resources for essential tasks.

Among the stages of sleep, **17 rapid eye movement (REM) sleep appears to be especially integral to higher-order thinking.** In this stage, brain activity resembles wakefulness, and research suggests that REM sleep enhances creativity and complex problem-solving. Experiments have shown, for instance, that **18 students who review academic material before sleeping are more likely to recall it accurately compared to those who remain awake for the same period.**

19 When sleep is disrupted, however, these benefits diminish. Sleep-deprived individuals often struggle with sustained attention and experience lapses in memory. Moreover, chronic deprivation has been linked to anxiety and depression. **20 Studying how sleep stages affect memory not only informs educational strategies but also provides insight into potential treatments for conditions such as Alzheimer's disease.**

깨어 있을 때 더 효율적으로 기능하도록 하여, 필수 과제에 인지 자원을 보존하게 한다.

수면의 여러 단계 중에서도 급속안구운동(REM) 수면은 고차원적 사고에 특히 필수적인 것으로 보인다. 이 단계에서 뇌 활동은 깨어 있을 때와 비슷하며, 연구에 따르면 REM 수면은 창의성과 복잡한 문제 해결 능력을 향상시킨다. 예를 들어, 학생들이 학습 자료를 잠자기 전에 복습하면 같은 시간 동안 깨어 있는 학생들보다 더 정확히 기억할 가능성이 높다는 실험 결과가 있다.

그러나 수면이 방해되면 이러한 이점은 줄어든다. 수면 부족에 시달리는 사람들은 지속적인 주의력을 유지하기 어려워하고, 기억의 단절을 경험한다. 또한 만성적인 수면 부족은 불안 및 우울증과 연관되어 있다. 수면 단계가 기억에 어떤 영향을 미치는지를 연구하는 것은 교육 전략에 정보를 제공할 뿐 아니라 알츠하이머병과 같은 질환 치료에도 통찰을 제공한다.

어휘

merely adv 단순히 | **fundamental** adj 근본적인 | **consolidate** v 공고히 하다, 강화하다 | **neural** adj 신경의 | **selectively** adv 선택적으로 | **acquire** v 습득하다, 획득하다 | **filter out** 걸러내다 | **retention** n 유지, 보존 | **cognitive** adj 인지의 | **resource** n 자원 | **rapid eye movement (REM)** 급속안구운동 | **integral** adj 필수적인 | **enhance** v 향상시키다 | **complex** adj 복잡한 | **recall** v 기억하다 n 회상 | **disrupt** v 방해하다 | **sustained** adj 지속적인, 한결 같은 | **lapse** n (기억·주의력의) 일시적 상실 | **chronic** adj 만성적인 | **deprivation** n 박탈, 부족

---

16. Which of the following best states a main idea of the passage?

Ⓐ The connection between REM sleep and emotional stability
Ⓑ **The critical role of sleep in strengthening memory and learning**
Ⓒ The scientific methods used to measure neural activity during rest
Ⓓ The health problems that result from long-term sleep deprivation

16. 다음 중 본문의 주제를 가장 잘 나타낸 것은 무엇인가?

Ⓐ REM 수면과 정서 안정의 관계
Ⓑ 기억 강화와 학습에서 수면의 중요한 역할
Ⓒ 휴식 중 신경 활동을 측정하는 과학적 방법
Ⓓ 장기적인 수면 부족으로 인한 건강 문제

17. The word "integral" in the passage is closest in meaning to

  (A) **essential**
  (B) harmful
  (C) limited
  (D) temporary

18. Why does the author mention students who review academic material before sleeping?

  (A) To show how different study habits produce the same results
  (B) To argue that staying awake can be equally effective for recall
  (C) **To demonstrate that memory improves when rest follows learning**
  (D) To explain why REM sleep is unrelated to long-term retention

19. What is the relationship between paragraphs 2 and 3?

  (A) Paragraph 3 provides evidence contradicting the claims in paragraph 2.
  (B) Paragraph 3 offers an example of the ideas introduced in paragraph 2.
  (C) **Paragraph 3 describes the negative effects that result from paragraph 2.**
  (D) Paragraph 3 introduces alternative theories unrelated to paragraph 2.

20. What does the passage suggest about future applications of sleep research?

  (A) **It may contribute to educational practices and medical treatments.**
  (B) It is unlikely to reveal further details about how memory works.
  (C) It will focus mainly on reducing the need for nightly sleep.
  (D) It is expected to concentrate on improving creativity in adults.

17. 본문에서 "integral"이라는 단어의 의미와 가장 가까운 것은?

  (A) 필수적인
  (B) 해로운
  (C) 제한된
  (D) 일시적인

18. 저자가 잠자기 전에 학습 자료를 복습하는 학생들을 언급한 이유는?

  (A) 다른 학습 습관이 같은 결과를 낳는다는 것을 보여주기 위해
  (B) 깨어 있는 것이 기억에 똑같이 효과적임을 주장하기 위해
  (C) 학습 후 수면을 취하면 기억력이 향상된다는 것을 보여주기 위해
  (D) REM 수면이 장기 기억과 관련이 없음을 설명하기 위해

19. 2단락과 3단락의 관계는 무엇인가?

  (A) 3단락은 2단락의 주장과 모순되는 증거를 제공한다.
  (B) 3단락은 2단락에서 제시된 아이디어의 사례를 제공한다.
  (C) 3단락은 2단락의 결과로 나타나는 부정적 영향을 설명한다.
  (D) 3단락은 2단락과 관련 없는 대체 이론을 소개한다.

20. 수면 연구의 미래 응용 가능성에 대해 본문은 무엇을 시사하는가?

  (A) 교육과 의료 분야의 발전에 기여할 수 있다.
  (B) 기억이 어떻게 작동하는지에 대한 새로운 사실은 드러내지 못할 것이다.
  (C) 야간 수면의 필요성을 줄이는 데 주로 집중할 것이다.
  (D) 성인의 창의력 향상에만 집중할 것으로 예상된다.

Listening Module 1

01. C	02. A	03. B	04. D	05. D
06. A	07. A	08. B	09. C	10. A
11. B	12. C	13. B	14. A	15. B
16. C	17. A	18. D		

[1-8] Choose the best response.

1. M: Why was the budget review postponed?
   Ⓐ The accounting unit.
   Ⓑ Next Thursday.
   Ⓒ **The chair was out sick.**
   Ⓓ Yes, it was.

2. W: I thought the seminar was online—wasn't it?
   Ⓐ **Actually, it's in Room 204.**
   Ⓑ Let's attend the seminar online!
   Ⓒ No, it's a virtual session.
   Ⓓ Who's presenting?

3. M: I can't make the 10 a.m. briefing.
   Ⓐ See you then.
   Ⓑ **Join the noon one.**
   Ⓒ Room A.
   Ⓓ So am I.

4. W: How much is the late registration fee?
   Ⓐ At the registrar's office window.
   Ⓑ I'll process your papers this afternoon.
   Ⓒ It's for late entries only.
   Ⓓ **It won't exceed forty dollars.**

5. M: Could you sign off on my request today?
   Ⓐ In your inbox.
   Ⓑ It's already in the queue.
   Ⓒ It was signed last year.
   Ⓓ **I'll squeeze it in before three.**

6. W: The orientation requires advance booking.
   Ⓐ **No, it doesn't.**
   Ⓑ On the events page.
   Ⓒ Before Friday at noon.
   Ⓓ The admissions office.

7. M: Let's book the auditorium for tonight.
   Ⓐ **Is it even free tonight?**
   Ⓑ It's near the main entrance.
   Ⓒ I scheduled tomorrow's event already.
   Ⓓ I'll check tomorrow morning.

8. W: Where do I submit travel receipts?
   Ⓐ By Friday, if possible.
   Ⓑ **Upload them to the Finance portal.**
   Ⓒ Label the receipts clearly.
   Ⓓ Have your supervisor sign them.

[1–8] 가장 적절한 응답을 고르세요.

1. 남: 왜 예산 검토가 연기되었나요?
   Ⓐ 회계 부서요.
   Ⓑ 다음 주 목요일이요.
   Ⓒ **의장이 아파서 결석했어요.**
   Ⓓ 네, 그렇습니다.

2. 여: 세미나가 온라인에서 하는 줄 알았는데, 아닌가요?
   Ⓐ **사실은 204호에서 해요.**
   Ⓑ 온라인으로 세미나에 참석합시다!
   Ⓒ 그것은 온라인 세션이에요.
   Ⓓ 누가 발표하나요?

3. 남: 오전 10시 브리핑에는 참석할 수 없어요.
   Ⓐ 그때 봐요.
   Ⓑ **정오 브리핑에 참석하세요.**
   Ⓒ A실이요.
   Ⓓ 저도 그래요.

4. 여: 늦게 등록하면 수수료가 얼마나 되나요?
   Ⓐ 접수처 창구에서요.
   Ⓑ 오늘 오후에 서류 처리할게요.
   Ⓒ 늦은 등록자 전용이에요.
   Ⓓ **40달러는 안 넘을 거예요.**

5. 남: 오늘 제 요청서에 결재해 주시겠습니까?
   Ⓐ 당신 메일함이요.
   Ⓑ 이미 대기열에 있습니다.
   Ⓒ 작년에 결재되었습니다.
   Ⓓ **오후 3시 전에 처리해 드리겠습니다.**

6. 여: 오리엔테이션은 사전 예약이 필요해요.
   Ⓐ **아니요, 그렇지 않습니다.**
   Ⓑ 행사 페이지요.
   Ⓒ 금요일 정오 전까지요.
   Ⓓ 입학처요.

7. 남: 오늘 밤 강당을 예약합시다.
   Ⓐ **오늘 밤에 정말 비어 있나요?**
   Ⓑ 그것은 정문 근처에 있습니다.
   Ⓒ 이미 내일 행사를 예약했습니다.
   Ⓓ 내일 아침 시간을 확인할게요.

8. 여: 출장 영수증은 어디에 제출하나요?
   Ⓐ 가능하면 금요일까지요.
   Ⓑ **재무 포털에 업로드하세요.**
   Ⓒ 영수증에 잘 보이게 라벨을 붙이세요.
   Ⓓ 상사에게 서명을 받으세요.

어휘

1. **budget** n 예산 | **review** n 검토, 심사 | **postpone** v 연기하다
2. **seminar** n 세미나, 학술 모임 | **online** adj 온라인의 adv 온라인으로 | **virtual** adj 가상의
3. **briefing** n 보고, 브리핑 | **make** v (시간·약속에) 참석하다, 맞추다 | **noon** n 정오
4. **registration** n 등록 | **fee** n 수수료 | **exceed** v 초과하다
5. **sign off** 결재하다, 승인하다 | **request** n 요청, 신청 | **queue** n 대기열 | **squeeze in** (~을 하기 위해) 짬을 내다
6. **orientation** n 오리엔테이션, 설명회 | **require** v 요구하다, 필요로 하다 | **advance** adj 사전의
7. **book** v 예약하다 | **auditorium** n 강당 | **schedule** v 일정을 잡다
8. **submit** v 제출하다 | **receipt** n 영수증 | **portal** n 포털, 접속 창구 | **label** v 라벨을 붙이다 n 라벨

[9-10] Listen to a conversation.

W Academic Advising, this is Dr. Patel.

M Hi, I'm outside your office. My appointment's at noon, but the door's locked.

W My calendar shows you at 3 p.m. Are you sure about the time?

M I'm looking at the confirmation e-mail—12:00 sharp.

W **9** **We migrated to a new booking app yesterday. Some slots defaulted to a different time zone.**

M That explains why your calendar looked empty all morning.

W I can open a quick video slot at 12:15, or we can meet tomorrow at 9.

M A quick virtual today would be really helpful.

W Great. **10** I'll send you a meeting link right now.

어휘

appointment n 약속, 예약 | **confirmation** n 확인, 확정 | **migrate** v (시스템·데이터를) 이전하다 | **slot** n 예약 시간대, 자리 | **time zone** 표준 시간대

---

9. Why does the man say, "That explains why your calendar looked empty all morning"?

(A) He realized the advisor stopped offering in-person meetings today.
(B) He learned her schedule was taken over by another office.
(C) **He discovered a time-zone setting caused the mismatch.**
(D) He thinks the advisor canceled all noon appointments.

10. What will the woman probably do next?
    Ⓐ **Start a brief video meeting with the man.**
    Ⓑ Reschedule the entire afternoon.
    Ⓒ Ask the man to return next week.
    Ⓓ File a service request with campus IT.

10. 여자가 아마도 다음에 할 일은 무엇인가?
    Ⓐ 남자와 짧은 화상 상담을 시작할 것이다.
    Ⓑ 오후 일정을 전부 다시 잡을 것이다.
    Ⓒ 남자에게 다음 주에 다시 오라고 할 것이다.
    Ⓓ 교내 IT팀에 서비스 요청서를 제출할 것이다.

[11-12] Listen to a conversation.

W ⑪ Hi. I'm calling because I got a "Ready for Pickup" text from your bookstore, but the counter is closed.
M After hours, we place orders in the side-entrance lockers.
W ⑫ Do I need staff to retrieve it?
M No. Enter your order number and the last four digits of your phone; the door pops open.
W Great, I'll grab it on my way to the dorm.

[11-12] 대화를 들으세요.

여 안녕하세요. 서점에서 "수령 준비 완료"라는 문자를 받았는데, 카운터가 닫혀 있네요.
남 영업시간 이후에는, 주문품을 측면 출입구 사물함에 보관합니다.
여 직원이 꺼내줘야 하나요?
남 아니요. 주문 번호와 휴대폰 뒷자리 네 자리를 입력하면 문이 열려요.
여 좋아요. 기숙사 가는 길에 찾아갈게요.

📘 어휘

pickup n 수령, 인도 | **counter** n 계산대, 카운터 | **after hours** 영업시간 이후 | **locker** n 사물함 | **retrieve** v 찾아오다, 회수하다

11. Why did the woman call the bookstore?
    Ⓐ To cancel a back-ordered item
    Ⓑ **To pick up an order after hours**
    Ⓒ To ask about price matching
    Ⓓ To change a payment method

11. 여자가 서점에 전화한 이유는 무엇인가?
    Ⓐ 예약 주문 상품을 취소하기 위해
    Ⓑ 영업시간 이후 주문품을 수령하기 위해
    Ⓒ 가격 비교에 대해 문의하기 위해
    Ⓓ 결제 방법을 변경하기 위해

12. What does the man imply that the woman can do?
    Ⓐ Reschedule pickup for next week
    Ⓑ Pay a late-pickup fee at the counter
    Ⓒ **Use a locker code to get the order**
    Ⓓ Transfer the order to another campus

12. 남자가 여자가 할 수 있다고 암시한 것은 무엇인가?
    Ⓐ 다음 주로 수령 일정을 다시 잡을 수 있다
    Ⓑ 카운터에서 수령 지체 수수료를 낼 수 있다
    Ⓒ 사물함 코드를 이용해 주문품을 받을 수 있다
    Ⓓ 주문품을 다른 캠퍼스로 옮길 수 있다

[13-14] Listen to an announcement in a university library.

[13-14] 대학 도서관에서의 안내방송을 들으세요.

Librarian: ⑬ Quick reminder about laptop loans. Devices check out at the front desk with student ID only. ⑭ The loan is four hours, renewable once if units are available. Please save work to cloud storage; files on the desktop are wiped upon

사서: 노트북 대여에 관한 간단한 알림입니다. 기기는 학생증만 있으면 안내 데스크에서 대여할 수 있습니다. 대여 기간은 4시간이며, 기기가 남아 있을 경우 한 번 연장할 수 있습니다. 작업은 반드시 클라우드 저장소에 저장하세요. 데스크톱에 저장된 파일은 반납 시 삭제됩

return. Report damage right away so we can swap a device. **14 These rules help more students borrow laptops during peak study times.**

니다. 손상은 즉시 보고해 주셔야 기기를 교체할 수 있습니다. 이러한 규칙은 학습이 집중되는 시간대에 더 많은 학생들이 노트북을 대여할 수 있도록 돕습니다.

어휘

loan n 대여, 대출 | **renewable** adj 갱신 가능한, 연장 가능한 | **wipe** v 지우다, 삭제하다 | **swap** v 교체하다, 바꾸다 | **peak** adj 절정의 n 절정기

---

13. What is the main purpose of the announcement?
Ⓐ New software update
Ⓑ Laptop checkout rules
Ⓒ Workshop event notice
Ⓓ Lost device report

13. 이 안내 방송의 주된 목적은 무엇인가?
Ⓐ 새로운 소프트웨어 업데이트 공지
Ⓑ 노트북 대여 규칙 안내
Ⓒ 워크숍 행사 알림
Ⓓ 분실 기기 보고

14. Why does the speaker mention "four hours"?
Ⓐ It is to help manage demand.
Ⓑ It is to match the lab schedule.
Ⓒ It is to track equipment inventory.
Ⓓ It is to discourage theft.

14. 화자가 "4시간"이라고 언급한 이유는 무엇인가?
Ⓐ 수요 관리를 돕기 위해
Ⓑ 실습실 일정에 맞추기 위해
Ⓒ 장비 재고를 추적하기 위해
Ⓓ 도난을 방지하기 위해

[15-18] Listen to a talk on a podcast about work and well-being.

[15-18] 일과 웰빙에 관한 담화를 들으세요.

Podcast Host: **15 If you want more creative problem-solving without adding hours to the day, try "micro-breaks." These are short, low-input pauses that reset attention without pulling you into another task.** Standing to stretch, watering a plant, or gazing out a window for three minutes can quiet mental noise just enough for ideas to surface. **16 In contrast, input-heavy pauses—checking a news feed or hopping into chat—often load the brain with fresh demands and leave you more scattered.** Field teams that pilot one micro-break every thirty minutes report steadier focus and fewer loops of "fake work," like rereading the same line. **17 Managers are sometimes skeptical—breaks can look like slacking—so I frame them as a precision tool: quick, physical, and time-boxed.** We also set norms so no one feels guilty stepping away briefly. I'm not anti-screen; I'm pro-recovery. Screens can help, but some pauses restore attention while others consume it. If you want a starting recipe, pick one physical action, schedule it, and evaluate

진행자: 하루에 시간을 더 늘리지 않고도 창의적인 문제 해결력을 원한다면, "마이크로 브레이크"를 시도해 보세요. 이것은 주의를 다른 일로 끌어가지 않으면서도 집중을 재설정해 주는 짧고 단순한 휴식입니다. 일어나서 스트레칭을 하거나, 화분에 물을 주거나, 창밖을 3분간 바라보는 것만으로도 정신적 잡음을 가라앉혀 아이디어가 떠오르게 할 수 있습니다. 반대로, **뉴스 피드를 확인하거나** 채팅에 참여하는 것 같은 입력량이 많은 휴식은 뇌에 새로운 부담을 안겨 주어 더 산만하게 만듭니다. 현장 팀들이 30분마다 마이크로 브레이크를 한 번씩 도입해 본 결과, 집중력이 더 안정되고 같은 문장을 반복해서 읽는 "가짜 일"의 반복이 줄어들었다고 보고했습니다. 관리자들은 때때로 회의적입니다—휴식이 게으름처럼 보일 수 있기 때문이죠—그래서 저는 이를 정밀한 도구라고 설명합니다: 짧고, 신체적이며, 시간 제한이 있습니다. 또한 누구도 잠시 자리를 비우는 것에 죄책감을 느끼지 않도록 규범을 세웁니다. 저는 "반(反) 스크린"이 아닙니다. 저는 "회복"을 지지합니다. 스크린도 도움이 될 수 있지만, 어떤 휴식은 주의를 회복시키고 어떤 휴식은 오히려 주의를 소모합니다. 시작 방법을 원한다면, 신체적 활동 하나를 고르고, 그

after a week. Track simple metrics—error rates, time to restart a task—to keep this practical. **18 Next episode, we'll talk about rolling this out: how to present data, answer objections, and adapt the rhythm for different roles and shift patterns.**

것을 일정에 넣은 다음, 일주일 후에 평가해 보세요. 단순한 지표—실수율, 업무 재시작 시간—를 추적해 실용성을 유지하세요. **다음 에피소드에서는 이것을 실제로 적용하는 방법: 데이터를 제시하고, 반대 의견에 답하며, 직무 유형과 근무 패턴에 맞게 리듬을 조정하는 방법에 대해 이야기하겠습니다.**

어휘

micro-break n 짧은 휴식, 미니 휴식 | **pause** n 잠깐 멈춤, 휴식 | **reset** v 다시 설정하다, 초기화하다 | **mental noise** 정신적 잡음, 산만함 | **surface** v (생각·감정이) 떠오르다, 드러나다 | **input-heavy** adj 입력량이 많은, 자극이 큰 | **scattered** adj 산만한, 집중하지 못하는 | **field team** 현장 팀, 협업 팀 | **steady** adj 안정적인 | **loop** n 반복, 순환 | **skeptical** adj 회의적인 | **slacking** n 게으름, 태만 | **precision** adj 정밀한 n 정확성 | **time-boxed** adj 시간 제한이 있는 | **metrics** n 측정 지표

---

15. What is the talk mainly about?
    Ⓐ Longer vacations as the main cure for burnout
    Ⓑ **How short pauses can restore focus and creativity**
    Ⓒ Whether removing screens increases office productivity
    Ⓓ Training personality traits to raise workplace innovation

16. Why does the host mention "checking a news feed"?
    Ⓐ To suggest regular news checks during the workday
    Ⓑ To claim digital tools always improve efficiency
    Ⓒ **To show a pause that fails to restore attention**
    Ⓓ To argue for stricter rules on social media

17. What does the host imply about managers' concerns?
    Ⓐ **Strict time limits can reduce skepticism.**
    Ⓑ Their worries are baseless and should be ignored.
    Ⓒ Only top leaders may approve micro-break policies.
    Ⓓ Persistent doubts mean the idea should be abandoned.

18. What will the host most likely discuss next?
    Ⓐ A history of corporate health promotion programs
    Ⓑ Calculating costs of well-being initiatives at work
    Ⓒ Brain research on memory with lab experiments
    Ⓓ **How to adapt micro-break schedules by job type**

15. 이 강연의 주된 내용은 무엇인가?
    Ⓐ 탈진을 치료하는 주요 방법으로 긴 휴가
    Ⓑ **짧은 휴식이 집중력과 창의성을 회복시키는 방법**
    Ⓒ 스크린 사용을 줄이는 것이 사무실 생산성을 높이는지 여부
    Ⓓ 직장에서 혁신을 높이기 위해 성격 특성을 훈련하는 것

16. 진행자가 "뉴스 피드 확인"을 언급한 이유는?
    Ⓐ 근무 중 정기적인 뉴스 확인을 권장하기 위해
    Ⓑ 디지털 도구가 항상 효율성을 높인다고 주장하기 위해
    Ⓒ **주의를 회복하지 못하는 휴식 사례를 보여주기 위해**
    Ⓓ 소셜 미디어에 대한 더 엄격한 규제를 주장하기 위해

17. 진행자가 관리자들의 우려에 대해 암시한 것은?
    Ⓐ **시간 제한을 엄격히 두면 회의론을 줄일 수 있다.**
    Ⓑ 그들의 우려는 근거가 없으므로 무시해야 한다.
    Ⓒ 최고 관리자만 마이크로 브레이크 정책을 승인할 수 있다.
    Ⓓ 지속적인 의심은 이 아이디어를 포기해야 함을 뜻한다.

18. 진행자가 다음에 다룰 주제로 가장 가능성이 높은 것은?
    Ⓐ 기업 건강 증진 프로그램의 역사
    Ⓑ 직장 웰빙 이니셔티브의 비용 계산
    Ⓒ 실험실에서의 기억 관련 뇌 연구
    Ⓓ **직무 유형별로 마이크로 브레이크 일정을 조정하는 방법**

Listening Module 2

01. Ⓑ	02. Ⓒ	03. Ⓐ	04. Ⓓ	05. Ⓒ
06. Ⓐ	07. Ⓐ	08. Ⓑ	09. Ⓑ	10. Ⓓ
11. Ⓓ	12. Ⓒ	13. Ⓐ	14. Ⓑ	15. Ⓒ
16. Ⓓ				

[1-8] Choose the best response.

1. M: What's the point of contact for lab safety training?
   - Ⓐ In the main lab.
   - **Ⓑ The administration office is.**
   - Ⓒ I do.
   - Ⓓ By next Monday, please.

2. W: I can't find my exam room.
   - Ⓐ No, a lot of students get lost.
   - Ⓑ Ask the registrar if your enrollment went through.
   - **Ⓒ Check the assignment board by Hall C.**
   - Ⓓ Rooms change after check-in.

3. M: Where do I pick up my conference badge?
   - **Ⓐ Outside Hall 2 at Registration Desk B.**
   - Ⓑ After the opening ceremony ends.
   - Ⓒ No, it's already been mailed to you.
   - Ⓓ In the hotel gym on the basement floor.

4. W: Doesn't my lab-safety certificate appear automatically once the training is logged?
   - Ⓐ I thought you were going to submit the form in person.
   - Ⓑ You probably mean the fire-safety record.
   - Ⓒ Yes, the training is mandatory.
   - **Ⓓ That's right—Isn't it showing up?**

5. M: How about moving the poster session outside if it stays sunny?
   - Ⓐ I moved last week's session already.
   - Ⓑ It's scheduled in the atrium lobby.
   - **Ⓒ Only if facilities can set up stands.**
   - Ⓓ Let's run the display outside tonight!

6. W: You don't happen to have the syllabus link, do you?
   - **Ⓐ I do—I'll send it now.**
   - Ⓑ It's printed in the course reader.
   - Ⓒ Yes, I don't have it.
   - Ⓓ After the add/drop period ends.

[1-8] 가장 적절한 응답을 고르세요.

1. 남: 실험실 안전 교육의 담당부서는 어디인가요?
   - Ⓐ 본관 실험실이에요.
   - Ⓑ 행정 사무실입니다.
   - Ⓒ 제가요.
   - Ⓓ 다음 주 월요일까지 해주세요.

2. 여: 제 시험장을 찾을 수가 없어요.
   - Ⓐ 아니요, 많은 학생들이 길을 잃어요.
   - Ⓑ 등록이 완료되었는지 교무처에 물어보세요.
   - Ⓒ Hall C 옆 배정 게시판을 확인하세요.
   - Ⓓ 체크인 후에 강의실이 바뀝니다.

3. 남: 제 학회 배지는 어디서 받나요?
   - Ⓐ Hall 2 바깥쪽 등록 데스크 B에서 받으세요.
   - Ⓑ 개회식이 끝난 후에요.
   - Ⓒ 아니요, 이미 우편으로 발송됐어요.
   - Ⓓ 호텔 지하층의 체육관에서요.

4. 여: 제 실험실 안전 수료증은 훈련이 기록되면 자동으로 표시되지 않나요?
   - Ⓐ 직접 양식을 제출하려고 한 줄 알았어요.
   - Ⓑ 아마도 화재 안전 기록을 말씀하신 것 같네요.
   - Ⓒ 네, 그 교육은 의무입니다.
   - Ⓓ 맞아요 – 지금 표시되지 않나요?

5. 남: 날씨가 계속 맑으면 포스터 세션을 밖으로 옮기는 건 어때요?
   - Ⓐ 지난주 세션은 이미 옮겼습니다.
   - Ⓑ 아트리움 로비에서 열릴 예정이에요.
   - Ⓒ 시설팀이 스탠드를 설치할 수 있어야만 가능합니다.
   - Ⓓ 오늘 밤 전시를 밖에서 진행합시다!

6. 여: 혹시 강의계획서 링크를 가지고 계신가요?
   - Ⓐ 가지고 있어요—지금 보내드릴게요.
   - Ⓑ 교재에 인쇄되어 있어요.
   - Ⓒ 네, 저는 가지고 있지 않아요.
   - Ⓓ 수강 변경 기간이 끝난 후에요.

7. W: What time is the rec center class?
   - (A) **It begins right after the 6 p.m. orientation.**
   - (B) Court B is booked during the evening slot.
   - (C) Check-ins for that class close at five-thirty.
   - (D) The posted schedule shows Tuesdays only.

8. M: We're still on for the advising session at one, aren't we?
   - (A) Room 214 near the stairs.
   - (B) **Actually, it was shifted to one-thirty.**
   - (C) Yes, all four of them are here.
   - (D) I booked tomorrow afternoon.

7. 여: 레크리에이션 센터 수업은 몇 시인가요?
   - (A) 오후 6시 오리엔테이션 직후 시작합니다.
   - (B) 저녁 시간대에 B코트가 예약되어 있습니다.
   - (C) 그 수업의 체크인은 5시 30분에 마감합니다.
   - (D) 게시된 일정에는 화요일만 나와 있습니다.

8. 남: 우리 상담 세션은 오후 1시에 그대로 진행하는 거죠?
   - (A) 계단 근처 214호실입니다.
   - (B) 사실 1시 30분으로 변경되었습니다.
   - (C) 네, 그들 네 명 모두 여기 있어요.
   - (D) 저는 내일 오후로 예약했습니다.

어휘

1. **point of contact** 연락 담당자[부서] | **lab safety** 실험실 안전 | **administration** n 행정
2. **exam room** 시험장 | **registrar** n 교무처 직원, 등록 담당자 | **enrollment** n 등록, 입학 절차 | **assignment board** 배정 게시판
3. **conference badge** 학회 참가 배지 | **registration desk** 등록 데스크 | **QR-code kiosk** QR코드 키오스크
4. **certificate** n 수료증, 증명서 | **automatically** adv 자동으로
5. **atrium** n 아트리움(유리 지붕 구조물 중앙의 넓은 공간) | **facilities** n 시설(팀) | **set up** 설치하다
6. **syllabus** n 강의계획서 | **reader** n 교재 모음집, 자료집 | **add/drop period** 수강 변경 기간
7. **rec center** 레크리에이션 센터 | **orientation** n 오리엔테이션, 설명회 | **slot** n 시간대, 자리
8. **advising session** 상담 세션 | **shift** v 옮기다, 변경되다 | **book** v 예약하다

[9-10] Listen to a conversation.

- W: IT support, this is Lena.
- M: Hi, **⑨ my e-mail keeps bouncing. A 38 megabyte PDF isn't getting sent to a client.**
- W: **⑨ Most mailboxes cap attachments at 25 megabytes.**
- M: I tried zipping it, but I can't install any tools on this laptop.
- W: No need. **⑩ Upload it to the team's shared drive;** you'll get a view-only link.
- M: Can the client download without logging in?
- W: Yes, **⑩ choose "anyone with the link" and allow download.**
- M: Great. I'll replace the attachment with the link.

[9-10] 대화를 들으세요.

- 여: IT 지원팀, 레나입니다.
- 남: 안녕하세요. 제 이메일이 계속 반송돼요. 38메가바이트짜리 PDF가 고객에게 전송되지 않아요.
- 여: 대부분의 메일함은 첨부파일 용량 제한이 25메가바이트입니다.
- 남: 압축해 보려고 했는데, 이 노트북에는 아무 도구도 설치할 수 없어요.
- 여: 그럴 필요 없어요. 팀 공유 드라이브에 업로드하면 보기 전용 링크가 생깁니다.
- 남: 고객이 로그인 없이 다운로드할 수 있나요?
- 여: 네, "링크가 있는 사람 누구나"를 선택하고 다운로드 허용을 하면 돼요.
- 남: 좋네요. 첨부파일 대신 그 링크를 넣을게요.

어휘

bounce v (이메일이) 반송되다, 되돌아오다 | **megabyte** n 메가바이트 (디지털 데이터 용량 단위) | **zip** v (파일을) 압축하다 | **upload** v 업로드하다, (파일을) 올리다 | **download** v 다운로드하다, (파일을) 받다

9. What problem are they trying to solve?
   - (A) Recovering a deleted folder
   - **(B) Emailing an oversized file**
   - (C) Fixing a broken keyboard
   - (D) Resetting a Wi-Fi password

10. What does the woman suggest the man do?
    - (A) Install a compressor app
    - (B) Wait for IT to raise the limit
    - (C) Print and mail the file
    - **(D) Use the shared drive link**

9. 그들이 해결하려는 문제는 무엇인가?
   - (A) 삭제된 폴더 복구
   - (B) 너무 큰 파일 이메일 전송
   - (C) 고장 난 키보드 수리
   - (D) 와이파이 비밀번호 재설정

10. 여자는 남자에게 무엇을 하라고 제안하는가?
    - (A) 압축 앱을 설치하라고
    - (B) IT팀이 용량 제한을 늘릴 때까지 기다리라고
    - (C) 파일을 출력해 우편으로 보내라고
    - (D) 공유 드라이브 링크를 사용하라고

[11-12] Listen to an announcement from Campus Safety.

[11-12] 캠퍼스 보안팀의 안내방송을 들으세요.

Announcer: **11 Beginning next month, two-factor sign-in will be required for all student accounts.** You can choose the authenticator app or text codes; either option works on phones you already have. This change follows several phishing attempts that targeted inboxes last week. **12 Before the deadline, please enroll through the security portal**, test a backup method, and update your recovery email. After setup, you'll enter your password and a one-time code to access mail, the LMS, and library databases. If you lose your phone, the help desk can issue temporary codes with ID.

안내원: 다음 달부터 모든 학생 계정에 대해 2단계 로그인이 필요합니다. 인증 앱이나 문자 메시지 코드를 선택할 수 있으며, 둘 다 이미 가지고 있는 휴대전화에서 사용 가능합니다. 이번 변경은 지난주 받은편지함을 노린 여러 차례의 피싱 공격 이후에 이루어지는 것입니다. **마감일 전에 보안 포털에서 등록하고,** 예비 방법을 시험해 보고, 복구 이메일을 업데이트하시기 바랍니다. 설정이 완료되면, 비밀번호와 일회용 코드를 입력해야 메일, 학습 관리 시스템, 그리고 도서관 데이터베이스에 접근할 수 있습니다. 휴대전화를 잃어버린 경우, 도움 창구에서 신분증을 제시하면 임시 코드를 발급받을 수 있습니다.

어휘

two-factor adj 이중 요소의, 2단계의 | **sign-in** n 로그인 | **authenticator** n 인증기, 인증 앱 | **phishing** n 피싱 (사기성 정보 탈취 행위) | **inbox** n 받은편지함 | **enroll** v 등록하다, 가입하다 | **portal** n 포털, 접속 창구[사이트] | **recovery** n 복구, 회복 | **temporary** adj 임시의

11. What is the announcement about?
    - (A) Longer help-desk hours
    - (B) A new campus browser
    - (C) Free antivirus software
    - **(D) Mandatory account verification**

12. What does the speaker ask students to do first?
    - (A) Ignore phishing emails
    - (B) Replace their phones
    - **(C) Register on the security site**
    - (D) Delete recovery emails

11. 이 공지는 무엇에 관한 것인가?
    - (A) 도움 창구 운영 시간 연장
    - (B) 새로운 캠퍼스 브라우저
    - (C) 무료 백신 소프트웨어
    - (D) 의무적인 계정 인증

12. 화자가 학생들에게 가장 먼저 하라고 요청한 것은 무엇인가?
    - (A) 피싱 이메일을 무시하라고
    - (B) 휴대전화를 교체하라고
    - (C) 보안 사이트에 등록하라고
    - (D) 복구 이메일을 삭제하라고

[13-16] Listen to a talk in a biology class.

Professor: Every year, millions of birds travel thousands of kilometers to feeding or breeding grounds. **13** **The question is how they navigate with such accuracy.** One explanation is that they use the night sky. Birds read the pattern of stars, especially constellations near the North Star, to keep a steady heading. The sun also works as a guide, but only if a bird has an internal clock that corrects for the sun's movement across the sky. **14** **More recently, researchers found evidence for a magnetic sense.** **15** **Certain proteins in the eye appear sensitive to Earth's magnetic field, giving birds an internal compass.** Experiments in planetariums support the idea of complex calculations: when star patterns were shifted, the birds changed orientation, which tells us they rely on multiple cues and can switch among them. **16** **Migration carries real risks.** Climate change can shift seasonal timing, so some birds arrive before food is available. Bright city lights at night can disorient flocks and increase collisions with buildings. **16** **Those problems lead directly to conservation questions about lighting policy and habitat protection.** Later this semester, we will examine case studies in which routes have changed with warming trends, and we will look at tracking data from satellite tags. Next time, we will compare how star cues, sun position, and magnetic input interact under different weather and light conditions.

[13-16] 생물학 수업 강의를 들으세요.

교수: 매년, 수백만 마리의 새들이 먹이나 번식지를 찾아 수천 킬로미터를 이동합니다. **문제는 그들이 어떻게 그렇게 정확하게 길을 찾는가 하는 것입니다.** 한 가지 설명은 밤하늘을 이용하는 것입니다. 새들은 별의 배열, 특히 북극성 근처의 별자리를 읽어 일정한 방향을 유지합니다. 태양도 길잡이 역할을 하지만, 이는 새가 하늘을 가로지르는 태양의 움직임을 보정할 수 있는 내부 시계를 가지고 있을 때만 가능합니다. 최근에는 자기 감각에 대한 증거도 발견되었습니다. 눈 속의 특정 단백질이 지구 자기장에 민감하게 반응하여, 새들에게 일종의 내부 나침반을 제공합니다. 플라네타륨 실험이 이러한 복잡한 계산 이론을 뒷받침합니다. 별자리 배열을 바꾸자, 새들이 방향을 바꾸었고, 이는 새들이 여러 신호를 활용하며 필요에 따라 전환할 수 있음을 보여줍니다. **이동은 실제로 위험을 동반합니다.** 기후 변화는 계절적 시기를 바꿀 수 있어, 일부 새들은 먹이가 나오기 전에 도착하기도 합니다. 밤의 도시 불빛은 무리를 혼란스럽게 하여 건물 충돌을 늘릴 수 있습니다. **이런 문제들은 곧바로 조명 정책과 서식지 보호 같은 보존 문제로 이어집니다.** 이번 학기 후반에는 따뜻해지는 기후에 따라 경로가 바뀐 사례를 살펴보고, 위성 태그를 이용한 추적 데이터를 분석할 것입니다. 다음 시간에는 별자리, 태양 위치, 자기 신호가 날씨와 빛 조건에 따라 어떻게 상호 작용하는지를 비교해 보겠습니다.

어휘

navigate v 항해하다, 길을 찾다 | **accuracy** n 정확성 | **constellation** n 별자리 | **heading** n 진행 방향 | **internal** adj 내부의 | **correct** v 수정하다, 보정하다 | **magnetic** adj 자기의, 자성의 | **protein** n 단백질 | **compass** n 나침반 | **orientation** n 방향 설정, 지향 | **cue** n 단서, 신호 | **disorient** v 방향 감각을 잃게 하다 | **collision** n 충돌 | **conservation** n 보존, 보호 | **satellite** n 위성

---

13. What topic does the professor mainly talk about?
    Ⓐ **Factors that guide long-distance bird migration**
    Ⓑ How urban lighting affects building safety
    Ⓒ Why predators follow seasonal changes
    Ⓓ Procedures for conditioning captive flocks

14. What does the professor discuss after traditional explanations?
    Ⓐ Student opinions on research priorities
    Ⓑ **Recent discoveries about navigation mechanisms**

13. 교수가 주로 논의하는 주제는 무엇인가?
    Ⓐ 장거리 철새 이동을 이끄는 요인들
    Ⓑ 도시 조명이 건물 안전에 미치는 영향
    Ⓒ 왜 포식자들이 계절 변화를 따라가는지
    Ⓓ 사육된 새 무리를 훈련하는 절차

14. 교수에 따르면, 전통적 설명 다음에 그가 논의하는 것은 무엇인가?
    Ⓐ 연구 우선순위에 대한 학생 의견
    Ⓑ 길찾기 메커니즘에 대한 최근 발견

  © Conservation campaigns before basic concepts
  ⒟ Field reports prior to experimental results

15. According to the professor, how does Earth's magnetic field assist migrants?
  Ⓐ Heat storage enables slow release after sunset.
  Ⓑ Nighttime winds increase between buildings.
  Ⓒ It provides an internal compass for orientation.
  Ⓓ Moisture uptake promotes longer rest during travel.

16. What does the professor imply about migration risks?
  Ⓐ They show migration is no longer necessary.
  Ⓑ They are minor compared with other issues.
  Ⓒ They are mostly solved by current tools.
  Ⓓ They highlight urgent need for conservation action.

15. 교수에 따르면, 지구 자기장은 이동하는 새들에게 어떻게 도움이 되는가?
  Ⓐ 열 저장이 해가 진 뒤 천천히 방출되도록 한다.
  Ⓑ 야간 바람이 건물 사이에서 증가한다.
  Ⓒ 방향을 잡기 위한 내부 나침반을 제공한다.
  Ⓓ 수분 흡수가 여행 중 더 긴 휴식을 가능하게 한다.

16. 교수는 이동의 위험성에 대해 무엇을 시사하는가?
  Ⓐ 이는 더 이상 이동이 필요 없음을 보여준다.
  Ⓑ 이는 다른 문제들에 비하면 사소하다.
  Ⓒ 이는 현재의 도구로 대부분 해결되었다.
  Ⓓ 이는 보존 조치의 긴급한 필요성을 강조한다.

Writing

[1-10] Make an appropriate sentence.

[1–10] 알맞은 문장을 만드세요.

1. Why was the event postponed?
  It <u>was</u> <u>the severe weather</u> <u>that</u> <u>forced</u> <u>the organizers</u> <u>to delay it</u>.

1. 행사가 왜 연기되었나요?
  심한 날씨 때문에 주최 측이 연기할 수밖에 없었습니다.

2. I'm updating the calendar now.
  <u>Could</u> <u>you</u> <u>let me know</u> <u>whether</u> <u>the meeting has been rescheduled</u>?

2. 지금 달력을 업데이트하고 있어요.
  회의 일정이 변경되었는지 알려주실 수 있나요?

3. We're preparing for the conference.
  <u>Who</u> <u>is in charge of</u> <u>coordinating</u> <u>the guest speakers</u>?

3. 우리는 학회를 준비하고 있어요.
  초청 연사를 조율하는 책임자는 누구인가요?

4. The professor mentioned an alternative assignment.
  <u>Do</u> <u>you</u> <u>know</u> <u>when</u> <u>the new guidelines</u> <u>will be posted</u>?

4. 교수님이 대체 과제를 말씀하셨어요.
  새로운 지침이 언제 게시될지 아시나요?

5. I couldn't access the dataset last night.
  The link <u>that</u> <u>you</u> <u>sent</u> <u>me</u> <u>no longer</u> <u>works</u>.

5. 어젯밤에 데이터셋에 접속할 수 없었어요.
  당신이 보내준 링크가 더 이상 작동하지 않아요.

6. I need to improve my writing.
  It <u>helps</u> <u>to outline</u> <u>the main points</u> <u>before</u> <u>drafting</u>.

6. 제 글쓰기를 향상시킬 필요가 있어요.
  초안을 쓰기 전에 요점을 개요로 정리하면 도움이 돼요.

7. My laptop keeps freezing during tutorials.
  <u>Have</u> <u>you</u> <u>tried</u> <u>updating</u> <u>the graphics</u> <u>driver</u>?

7. 제 노트북이 강의 중에 계속 멈춰요.
  그래픽 드라이버를 업데이트해 보셨나요?

8. We arrived late to the station.
   By the time we got there, the last train had left.

9. What did the advisor recommend?
   She suggested that I take a lighter course load.

10. How did you handle the complaint?
    I apologized and offered to replace the damaged item.

[11] Write an Email.

Yesterday afternoon, the campus lab was closed without prior notice for maintenance. You had scheduled time to collect data for an assignment due later this week, but you could not finish the required trials. The equipment you need is only available in that lab, and your schedule limits rescheduling.

Write an email to your instructor. In your email, do the following.

- Explain the lab closure and missed trials.
- Request a short extension with a new date.
- Ask about acceptable alternatives for submission.

Write as much as you can and in complete sentences.

Sample Answer
Your Response:
To: Prof. Nguyen
Subject: Lab Closure and Assignment Timeline

Dear Professor Nguyen,

Yesterday afternoon, the Biology Methods Lab (Room 2B) closed without notice for maintenance from about 2:30 to 5:00. I had reserved that time to run spectrophotometer trials for this week's assignment, but I completed only two of the five required runs. The equipment I need is only available there, and my schedule left no way to reschedule yesterday.

May I request a short extension until Friday, September 19, 6 p.m., to finish the remaining trials and submit a complete report? If an extension is not possible, could you recommend an alternative—submitting partial results with notes, using sample data, or adapting the procedure with available equipment?

I appreciate your guidance and will follow your preferred plan.

Sincerely,
TJ Kim
BIO 302, Section 1

---

[12] Write for an Academic Discussion.

Your professor is teaching a class on educational technology. Write a post responding to the professor's question.

In your response, you should do the following.
- Express and support your opinion.
- Make a contribution to the discussion in your own words.

An effective response will contain at least 100 words.

Professor: Many courses now intersect with generative AI tools. Some universities are considering strict limits to protect academic integrity and skill development, while others argue that guided use reflects real-world practice. In your view, should universities ban generative AI in coursework or teach responsible use? Explain your position.

Student A: I think universities should teach responsible use of AI. These tools are already part of workplaces, so students need to learn how to cite outputs, check accuracy, and distinguish their own ideas. Clear guidelines can prevent misuse, while outright bans may simply push students to use AI secretly.

Student B: I support limited use, especially in early writing courses. Beginners need to develop basic skills like planning and revising without shortcuts. Later, instructors could allow AI under strict policies, requiring drafts and disclosure of prompts. A phased approach ensures assessment fairness while still preparing students for real-world practice.

Sample Answer

Universities should teach responsible use of AI, not ban it. Bans push activity underground, and fail to prepare students for workplaces where AI appears. With clear rules, AI can support learning rather than replace it. Require disclosure of prompts and outputs, a brief reflection on what the tool contributed and how facts were checked, and occasional spot-checks. I share Student B's concern about first-year courses: early overreliance can short-circuit drafting skills. A phased policy works: AI-free checkpoints (in-class outline or first paragraph,) then limited, documented use for brainstorming or revision—not full drafts. Process drafts or version histories let instructors see the students' thinking. This approach protects integrity, builds foundational skills, and mirrors real professional practice, which is the point of higher education.

예시 답변

대학은 AI를 금지하는 것이 아니라 책임 있는 사용을 가르쳐야 합니다. 금지는 활동을 비밀스럽게 몰아가며, AI가 등장하는 직장에 학생들을 준비시키는 데 실패합니다. 명확한 규칙이 있으면, AI는 학습을 대체하는 것이 아니라 학습을 지원할 수 있습니다. 프롬프트와 산출물을 공개하도록 요구하고, 도구가 기여한 바와 사실이 어떻게 확인되었는지에 대한 짧은 성찰문을 제출하게 하며, 가끔 무작위 점검을 실시해야 합니다. 저는 1학년 과정에 대한 학생 B의 우려에 공감합니다. 초기부터 지나치게 의존하면 초안 작성 기술이 단축될 수 있습니다. 단계적인 정책이 효과적입니다. 즉, AI를 사용하지 않는 점검 지점(수업 중 개요 작성이나 첫 단락 작성), 그 다음은 브레인스토밍이나 수정에 한정된 기록된 사용—전체 초안은 아님—으로 나아가는 것입니다. 과정 초안이나 버전 기록을 통해 교수들은 학생의 사고 과정을 볼 수 있습니다. 이러한 접근은 성실성을 지키고, 기초적인 기술을 구축하며, 실제 전문적 관행을 반영합니다. 이것이 바로 고등 교육의 핵심 목적입니다.

Speaking

[1–7] Listen and Repeat.

You are learning how to greet visitors at a community library. Listen to the staff trainer and repeat what she says. Repeat only once.

1. **Trainer:** Welcome to the Community Library.
2. **Trainer:** New books are displayed near the entrance for visitors to browse.
3. **Trainer:** Study rooms can be reserved online or at the front desk.
4. **Trainer:** Please speak quietly and set your phone to silent mode.
5. **Trainer:** Food is not allowed, but drinks with secure lids are permitted.
6. **Trainer:** Children's programs are held downstairs every afternoon, offering fun reading and art activities.

[1–7] 듣고 따라 말하세요.

당신은 지역 도서관에서 방문객들에게 인사하는 방법을 배우고 있습니다. 직원 교육관의 말을 듣고 그녀가 말하는 것을 따라 하세요. 단 한 번만 반복하세요.

1. **교육관:** 커뮤니티 도서관에 오신 것을 환영합니다.
2. **교육관:** 새 책들은 방문객들이 볼 수 있도록 입구 근처에 진열되어 있습니다.
3. **교육관:** 스터디룸은 온라인이나 안내 데스크에서 예약할 수 있습니다.
4. **교육관:** 조용히 말씀해 주시고 휴대전화는 무음 모드로 설정해 주십시오.
5. **교육관:** 음식은 허용되지 않지만, 뚜껑이 있는 음료는 허용됩니다.
6. **교육관:** 어린이 프로그램은 매일 오후 아래층에서 열리며, 재미있는 독서와 미술 활동이 포함되어 있습니다.

7. Trainer: If you need help locating materials, ask a librarian—they'll be happy to guide you to the right section.

7. 교육관: 자료를 찾는 데 도움이 필요하면 사서에게 물어보세요. 친절히 올바른 구역으로 안내해 드릴 것입니다.

[8-11] Take an Interview.

You have agreed to take part in a research study about healthy eating. You will have a short online interview with a researcher. The researcher will ask you some questions.

[8-11] 인터뷰에 응하세요.

당신은 건강한 식습관에 관한 연구에 참여하기로 동의하셨습니다. 연구자와 짧은 온라인 인터뷰를 하게 됩니다. 연구자가 몇 가지 질문을 할 것입니다.

8. Interviewer: Thank you for participating in our study on healthy eating. I would like to ask you some questions about food choices and lifestyle. To start, do you consider your current diet healthy or unhealthy overall? Please explain briefly why you think so.

8. 면접관: 건강한 식습관에 관한 저희 연구에 참여해 주셔서 감사합니다. 식품 선택과 생활 방식에 대해 몇 가지 질문을 드리고자 합니다. 먼저, 현재 본인의 식단이 전반적으로 건강하다고 생각하시나요, 아니면 건강하지 않다고 생각하시나요? 그렇게 생각하시는 이유를 간단히 설명해 주세요.

Sample Answer

I would describe my diet as moderately healthy. I eat vegetables and fruits every day, and I try to limit fast food. However, I sometimes skip breakfast when I am busy, which I know is not good. Overall, I think I am doing better than before, but I still have room to improve.

예시 답변

저는 제 식단을 적당히 건강하다고 설명할 수 있습니다. 저는 매일 채소와 과일을 먹고, 패스트푸드 섭취를 줄이려고 노력합니다. 그러나 바쁠 때는 아침을 거르기도 하는데, 그것이 좋지 않다는 것을 알고 있습니다. 전반적으로, 저는 예전보다 더 잘하고 있다고 생각하지만, 여전히 개선할 여지가 있습니다.

9. Interviewer: Interesting. Many people see healthy eating as a challenge, especially in busy modern life. Some say it gives them energy and improves their mood, while others think it is costly and difficult to maintain. What is your personal reaction to healthy eating? Why?

9. 면접관: 흥미롭네요. 많은 사람들이, 특히 바쁜 현대 생활에서, 건강한 식습관을 하나의 도전으로 봅니다. 어떤 이들은 그것이 에너지를 주고 기분을 향상시킨다고 말하는 반면, 다른 이들은 비용이 많이 들고 유지하기 어렵다고 생각합니다. 당신은 건강한 식습관을 개인적으로 어떻게 받아들이나요? 왜 그렇게 생각하시나요?

Sample Answer

Personally, I feel positive about healthy eating. When I eat balanced meals, I have more energy to study and I feel less tired in the afternoon. It also improves my mood because I don't feel heavy or uncomfortable. Even though preparing healthy meals can take more time, I think the benefits are greater than the inconvenience.

예시 답변

개인적으로 저는 건강한 식습관에 대해 긍정적으로 느낍니다. 균형 잡힌 식사를 할 때 저는 공부할 에너지가 더 생기고, 오후에 덜 피곤합니다. 또한 무겁거나 불편하지 않기 때문에 제 기분도 좋아집니다. 비록 건강한 식사를 준비하는 데 시간이 더 걸리긴 하지만, 저는 그 불편보다 이점이 더 크다고 생각합니다.

10. Interviewer: Good. Now I want to ask your opinion. Some argue that healthy eaters live longer, more productive lives, since they avoid illness and stay active. Do you agree that maintaining a healthy diet directly leads to a more fulfilling life? Why or why not?

Sample Answer

Yes, I agree. Eating healthy foods can prevent diseases like obesity or diabetes, which means people can enjoy their lives without health problems. Also, a nutritious diet helps people stay active, so they can travel, play sports, and enjoy hobbies longer. For me, having the energy to do what I love makes life more fulfilling.

11. Interviewer: That makes sense. Finally, I want to ask about government policy. Do you think city governments should support healthier eating by offering more farmers' markets, nutrition programs, or cooking classes? Why or why not? Give one clear reason for your answer.

Sample Answer

Yes, I think governments should support healthier eating. Not everyone knows how to cook or has access to fresh food. Farmers' markets and nutrition programs can make fruits and vegetables cheaper and easier to buy. If cooking classes are available, people can learn simple, healthy recipes. This kind of support would improve public health in the long term.

10. 면접관: 좋습니다. 이제 당신의 의견을 묻고 싶습니다. 몇몇 사람들은, 건강하게 식사하는 사람들이 질병을 피하고 활동적으로 지내기 때문에 더 오래, 더 생산적인 삶을 산다고 주장합니다. 건강한 식단을 유지하는 것이 직접적으로 더 충만한 삶으로 이어진다고 보시나요? 그렇다고 보시는 이유 또는 그렇지 않다고 보시는 이유를 말씀해 주세요.

예시 답변

네, 저는 동의합니다. 건강한 음식을 먹는 것은 비만이나 당뇨병과 같은 질병을 예방할 수 있으며, 이는 사람들이 건강 문제 없이 삶을 즐길 수 있다는 뜻입니다. 또한, 영양가 있는 식단은 사람들이 활동적으로 지낼 수 있도록 도와주기 때문에, 여행을 하거나 스포츠를 즐기거나 취미 생활을 더 오래 이어갈 수 있습니다. 저에게는 제가 좋아하는 일을 할 수 있는 에너지를 갖는 것이 삶을 더 충만하게 만듭니다.

11. 면접관: 타당한 말씀이네요. 마지막으로, 정부 정책에 대해 묻고 싶습니다. 시 정부가 더 많은 파머스 마켓(농산물 직거래 장터), 영양 프로그램, 혹은 요리 수업을 제공하는 방식으로 더 건강한 식습관을 지원해야 한다고 생각하시나요? 왜 그렇게 생각하시나요, 또는 왜 그렇지 않다고 생각하시나요? 당신의 답을 뒷받침하는 명확한 이유 한 가지를 제시해 주세요.

예시 답변

네, 저는 정부가 더 건강한 식습관을 지원해야 한다고 생각합니다. 모든 사람들이 요리를 할 줄 아는 것도 아니고, 신선한 식품에 접근할 수 있는 것도 아닙니다. 파머스 마켓이나 영양 프로그램은 과일과 채소를 더 저렴하고 쉽게 살 수 있도록 해줍니다. 요리 수업이 제공된다면, 사람들은 간단하고 건강한 요리법을 배울 수 있습니다. 이러한 지원은 장기적으로 공중 보건을 향상시킬 것입니다.

Actual Test 2

Reading Module 1

01. prod<u>uce</u>	02. ca<u>lls</u>	03. tra<u>vel</u>	04. dist<u>ances</u>	05. gro<u>ups</u>
06. <u>stay</u>	07. <u>even</u>	08. wid<u>ely</u>	09. S<u>uch</u>	10. g<u>uide</u>
11. ⓓ	12. ⓑ	13. ⓑ	14. ⓐ	15. ⓓ
16. ⓑ	17. ⓓ	18. ⓐ	19. ⓒ	20. ⓐ

[1-10] Fill in the missing letters in the paragraph.

Whales use acoustic signals to interact across vast ocean spaces, demonstrating advanced biological adaptations for underwater communication. They prod<u>uce</u> low-frequency ca<u>lls</u> that tra<u>vel</u> long dist<u>ances</u>, allowing gro<u>ups</u> to st<u>ay</u> connected ev<u>en</u> when wid<u>ely</u> separated. S<u>uch</u> sounds g<u>uide</u> migration, strengthen social bonds, and help whales coordinate cooperative behaviors in the deep sea. Marine biologists analyze these vocalizations to learn about population dynamics, environmental conditions, and marine ecological relationships. Continued research on whale sounds highlights the complexity of animal communication and the importance of preserving marine ecosystems.

[1-10] 문단에서 빠진 글자들을 채워 넣으세요.

고래들은 음향 신호를 사용하여 광활한 바다 공간에서 서로 상호작용하며, 수중 의사소통을 위한 고도의 생물학적 적응을 보여준다. 그들은 저주파 소리를 내는데, 이 소리는 먼 거리를 이동하여 무리가 멀리 떨어져 있어도 서로 연결된 상태를 유지할 수 있게 한다. 이러한 소리는 이동 경로를 안내하고, 사회적 유대를 강화하며, 깊은 바다에서 고래들이 협력적 행동을 조정하는 데 도움을 준다. 해양 생물학자들은 이러한 발성을 분석하여 개체군 역학, 환경 조건, 그리고 해양 생태 관계에 대해 배운다. 고래 소리에 대한 지속적인 연구는 동물 의사소통의 복잡성과 해양 생태계 보존의 중요성을 부각시킨다.

어휘
acoustic adj 음향의, 소리의 | **signals** n 신호 | **demonstrate** v 보여주다, 입증하다 | **adaptations** n 적응, 적응 현상 | **frequency** n 주파수 | **migration** n 이동, (동물의) 이동 현상 | **cooperative** adj 협력적인 | **vocalizations** n 발성, 발성 행위 | **dynamics** n 역학, 변화 양상 | **ecosystems** n 생태계

[11-12] Read a flyer.

Community Theater – Summer Film Festival

Experience three evenings of international films at the Community Theater from July 10 to 12. Each screening commences at 7:00 P.M. Advance tickets cost $8, while ⑪ admission at the door is $10. Students presenting valid identification will receive a $1 discount. ⑫ Following every showing, a moderated session with local critics is scheduled in the lobby.

[11-12] 전단을 보세요.

커뮤니티 극장 – 여름 영화제

7월 10일부터 12일까지 커뮤니티 극장에서 열리는 세 번의 국제 영화 저녁 상영을 경험하세요. 각 상영은 오후 7시에 시작됩니다. 사전 예매 티켓은 8달러이고, 현장 입장은 10달러입니다. 유효한 신분증을 제시하는 학생은 1달러 할인을 받습니다. 모든 상영 후에는 지역 평론가들이 진행하는 좌담회가 로비에서 예정되어 있습니다.

어휘

flyer n 전단 | festival n 축제 | international adj 국제적인 | screening n 상영, 시사회 | commence v 시작하다 | advance adj 사전의, 미리 하는 | admission n 입장, 입장료 | identification n 신분증, 신원 확인 | discount n 할인 | moderated adj 사회자가 진행하는, 조정된

---

11. How much will a student without proper ID pay at the door?
ⓐ $7
ⓑ $8
ⓒ $9
ⓓ **$10**

12. What is scheduled to occur immediately after each screening?
ⓐ A reception for visiting filmmakers
ⓑ **A talk led by local critics**
ⓒ A concert by the theater orchestra
ⓓ A guided tour of backstage areas

11. 유효한 신분증이 없는 학생은 현장에서 얼마를 지불해야 하는가?
ⓐ 7달러
ⓑ 8달러
ⓒ 9달러
ⓓ **10달러**

12. 각 상영 직후에 예정된 것은 무엇인가?
ⓐ 초청 영화 제작자를 위한 리셉션
ⓑ **지역 평론가들이 이끄는 토론회**
ⓒ 극장 오케스트라의 연주회
ⓓ 무대 뒤 안내 투어

[13-15] Read an e-mail.

To: allstudents@westfield.edu
From: housingoffice@westfield.edu
Date: August 12
Subject: Oak Hall Renovation Notice

Dear Students,

13 **Renovations in Oak Hall are scheduled to begin on September 1 and are expected to continue through October 15.** During this period, the first-floor lounge and the laundry room will be closed to residents. To minimize inconvenience, several temporary laundry machines will be installed in the basement of Pine Hall, while **14** **additional seating has been arranged in the main cafeteria so that students still have a comfortable place to gather.**

15 **Construction activities will be concentrated between 9:00 A.M. and 5:00 P.M.; however, deliveries of equipment and minor adjustments may occasionally take place outside those hours.** Because of the likelihood of disruptive noise, students who need quiet spaces for study are encouraged to use the library, which has extended

[13-15] 이메일을 보세요.

수신: allstudents@westfield.edu
발신: housingoffice@westfield.edu
날짜: 8월 12일
제목: 오크 홀 보수공사 안내

학생 여러분께,

오크 홀의 보수 공사가 9월 1일에 시작되어 10월 15일까지 진행될 예정입니다. 이 기간 동안 1층 라운지와 세탁실은 사용이 중지됩니다. 불편을 최소화하기 위해 파인 홀 지하에 임시 세탁기를 설치하고, 학생들이 편하게 모일 수 있도록 중앙 식당의 좌석을 추가로 마련했습니다.

공사 작업은 오전 9시~오후 5시에 집중되지만, 장비 반입이나 소규모 조정은 시간 외에 이루어질 수 있습니다. 소음 가능성이 있으므로, 조용한 학습 공간이 필요한 학생은 도서관(오후 11시까지 연장 운영) 또는 메이플 홀의 스터디룸을 이용하시기 바랍니다. 문의 사항은 주거지원팀(내선 203)으로 연락 주세요.

its evening hours until 11:00 P.M., or the study rooms in Maple Hall. For further questions, please contact the Housing Office at extension 203.

Thank you for your cooperation.

Housing Office

협조에 감사 드립니다.

주거지원팀

어휘

renovation n 보수 공사 | **resident** n 거주자, 주민 | **temporary** adj 임시의 | **basement** n 지하실 | **delivery** n (물품) 배송 | **adjustment** n 조정, 조절 | **disruptive** adj 방해가 되는 | **encourage** v 권장하다 | **extension** n (전화) 내선번호

---

13. What is the main purpose of the e-mail?
    - (A) To announce the opening of new housing facilities
    - **(B) To inform students about upcoming renovations**
    - (C) To invite students to participate in construction projects
    - (D) To provide details about changes to library operating hours

14. Which facility will continue to be available to students during the renovation?
    - **(A) The cafeteria**
    - (B) The first-floor lounge
    - (C) The laundry room in Oak Hall
    - (D) The Oak Hall lobby

15. What is indicated about the construction schedule?
    - (A) It may occur less frequently than expected.
    - (B) It may be completed before September 1.
    - (C) It may not cause any significant noise problems.
    - **(D) It may continue outside regular daytime hours.**

13. 이 이메일의 주요 목적은 무엇인가?
    - (A) 새로운 기숙사 시설 개장을 알리기 위해
    - (B) 다가오는 보수 공사에 대해 학생들에게 알리기 위해
    - (C) 학생들을 건설 프로젝트에 참여시키기 위해
    - (D) 도서관 운영 시간 변경에 대한 세부 사항을 제공하기 위해

14. 보수공사 기간 동안 학생들이 계속 이용할 수 있는 시설은 무엇인가?
    - (A) 식당
    - (B) 1층 라운지
    - (C) 오크 홀 세탁실
    - (D) 오크 홀 로비

15. 공사 일정에 대해 알 수 있는 것은?
    - (A) 예상보다 덜 자주 이루어질 수 있다.
    - (B) 9월 1일 이전에 끝날 수 있다.
    - (C) 큰 소음 문제를 일으키지 않을 수 있다.
    - (D) 일반 주간 시간대 외에도 진행될 수 있다.

[16-20] Papermaking along the Silk Road

[16-20] 실크로드를 통한 제지술

16 **Among the many cultural exchanges along the Silk Road, the transmission of papermaking from China to the West was one of the most influential.** Developed during the Han Dynasty, Chinese papermaking relied on plant fibers that produced a durable writing surface. **17** **For centuries, this innovation remained largely confined to East Asia.** However, as trade and travel expanded, knowledge of papermaking began to move

실크로드를 따라 이루어진 많은 문화 교류 중에서, 중국에서 서방으로의 제지술 전파는 가장 영향력 있는 것 중 하나였다. 한(漢) 왕조 시기에 개발된 중국 제지술은 내구성이 강한 기록용 표면을 만들어내는 식물 섬유에 의존했다. **수 세기 동안, 이 혁신은 주로 동아시아에 국한되어 있었다.** 그러나 교역과 여행이 확대되면서, 제지술에 대한 지식은 서쪽으로 전파되기 시작했고, 멀리 떨어진 사회들 간의 의사소통 방식을 변화시켰다.

westward, transforming communication in distant societies.

19 **A turning point came in the eighth century, when papermaking techniques reached the Islamic world.** Cities such as Samarkand and Baghdad became centers of production, adapting Chinese methods to local materials. **19** **Paper soon replaced parchment as the dominant medium for recording information.** This shift supported advances in scholarship, bureaucracy, and literature. **18 19** **Libraries flourished, and texts could be copied and distributed with greater efficiency, spreading knowledge more widely than ever before.**

From the Islamic world, papermaking eventually reached Europe by the twelfth century. The technology laid the foundation for later innovations such as the printing press, which revolutionized education and communication. **20** **Historians argue that the movement of papermaking through the Silk Road illustrates how a single technology, when transmitted across cultures, can reshape intellectual life on a global scale.**

전환점은 8세기에 찾아왔다. 제지 기술이 이슬람 세계에 도달했을 때였다. 사마르칸트와 바그다드 같은 도시들은 생산의 중심지가 되었고, 중국의 제지 방식을 지역 재료에 맞게 적용했다. 곧 종이는 양피지를 대신하여 기록의 주된 매체가 되었다. 이러한 변화는 학문, 행정, 문학의 발전을 뒷받침했다. 도서관이 번성했고, 문헌은 더 효율적으로 복사되고 배포될 수 있었으며, 지식은 그 어느 때보다 널리 퍼졌다.

이슬람 세계에서 제지술은 결국 12세기에 유럽에 도달했다. 이 기술은 인쇄술과 같은 후대의 혁신을 위한 토대를 마련했으며, 이는 교육과 의사소통을 혁신시켰다. 역사가들은 제지술이 실크로드를 통해 전파된 것은 하나의 기술이 문화를 넘어 전해질 때 어떻게 세계적 차원에서 지적 생활을 재구성할 수 있는지를 보여준다고 주장한다.

어휘

transmission n 전파, 전달 | **influential** adj 영향력 있는 | **dynasty** n 왕조 | **fiber** n 섬유 | **durable** adj 내구성 있는 | **innovation** n 혁신 | **confined** adj 제한된, 국한된 | **transform** v 변화시키다 | **turning point** 전환점 | **techniques** n 기술, 기법 | **center** n 중심지 | **adapt** v 적응하다, 맞추다 | **parchment** n 양피지 | **dominant** adj 지배적인, 주요한 | **bureaucracy** n 관료 제도, 행정 체계 | **flourish** v 번성하다, 번창하다 | **distribute** v 배포하다 | **foundation** n 토대, 기반 | **revolutionize** v 혁명적으로 바꾸다 | **reshape** v 재구성하다, 다시 형성하다

---

16. What is the passage mainly about?
    - Ⓐ The development of scholarship in medieval Islamic libraries
    - Ⓑ **The spread of papermaking technology from China to other regions**
    - Ⓒ The invention of the printing press in Europe during the twelfth century
    - Ⓓ The replacement of parchment with silk as a writing material

17. The word "confined" in the passage is closest in meaning to
    - Ⓐ shared
    - Ⓑ surrounded

16. 이 글의 주제는 무엇인가?
    - Ⓐ 중세 이슬람 도서관의 학문 발달
    - Ⓑ **중국에서 다른 지역으로 전파된 제지 기술**
    - Ⓒ 12세기 유럽에서의 인쇄술 발명
    - Ⓓ 필기 재료로서 양피지를 비단으로 대체한 것

17. 본문에서 "confined"라는 단어의 의미와 가장 가까운 것은?
    - Ⓐ 공유된
    - Ⓑ 둘러싸인

C recorded
D **restricted**

18. Why did papermaking contribute to advances in scholarship in the Islamic world?
    A **It made the production of written texts more efficient.**
    B It encouraged the replacement of silk with parchment for writing.
    C It limited access to knowledge to government officials only.
    D It prevented the spread of literature beyond large cities.

19. According to the passage, all of the following are true about papermaking EXCEPT:
    A It was introduced to the Islamic world in the eighth century.
    B It replaced parchment as the primary writing material.
    C **It was first developed in Europe during the twelfth century.**
    D It supported the growth of libraries and scholarship.

20. What can be inferred about the historical impact of papermaking?
    A **It played a pivotal role in expanding access to knowledge across cultures.**
    B Its primary effect was to support administrative growth beyond its place of origin.
    C It contributed to later innovations but was not the main driving force.
    D It offered limited benefits and did not shape intellectual life broadly.

18. 제지술은 왜 이슬람 세계에서 학문의 발전에 기여했는가?
    A **문헌의 생산을 더 효율적으로 만들었기 때문이다.**
    B 필기를 위해 비단을 양피지로 대체하도록 장려했기 때문이다.
    C 지식 접근을 정부 관리들에게만 제한했기 때문이다.
    D 문학이 대도시를 넘어 퍼지는 것을 막았기 때문이다.

19. 본문에 따르면, 다음 중 제지술에 대한 사실이 아닌 것은 무엇인가?
    A 8세기에 이슬람 세계에 도입되었다.
    B 기록의 주된 매체로 양피지를 대체했다.
    C **12세기에 유럽에서 처음 개발되었다.**
    D 도서관과 학문의 성장을 지원했다.

20. 제지술의 역사적 영향에 대해 추론할 수 있는 것은?
    A **문화 간 지식 접근 확대에 핵심적인 역할을 했다.**
    B 그 기원지를 넘어 행정적 성장을 지원했다.
    C 후대의 혁신에 기여했지만 주요 원동력은 아니었다.
    D 제한적인 혜택만 제공했으며 지적 생활을 널리 형성하지는 않았다.

Reading Module 2

01. carved	02. blocks	03. applied	04. over	05. surface
06. pressing	07. carefully	08. the	09. process	10. books
11. C	12. C	13. B	14. B	15. D
16. B	17. C	18. A	19. C	20. A

[1-10] Fill in the missing letters in the paragraph.

During the Tang Dynasty, artisans developed woodblock printing as a practical method for reproducing Buddhist scriptures and administrative documents. Craftsmen ca_rved_ wooden blo_cks_ but app_lied_ ink ov_er_ the su_rface_ before pre_ssing_ paper care_fully_ onto t_he_ design. This pro_cess_ allowed bo_oks_ to be copied in large quantities for broader distribution to scholars and institutions. The technique significantly reduced copying errors and preserved classical texts with greater accuracy. As printing spread, it encouraged literacy, promoted scholarship, and laid the foundation for the cultural and intellectual flourishing of later centuries.

[1-10] 문단에서 빠진 글자들을 채워 넣으세요.

당나라 시대에 장인들은 불경과 행정 문서를 복제하기 위한 실용적인 방법으로 목판 인쇄술을 개발했다. 장인들은 나무판을 새긴 후 표면에 잉크를 바르고, 종이를 조심스럽게 새긴 무늬 위에 눌렀다. 이 과정은 책을 대량으로 복사하여 학자들과 기관에 더 널리 배포할 수 있게 했다. 이 기술은 필사 오류를 크게 줄였고, 고전 문헌을 더 정확하게 보존할 수 있었다. 인쇄가 확산되면서, 이는 문해력을 장려하고 학문을 촉진했으며, 후대의 문화적 · 지적 번영을 위한 토대를 마련했다.

어휘

artisan n 장인, 숙련된 기술자 | **woodblock printing** 목판 인쇄술 | **practical** adj 실용적인 | **scripture** n 경전, 성서 | **administrative** adj 행정의 | **quantity** n 양, 분량 | **distribution** n 배포, 분배 | **accuracy** n 정확성 | **flourishing** n 번영, 번성 adj 번영하는

[11-12] Read an e-mail.

To: clubmembers@hillvalley.edu
From: debateclub@hillvalley.edu
Date: November 2
Subject: Debate Club Meeting – Rescheduled Date

Dear Members,

11 12 Please note that our next Debate Club meeting, originally set for Thursday, November 9, has been moved to Tuesday, November 14 at 6:00 P.M. in Lecture Hall B of the Humanities Building. **12** Members will receive an e-mail two days before the gathering with additional details. Signs will also be posted near the main entrance of the building. Refreshments will be provided after the meeting.

Debate Club Committee

[11-12] 이메일을 보세요.

수신: clubmembers@hillvalley.edu
발신: debateclub@hillvalley.edu
날짜: 11월 2일
제목: 토론 동아리 모임 – 변경된 날짜

회원 여러분께,

다음 토론 동아리 모임은 원래 11월 9일 목요일로 예정되어 있었으나, 11월 14일 화요일 오후 6시에 인문관 강의실 B에서 열리게 되었습니다. 회원들은 모임 이틀 전에 추가 세부 사항이 담긴 이메일을 받게 될 것입니다. 건물 정문 근처에도 안내 표지가 게시될 예정입니다. 모임 후에는 다과가 제공됩니다.

토론 동아리 운영위원회

어휘

rescheduled adj 다시 일정이 잡힌, 일정이 변경된 | **originally** adv 원래, 처음에 | **set** v 정하다, 예정하다 | **move** v 옮기다, 이동하다 | **Lecture Hall** 강의실 | **Humanities** n 인문관, 인문학 | **gathering** n 모임 | **additional** adj 추가적인 | **entrance** n 입구 | **refreshments** n 다과, 음료

11. Why did the committee send the e-mail to club members?
   Ⓐ To provide details about the change of meeting location
   Ⓑ To remind members to bring refreshments to the event
   Ⓒ **To confirm the arrangements for the revised schedule**
   Ⓓ To inform them about the placement of directional signs

12. When will members be reminded about the session?
   Ⓐ On November 2
   Ⓑ On November 9
   Ⓒ **On November 12**
   Ⓓ On November 14

[13-15] Read a social media post.

👤 City Library

Looking for your next great read? **13 Join us at the annual Autumn Book Fair, where shelves overflow with both timeless classics and exciting new releases.** Independent publishers will showcase rare editions and debut works, offering chances to discover new authors.

Beyond books, the fair features lively storytelling sessions, craft corners for children, and a reading lounge where visitors can relax. **14 Local cafés will provide complimentary samples of seasonal drinks,** filling the air with the scent of spiced tea and roasted coffee.

This event has grown into a cherished community tradition, drawing readers of every age. **13 15 More than just a marketplace, it celebrates imagination and shared stories.** Don't miss the chance to explore, connect, and leave with inspiration for your next reading journey.

👍 Like   💬 Comment

어휘
annual adj 매년의, 연례의 | **classic** n 고전 작품 | **showcase** v 선보이다, 전시하다 | **rare** adj 희귀한 | **debut** adj 첫 출간의 n 첫 작품 | **lively** adj 생동감 있는 | **complimentary** adj 무료의 | **seasonal** adj 계절의, 계절 한정의 | **cherished** adj 소중히 여겨지는 | **marketplace** n 시장, 장터

13. What is the main purpose of the post?
    Ⓐ To highlight the library's efforts to preserve rare editions
    Ⓑ To invite the community to an event that celebrates reading
    Ⓒ To explain the rules of participation in library programs
    Ⓓ To encourage donations for the library's annual fundraiser

14. What unique feature distinguishes the fair?
    Ⓐ Guests can listen to authors present their own debut works.
    Ⓑ Visitors can sample seasonal drinks from nearby cafés.
    Ⓒ Children are given complimentary books from the library.
    Ⓓ Readers can participate in novel-writing contests.

15. What can be inferred about the Autumn Book Fair?
    Ⓐ It is described as a specialized event for book collectors.
    Ⓑ It is seen mainly as a commercial event for publishers.
    Ⓒ It functions primarily as entertainment for children.
    Ⓓ It serves as a cultural gathering, not merely a marketplace.

13. 이 게시물의 주된 목적은 무엇인가?
    Ⓐ 도서관의 희귀본 보존 노력을 강조하기 위해
    Ⓑ 독서를 기념하는 행사에 지역 사회를 초대하기 위해
    Ⓒ 도서관 프로그램 참여 규칙을 설명하기 위해
    Ⓓ 도서관 연례 기금 모금을 장려하기 위해

14. 박람회를 차별화하는 독특한 특징은 무엇인가?
    Ⓐ 손님들이 작가의 첫 출간 작품 발표를 들을 수 있다.
    Ⓑ 방문객들이 인근 카페에서 계절 음료를 시음할 수 있다.
    Ⓒ 어린이들이 도서관에서 무료 책을 받는다.
    Ⓓ 독자들이 소설 집필 대회에 참여할 수 있다.

15. 가을 도서 박람회에 대해 추론할 수 있는 것은 무엇인가?
    Ⓐ 책 수집가를 위한 전문 행사로 묘사된다.
    Ⓑ 주로 출판사들을 위한 상업적 행사로 여겨진다.
    Ⓒ 주로 어린이를 위한 오락 행사의 기능을 한다.
    Ⓓ 단순한 시장이 아닌 문화적 모임의 역할을 한다.

[16-20] Social Bonds in Urban Life

⑯ Urbanization, the movement of populations from rural to urban areas, has been a defining feature of modern society. Cities often provide greater access to education, employment, and healthcare, which attracts people seeking opportunity. **⑯ Yet rapid urban growth can also produce social challenges, such as overcrowding and weakened community ties.** While villages typically maintain close-knit relationships, city life is often characterized by anonymity and reduced interaction among neighbors.

Nevertheless, urban areas also create new forms of connection. **⑱ Public spaces such as parks, libraries, and marketplaces can foster interaction**

[16-20] 도시 생활의 사회적 유대

도시화는 인구가 농촌 지역에서 도시 지역으로 이동하는 현상을 말하며, 현대 사회의 중요한 특징이 되어 왔다. 도시는 종종 더 큰 교육, 고용, 의료 접근성을 제공하며, 이는 기회를 찾는 사람들을 끌어들인다. 그러나 급속한 도시 성장은 과밀화와 공동체의 유대 약화와 같은 사회적 문제를 낳을 수도 있다. 마을은 보통 긴밀한 관계를 유지하는 반면, 도시 생활은 익명성과 이웃 간의 상호작용 감소로 특징지어지는 경우가 많다.

그럼에도 불구하고, 도시 지역은 새로운 형태의 연결을 만들어낸다. 공원, 도서관, 시장과 같은 공공 공간은 다양한 집단 간의 상호작용을 촉진할 수 있다. 또한, 기술

among diverse groups. Moreover, technological advances have allowed city residents to form digital communities that transcend physical boundaries. **17 These social networks can strengthen solidarity, encourage cultural exchange, and provide platforms for civic engagement.** However, the benefits of such connections are not equally distributed, as marginalized groups may still face barriers to participation.

19 Researchers studying urbanization argue that the relationship between population density and social bonds is complex. While cities may weaken traditional ties, they simultaneously generate opportunities for new affiliations. Understanding how urban environments shape human networks is critical for policymakers seeking to balance growth with social cohesion. **20 By designing inclusive spaces and promoting equal access to resources, cities can cultivate both diversity and unity within their populations.**

어휘

urbanization n 도시화 | **defining** adj 특징을 규정하는 | **feature** n 특징 | **opportunity** n 기회 | **overcrowding** n 과밀 | **anonymity** n 익명성 | **diverse** adj 다양한 | **transcend** v 초월하다 | **boundary** n 경계 | **solidarity** n 연대, 결속 | **civic** adj 시민의 | **engagement** n 참여, 관여 | **marginalized** adj 소외된 | **barrier** n 장벽 | **density** n 밀도 | **affiliation** n 결속, 소속 관계 | **cohesion** n 결속, 응집력 | **inclusive** adj 포용적인 | **cultivate** v 육성하다, 기르다 | **unity** n 통합, 단결

---

16. Which of the following best states a main idea of the passage?

Ⓐ The challenges of rural communities in maintaining social ties
Ⓑ **The influence of urbanization on social networks**
Ⓒ The role of digital technology in replacing face-to-face interaction
Ⓓ The economic benefits of living in large metropolitan areas

17. The word "solidarity" in paragraph 2 is closest in meaning to

Ⓐ independence
Ⓑ conflict
Ⓒ **cooperation**
Ⓓ autonomy

16. 다음 중 본문의 주제를 가장 잘 나타낸 것은 무엇인가?

Ⓐ 농촌 공동체가 사회적 유대를 유지하는 데 겪는 어려움
Ⓑ 도시화가 사회적 네트워크에 미치는 영향
Ⓒ 대면 상호작용을 대체하는 디지털 기술의 역할
Ⓓ 대도시 생활의 경제적 이점

17. 두 번째 단락에서 "solidarity"라는 단어의 의미와 가장 가까운 것은?

Ⓐ 독립
Ⓑ 갈등
Ⓒ 협력
Ⓓ 자율성

18. Why does the author mention public spaces such as parks and marketplaces?
    Ⓐ **To show how cities can create opportunities for interaction**
    Ⓑ To explain why rural areas maintain stronger family ties
    Ⓒ To argue that physical environments discourage social participation
    Ⓓ To provide evidence that urbanization reduces community engagement

19. What is the relationship between paragraphs 2 and 3?
    Ⓐ Paragraph 3 provides additional examples supporting claims in paragraph 2.
    Ⓑ Paragraph 3 introduces ideas that contradict the points made in paragraph 2.
    Ⓒ **Paragraph 3 explains the consequences of the issues introduced in paragraph 2.**
    Ⓓ Paragraph 3 suggests possible solutions to the problems described in paragraph 2.

20. What does the passage suggest about building stronger social networks in cities?
    Ⓐ **It requires creating inclusive spaces and equal access to resources.**
    Ⓑ It depends mainly on replacing public spaces with digital platforms.
    Ⓒ It can be achieved by increasing population density in all areas.
    Ⓓ It is only possible when traditional ties are completely preserved.

18. 저자가 공원이나 시장과 같은 공공 공간을 언급한 이유는?
    Ⓐ 도시가 상호작용 기회를 창출할 수 있는 방법을 보여주기 위해
    Ⓑ 농촌 지역이 더 강한 가족 유대를 유지하는 이유를 설명하기 위해
    Ⓒ 물리적 환경이 사회적 참여를 억제한다고 주장하기 위해
    Ⓓ 도시화가 공동체 유대를 줄인다는 증거를 제시하기 위해

19. 2단락과 3단락의 관계는 무엇인가?
    Ⓐ 3단락은 2단락의 주장들을 뒷받침하는 추가 예시를 제시한다.
    Ⓑ 3단락은 2단락에서 제기된 주장에 반대되는 생각을 소개한다.
    Ⓒ 3단락은 2단락에서 제기된 문제의 결과를 설명한다.
    Ⓓ 3단락은 2단락에서 설명된 문제의 해결책을 제안한다.

20. 본문에 따르면 도시에서 더 강한 사회적 네트워크를 구축하는 방법은 무엇인가?
    Ⓐ 포용적인 공간을 만들고 자원에 대한 평등한 접근을 제공하는 것이다.
    Ⓑ 공공 공간을 디지털 플랫폼으로 대체하는 데 주로 의존하는 것이다.
    Ⓒ 모든 지역에서 인구 밀도를 높임으로써 이루어질 수 있다.
    Ⓓ 전통적 유대가 완전히 보존될 때만 가능한 것이다.

Listening Module 1

01. Ⓐ	02. Ⓒ	03. Ⓒ	04. Ⓐ	05. Ⓐ
06. Ⓑ	07. Ⓓ	08. Ⓐ	09. Ⓑ	10. Ⓐ
11. Ⓓ	12. Ⓑ	13. Ⓒ	14. Ⓑ	15. Ⓐ
16. Ⓒ	17. Ⓑ	18. Ⓓ		

[1-8] Choose the best response.

1. M: Did you attend the career talk?
   Ⓐ **I missed it.**
   Ⓑ Yes, I would.
   Ⓒ After the lecture.
   Ⓓ It's a talk.

[1-8] 가장 적절한 응답을 고르세요.

1. 남: 경력 설명회에 참석했나요?
   Ⓐ 저는 놓쳤어요.
   Ⓑ 네, 그럴게요.
   Ⓒ 강의 후에요.
   Ⓓ 그건 설명회예요.

2. W: I don't have the Wi-Fi password.
   - (A) The library login desk.
   - (B) No, you don't.
   - **(C) It's printed on the router.**
   - (D) Tomorrow morning online.

3. W: Which office handles visiting-scholar visas?
   - (A) At the main gate information desk.
   - (B) By next Monday, if possible.
   - **(C) The International Programs Office does.**
   - (D) I handle those requests.

4. M: If no one objects, shall we move the colloquium online?
   - **(A) As long as captions are enabled.**
   - (B) The colloquium is at Hall C.
   - (C) I moved last month's session already.
   - (D) Why don't you check with the chair first?

5. W: Would it be possible to get your approval on the budget today?
   - **(A) I can sign right after lunch.**
   - (B) The panel starts at three o'clock.
   - (C) Please send a printed final version.
   - (D) It's already in the queue.

6. W: How often are study rooms cleaned?
   - (A) They're on Building C's second floor.
   - **(B) Do you mean the library or the dorms?**
   - (C) Yes, they get cleaned regularly.
   - (D) After closing, around midnight.

7. M: I was wondering if you could review my draft this morning.
   - (A) By tomorrow afternoon would be better.
   - (B) The review guidelines are on the portal.
   - (C) Your outline might need more sources.
   - **(D) I can carve out twenty minutes at ten.**

8. W: Doesn't the lab require closed-toe shoes?
   - **(A) Tours are exempt.**
   - (B) In the main lab, Room 310.
   - (C) Eye protection is mandatory at all times.
   - (D) The stockroom sells lab-approved footwear.

---

2. 여: 저는 와이파이 비밀번호가 없어요.
   - (A) 도서관 로그인 데스크요.
   - (B) 아니요, 없어요.
   - **(C) 라우터에 인쇄되어 있어요.**
   - (D) 내일 아침 온라인에서요.

3. 여: 어떤 사무실이 방문 학자 비자를 처리하나요?
   - (A) 정문 안내 데스크에서요.
   - (B) 가능하다면 다음 주 월요일까지요.
   - **(C) 국제 프로그램 사무실입니다.**
   - (D) 제가 그 요청들을 처리합니다.

4. 남: 아무도 이의가 없다면, 학술 모임을 온라인으로 옮길까요?
   - **(A) 자막이 켜져 있다면요.**
   - (B) 학술 모임은 C홀에서 열려요.
   - (C) 지난달 모임은 제가 이미 옮겼습니다.
   - (D) 의장에게 먼저 확인해 보시지요?

5. 여: 오늘 예산 승인을 받을 수 있을까요?
   - **(A) 점심 직후에 서명할 수 있습니다.**
   - (B) 패널은 세 시에 시작합니다.
   - (C) 인쇄된 최종본을 보내 주세요.
   - (D) 이미 대기열에 있습니다.

6. 여: 스터디룸은 얼마나 자주 청소되나요?
   - (A) 건물 C의 2층에 있어요.
   - **(B) 도서관 말인가요, 아니면 기숙사 말인가요?**
   - (C) 네, 정기적으로 청소됩니다.
   - (D) 문 닫은 후, 자정쯤에요.

7. 남: 오늘 아침 제 초안을 검토해 주실 수 있을까요?
   - (A) 내일 오후까지가 더 좋겠습니다.
   - (B) 검토 지침은 포털에 있습니다.
   - (C) 개요에 더 많은 자료가 필요할 수도 있어요.
   - **(D) 10시에 20분 정도 시간을 낼 수 있어요.**

8. 여: 연구실에서는 발가락이 덮인 신발이 필요하지 않나요?
   - **(A) 견학은 예외입니다.**
   - (B) 본 연구실, 310호에서요.
   - (C) 항상 눈 보호 장비가 의무입니다.
   - (D) 비품실에서 실험용으로 승인된 신발을 팝니다.

어휘

1 **attend** v 참석하다 | **career** n 경력, 직업 | **talk** n 강연, 설명회
2 **password** n 비밀번호 | **print** v 인쇄하다 | **router** n 라우터(네트워크 장치)
3 **handle** v 처리하다, 담당하다 | **visiting-scholar** 방문 학자 | **request** n 요청(서) v 요청하다
4 **object** v 반대하다, 이의를 제기하다 | **colloquium** n 학술 모임, 세미나 | **caption** n 자막
5 **approval** n 승인 | **budget** n 예산 | **queue** n 대기열
6 **dorm(=dormitory)** n 기숙사 | **regularly** adv 정기적으로 | **closing** n 마감
7 **review** v 검토하다 n 검토 | **draft** n 초안 | **carve out** (시간 등을) 따로 내다
8 **require** v 요구하다 | **closed-toe** adj 발가락이 덮인 | **exempt** adj 면제된 v 면제하다

[9-10] Listen to a conversation.

W Good morning. **9** I'd like to confirm my dinner reservation for tonight under Kim and change the seating, if possible.

M Let me check... Yes, a table for four at 7 p.m. on the terrace. Would you prefer the main dining room?

W Yes, please move us indoors now; **10** the forecast says heavy rain this evening, and one guest uses a cane.

M No problem. I'll switch you to the main room at 7, same party size, and note aisle access near the entrance.

[9-10] 대화를 들으세요.

여 안녕하세요. 오늘 저녁 제 이름 김으로 예약한 저녁 식사를 확인하고, 가능하다면 좌석을 변경하고 싶습니다.

남 확인해 보겠습니다… 네, 테라스에서 7시에 4인 테이블로 예약되어 있습니다. 메인 다이닝룸을 원하시나요?

여 네, 실내로 옮겨 주세요. 오늘 저녁에 폭우 예보가 있고, 한 손님은 지팡이를 사용해서요.

남 문제 없습니다. 같은 인원으로 7시에 메인룸으로 옮겨 드리고, 입구에서 가까운 통로 자리로 메모해 두겠습니다.

어휘

reservation n 예약 | **terrace** n 테라스, 야외 좌석 공간 | **forecast** n 예보 (특히 날씨) | **cane** n 지팡이 | **aisle** n 통로

---

9. What is the woman doing?
   Ⓐ Booking a hotel stay
   Ⓑ Adjusting a reservation
   Ⓒ Ordering full catering services
   Ⓓ Paying a banquet deposit

10. What reason does the woman give for her request?
    Ⓐ She expects heavy rain.
    Ⓑ She wants brighter lighting.
    Ⓒ She prefers live music.
    Ⓓ She needs extra parking.

9. 여자는 무엇을 하고 있는가?
   Ⓐ 호텔 숙박 예약
   Ⓑ 예약 조정
   Ⓒ 전체 케이터링 서비스 주문
   Ⓓ 연회 예약금 지불

10. 여자가 요청한 이유는 무엇인가?
    Ⓐ 그녀는 폭우를 예상한다.
    Ⓑ 그녀는 더 밝은 조명을 원한다.
    Ⓒ 그녀는 라이브 음악을 선호한다.
    Ⓓ 그녀는 추가 주차 공간이 필요하다.

[11-12] Listen to a conversation.

M **11** I just saw a notice that my health plan "rolled over." Did I miss open enrollment?

[11-12] 대화를 들으세요.

남 제 건강보험이 이월되었다는 공지를 방금 봤어요. 제가 가입 기간을 놓친 건가요?

W: **11** **It closed at midnight.** Some reminders landed in spam for a few employees.
M: That might be me—I never saw a single e-mail.
W: **11** **The system locked you into last year's plan so your coverage won't lapse.**
M: Can I still make changes? My wife starts a new job next month.
W: **12** **There's a one-day grace period. If you log in before 6 p.m., you can update your elections.**
M: I'll jump on it right after lunch.
W: If you run into issues, call me and I'll extend the session.

여: 자정에 마감됐습니다. 일부 직원들은 안내 메일이 스팸함에 들어갔어요.
남: 아마 저도 그랬나 봐요—메일을 한 통도 못 봤거든요.
여: 시스템이 당신을 작년 플랜에 그대로 묶어놔서 보장에 공백은 없을 겁니다.
남: 그래도 변경할 수 있나요? 제 아내가 다음 달에 새 일을 시작하거든요.
여: 하루 유예 기간이 있어요. 오후 6시 전에 로그인하면 선택 사항을 업데이트할 수 있습니다.
남: 점심 먹고 바로 하겠습니다.
여: 문제가 생기면 저한테 전화하세요. 제가 세션을 연장해 드릴게요.

어휘

roll over (자동으로) 이월시키다, 넘기다 | **enrollment** n 등록; 보험 가입 기간 | **coverage** n (보험에서) 보장 | **lapse** v (권리·보장 등이) 소멸하다 n 소멸, 중단 | **grace period** 유예 기간

11. What does the woman imply when she says, "The system locked you into last year's plan"?
    (A) His eligibility for coverage was lost.
    (B) His premiums will be waived this cycle.
    (C) His plan was automatically upgraded.
    (D) **His old choices stayed as default.**

12. What does the man most likely need to do?
    (A) Complete his direct-deposit details
    (B) **Log in and update his benefits today**
    (C) Provide a doctor's note to HR
    (D) Submit a medical claim for reimbursement

11. 여자가 "시스템이 당신을 작년 플랜에 묶어놨습니다"라고 말할 때, 그녀가 암시한 것은 무엇인가?
    (A) 그의 보장 자격이 상실되었다.
    (B) 이번 회차의 보험료가 면제될 것이다.
    (C) 그의 플랜이 자동으로 업그레이드되었다.
    (D) **작년 선택 사항이 기본값으로 유지되었다.**

12. 남자가 가장 해야 할 일은 무엇인가?
    (A) 본인 급여 계좌 정보를 작성한다
    (B) **오늘 로그인해서 복리후생을 업데이트한다**
    (C) 의사 진단서를 인사팀에 제출한다
    (D) 환급을 위해 의료비 청구서를 제출한다

[13-14] Listen to an announcement in a student service center.

Coordinator: **13** **If food costs are tight, the campus pantry is open to all students.** Bring your ID to check in; no income paperwork is required. You may choose items yourself, including fresh produce when available. **14** **If you prefer privacy, ask for discreet pickup at the service desk,** and a bag will be prepared. Pantry use does not affect aid eligibility. Details are posted on our website.

[13-14] 학생 서비스 센터의 안내 방송을 들으세요.

담당자: 식비가 빠듯하다면, 교내 식료품 보관소가 모든 학생들에게 열려 있습니다. 체크인을 위해 학생증만 가져오시면 됩니다. 소득 증빙 서류는 필요하지 않습니다. 신선한 농산물이 있을 경우, 이를 포함하여 직접 물건을 선택할 수 있습니다. 사생활 보호를 원한다면, 서비스 데스크에서 비공개 수령을 요청하시면, 가방이 준비될 것입니다. 보관소 이용은 재정 지원 자격에 영향을 주지 않습니다. 자세한 내용은 저희 웹사이트에 게시되어 있습니다.

| pantry n 식료품 저장실, 식료품 보관소 | produce n 농산물 (특히 신선한 과일·채소) | privacy n 사생활, 프라이버시 | discreet adj 신중한, 은밀한 | eligibility n 자격, 적격성 |

13. What is the main topic of the announcement?
    A A chef demonstration event
    B A dining hall closure
    C **A new campus pantry service**
    D A meal-plan price change

14. What should students do for privacy?
    A Use self-checkout
    B **Request a private pickup**
    C Email a counselor
    D Skip showing Identification

13. 이 안내 방송의 주된 주제는 무엇인가?
    A 요리 시연 행사
    B 학생 식당 폐쇄
    C **새로운 교내 식료품 보관소 서비스**
    D 식사 이용권 가격 변경

14. 학생들은 사생활 보호를 위해 무엇을 해야 하는가?
    A 셀프 계산대를 이용한다
    B **비공개 수령을 요청한다**
    C 상담사에게 이메일을 보낸다
    D 신분증 제시를 생략한다

[15-18] Listen to a talk in an urban environmental science class.

[15-18] 도시 환경 과학 수업 강의를 들으세요.

Professor: **15** **Today we'll examine urban heat islands—the tendency for cities to run hotter than nearby rural areas.** Dark, low-albedo surfaces such as asphalt and tar roofs absorb sunlight and store heat; dense building canyons then slow nighttime cooling. The result isn't just discomfort: higher cooling demand strains grids and worsens air quality. Mitigation is a portfolio, not a single fix. Trees help twice—shading pavement and cooling air through evapotranspiration. **16** **"Cool roofs" and high-albedo pavements reflect more sunlight, lowering surface temperatures and the heat released back into the air.** Green roofs add mass and moisture, moderating daily swings while improving stormwater control. **17** **Each option has trade-offs: bright surfaces can raise glare, green roofs add maintenance, and some measures carry higher upfront costs even if they cut energy bills later.** When people say they can feel the difference walking barefoot on a dark parking lot in summer, that's the albedo problem in miniature. **18** **In this course we'll compare two material properties. The first is albedo, which means how much sunlight a surface reflects. The second is emissivity, which means how much radiation a surface releases. Together, these two factors shape the heat balance of surfaces. Next week we'll quantify**

교수: 오늘은 도시 열섬 현상—즉, 도시가 인근 농촌 지역보다 더 뜨거워지는 경향—을 살펴보겠습니다. 아스팔트와 타르 지붕 같은 어두운 저알베도 표면은 햇빛을 흡수하고 열을 저장하며, 밀집된 건물 협곡은 야간 냉각을 늦춥니다. 그 결과는 단순한 불편함에 그치지 않습니다: 냉방 수요 증가가 전력망에 부담을 주고, 공기 질을 악화시킵니다. 완화책은 단일 해결책이 아닌 다양한 조합입니다. 나무는 두 가지 효과가 있습니다—보도를 그늘지게 하고 증산작용을 통해 공기를 식힙니다. "쿨 루프"와 고알베도 포장재는 더 많은 햇빛을 반사하여 표면 온도를 낮추고, 다시 공기 중으로 방출되는 열을 줄입니다. 녹색 지붕은 질량과 수분을 더해 일일 온도 변화를 완화하면서 빗물 관리도 개선합니다. 각 선택에는 장단점이 있습니다: 밝은 표면은 눈부심을 유발할 수 있고, 녹색 지붕은 유지 관리가 필요하며, 일부 대책은 나중에 에너지 비용을 절감하더라도 초기 비용이 더 많이 듭니다. 사람들이 여름에 어두운 주차장을 맨발로 걸을 때 차이를 느낀다고 하는 것은, 알베도 문제의 축소판입니다. 이 강의에서 우리는 두 가지 재료 특성을 비교할 것입니다. 첫 번째는 알베도, 이는 표면이 햇빛을 얼마나 반사하는지를 의미합니다. 두 번째는 방출률로, 이는 표면이 얼마나 많은 복사열을 방출하는지를 의미합니다. 이 두 요인은 함께 표면의 열 균형을 형성합니다. 다음 주에는 두 특성을 수치화하고, 블록 규모의 사례 연구에서 조합을 시험하여 왜 지역마다 나무, 지붕 코팅, 포장재 선택의 비율이 달라져야 하는지를 보여줄 것입니다.

both properties and test combinations in a block-scale case study to show why neighborhoods often need different mixes of trees, roof coatings, and paving choices.

어휘

urban heat island 도시 열섬 현상 | **albedo** n 반사율(표면이 햇빛을 반사하는 정도) | **asphalt** n 아스팔트 | **tar** n 타르, 역청 | **canyon** n 협곡 | **grid** n 전력망 | **mitigation** n 완화책, 경감 방법 | **portfolio** n 여러 선택지의 조합 | **pavement** n 포장, 도로 표면 | **evapotranspiration** n 증산작용 (식물이 물을 증발시키며 공기를 식히는 과정) | **trade-off** 장단점, 상충 관계 | **glare** n 눈부심 | **maintenance** n 유지 관리 | **upfront** adj 선행의, 초기의 | **emissivity** n 방출률(열 복사 방출 정도) | **case study** 사례 연구

---

15. What is the lecture mainly about?
    - (A) **Why urban areas heat up, with ways to cool them**
    - (B) Government aid for household energy bills in large cities
    - (C) The chemistry of ozone during summer smog events
    - (D) Old methods for paving roads in the twentieth century

16. According to the lecture, how do high-albedo surfaces help?
    - (A) By storing heat for slow release after sunset
    - (B) By increasing nighttime wind between tall buildings
    - (C) **By reflecting sunlight and lowering surface temperatures**
    - (D) By absorbing moisture and promoting evaporation downtown

17. What does the professor imply about mitigation choices?
    - (A) One uniform solution works best for city budgets.
    - (B) **Trade-offs require tailored mixes for each context.**
    - (C) Reflective coatings are unsuitable due to glare.
    - (D) Trees are less effective than resurfacing projects.

18. What will the professor most likely discuss next?
    - (A) Rules for rooftop maintenance crews in cities
    - (B) Wildlife impacts of rural heat waves in drought
    - (C) Marketing strategies for reflective-coating companies
    - (D) **How albedo compares with emissivity in case studies**

15. 이 강의의 주된 내용은 무엇인가?
    - (A) 도시 지역이 뜨거워지는 이유와 이를 식히는 방법들
    - (B) 대도시 가정의 에너지 요금에 대한 정부 지원
    - (C) 여름 스모그 현상에서 오존의 화학 반응
    - (D) 20세기의 오래된 도로 포장 방식

16. 강의에 따르면, 고알베도 표면은 어떻게 도움이 되는가?
    - (A) 열을 저장하여 일몰 후 천천히 방출함으로써
    - (B) 높은 건물 사이의 야간 바람을 증가시킴으로써
    - (C) 햇빛을 반사하고 표면 온도를 낮춤으로써
    - (D) 습기를 흡수하고 도심에서의 증발을 촉진함으로써

17. 완화책에 대해 교수가 암시한 것은 무엇인가?
    - (A) 하나의 동일한 해결책이 도시 예산상 최선이다.
    - (B) 장단점 때문에 상황별 맞춤형 조합이 필요하다.
    - (C) 반사 코팅은 눈부심 때문에 적합하지 않다.
    - (D) 나무는 재포장 프로젝트보다 효과가 덜하다.

18. 교수는 다음에 무엇을 얘기할 가능성이 가장 높은가?
    - (A) 도시 지붕 유지 관리 인력 규정
    - (B) 가뭄 시 농촌 지역 폭염이 야생에 미치는 영향
    - (C) 반사 코팅 회사들의 마케팅 전략
    - (D) 사례 연구에서 알베도와 방출률을 비교하는 방법

Listening Module 2

01. Ⓐ	02. Ⓒ	03. Ⓐ	04. Ⓑ	05. Ⓒ
06. Ⓒ	07. Ⓑ	08. Ⓓ	09. Ⓓ	10. Ⓒ
11. Ⓑ	12. Ⓓ	13. Ⓐ	14. Ⓒ	15. Ⓐ
16. Ⓑ				

[1-8] Choose the best response.

1. M: Isn't the seminar on Zoom?
   - Ⓐ **No, it's in Room 210.**
   - Ⓑ Yes, they probably are.
   - Ⓒ Tomorrow.
   - Ⓓ The syllabus.

2. M: The projector in Hall A keeps flickering.
   - Ⓐ The microphone is kept in the storage room.
   - Ⓑ It's near the podium in Hall A.
   - Ⓒ **I'll ask IT to swap it before class.**
   - Ⓓ Why don't you write the notes instead?

3. W: Let's open the pop-up booth outside if the wind dies down.
   - Ⓐ **Only if management agrees to it.**
   - Ⓑ It's scheduled for the lobby anyway.
   - Ⓒ I moved last week's booth already.
   - Ⓓ That area gets crowded in the afternoon.

4. W: Could you send me the data summary this morning?
   - Ⓐ The summary was uploaded last semester.
   - Ⓑ **Which format do you need?**
   - Ⓒ The charts are missing from it.
   - Ⓓ It's due by Friday.

5. M: The campus gym is under renovation this month.
   - Ⓐ The gym has brand-new treadmills.
   - Ⓑ Membership cards were reissued last month.
   - Ⓒ **No, it reopens next Monday.**
   - Ⓓ The library hours changed recently.

6. W: We can still submit it after midnight, can't we?
   - Ⓐ Yes, but that's for the draft version.
   - Ⓑ The registrar closes their office at five.
   - Ⓒ **Not unless you get an extension.**
   - Ⓓ The evaluation criteria are posted online.

[1-8] 가장 적절한 응답을 고르세요.

1. 남: 세미나가 줌으로 열리는 거 아니에요?
   - Ⓐ **아니요, 210호실에서 해요.**
   - Ⓑ 네, 아마 그렇겠죠.
   - Ⓒ 내일이에요.
   - Ⓓ 강의계획서요.

2. 남: A홀의 프로젝터가 계속 깜빡여요.
   - Ⓐ 마이크는 보관실에 있습니다.
   - Ⓑ A홀의 연단 옆에 있어요.
   - Ⓒ **수업 전에 IT팀에 교체 요청을 하겠습니다.**
   - Ⓓ 대신에 노트에 적는 게 어때요?

3. 여: 바람이 잦아들면 야외에 팝업 부스를 엽시다.
   - Ⓐ **시설팀의 승인이 난 후에만 가능합니다.**
   - Ⓑ 어차피 로비에서 하기로 예정되어 있어요.
   - Ⓒ 지난주 부스는 제가 이미 옮겼어요.
   - Ⓓ 그 구역은 오후에 붐빕니다.

4. 여: 오늘 아침에 데이터 요약본을 보내줄 수 있나요?
   - Ⓐ 요약본은 지난 학기에 업로드되었어요.
   - Ⓑ **어떤 형식으로 필요하세요?**
   - Ⓒ 차트가 거기에서 빠져 있어요.
   - Ⓓ 금요일까지 제출해야 합니다.

5. 남: 이번 달에 교내 체육관이 보수 중이에요.
   - Ⓐ 체육관에는 새 러닝머신이 있습니다.
   - Ⓑ 회원증은 지난달에 재발급됐습니다.
   - Ⓒ **아니요, 다음 주 월요일에 다시 열어요.**
   - Ⓓ 도서관 운영 시간이 최근에 바뀌었습니다.

6. 여: 자정 이후에도 제출할 수 있죠, 그렇죠?
   - Ⓐ 네, 하지만 초안 버전만 가능합니다.
   - Ⓑ 교무처는 5시에 문을 닫습니다.
   - Ⓒ **연장을 허가받지 않으면 안 돼요.**
   - Ⓓ 평가 기준표는 온라인에 게시되어 있습니다.

7. M: Can you tell me who approved the equipment purchase last semester?
   A In the main lab.
   B **Finance would know.**
   C Yes, I do.
   D By next Monday, please.

8. W: Doesn't this course require a lab component?
   A It's usually held in Room 3 for practice.
   B The syllabus only lists the lecture topics.
   C The midterm for this course is scheduled next Monday.
   D **That's only required for Biology majors this year.**

7. 남: 지난 학기에 누가 장비 구매를 승인했는지 알려줄 수 있나요?
   A 본 실험실에서요.
   B 재무팀이 알 거예요.
   C 네, 제가 알아요.
   D 다음 주 월요일까지 해주세요.

8. 여: 이 강의는 실험 수업이 꼭 필요한 거 아니에요?
   A 보통 실습은 3호실에서 진행돼요.
   B 강의계획서에는 강의 주제만 나와 있어요.
   C 이 강의의 중간고사는 다음 주 월요일로 예정되어 있어요.
   D 올해는 생물학 전공자들에게만 필수입니다.

어휘

1. **seminar** n 세미나, 학술 모임 | **Zoom** n 줌화상 회의 플랫폼 | **syllabus** n 강의계획서
2. **projector** n 프로젝터, 영상 투사기 | **flicker** v 깜빡거리다 | **swap** v 교체하다, 바꾸다
3. **pop-up** adj 임시로 설치된 n 팝업 매장·부스 | **booth** n 부스, 작은 임시 공간
4. **data** n 데이터, 자료 | **summary** n 요약, 요약본 | **format** n 형식, 형태
5. **gym** n 체육관 | **renovation** n 보수 | **reissue** v 재발급하다
6. **submit** v 제출하다 | **draft** n 초안 | **extension** n 연장, 유예
7. **approve** v 승인하다 | **equipment** n 장비, 기기 | **Finance** n 재무팀, 재무 부서
8. **require** v 요구하다, 필요로 하다 | **component** n 구성 요소, 부분 | **major** n 전공

[9-10] Listen to a conversation.

W: I'm checking on my interlibrary loan for *Regional Trade Patterns*. It's a week late.

M: **9 We've had courier disruptions—drivers went on strike regionally, so incoming parcels are slow.**

W: That explains it. I need two chapters for my seminar on Friday.

M: Let me see… **10 There's an e-book license through a partner database.**

W: Full text?

M: Yes—limited seats, but **10 you can read online and download chapters.**

W: Perfect. Could you send the access details?

M: I'll e-mail them with step-by-step login instructions.

[9-10] 대화를 들으세요.

여: Regional Trade Patterns에 대한 상호 대차를 확인 중인데요. 일주일 늦어졌거든요.

남: 택배 운송에 차질이 있었습니다—운전사들이 지역적으로 파업을 해서, 들어오는 소포가 늦어지고 있습니다.

여: 그렇군요. 이번 주 금요일 세미나에 두 개 챕터가 필요해서요.

남: 제가 확인해 보겠습니다… 파트너 데이터베이스를 통해 전자책 이용권이 있네요.

여: 전체 텍스트인가요?

남: 네—이용권이 제한되어 있지만, 온라인으로 읽어보고 챕터를 다운로드할 수 있습니다.

여: 정말 잘됐네요. 접속 정보를 보내주시겠어요?

남: 로그인 단계별 안내와 함께 이메일로 보내 드리겠습니다.

어휘

interlibrary loan 도서관 간 대출, 상호 대차 | **courier** n 운송업체, 택배 회사 | **disruption** n 혼란, 중단, 차질 | **license** n 이용권, 허가증 | **database** n 데이터베이스

9. Why is there a delay with the woman's request?
   Ⓐ The library closed for renovations.
   Ⓑ The journal is permanently out of print.
   Ⓒ The request went to the wrong campus.
   Ⓓ **The courier strike is slowing deliveries.**

10. What does the man recommend the woman do?
    Ⓐ Purchase a personal copy from the publisher
    Ⓑ Wait until the print copy arrives next month
    Ⓒ **Use the e-book version via another database**
    Ⓓ Switch her seminar topic this week

9. 여자의 요청이 지연된 이유는 무엇인가?
   Ⓐ 도서관이 보수 공사로 문을 닫았다.
   Ⓑ 저널이 영구적으로 절판되었다.
   Ⓒ 요청이 다른 캠퍼스로 전달되었다.
   Ⓓ 운송업체 파업으로 배송이 늦어지고 있다.

10. 남자가 여자에게 추천한 것은 무엇인가?
    Ⓐ 출판사에서 개인용 책을 구입한다
    Ⓑ 인쇄본이 다음 달에 도착할 때까지 기다린다
    Ⓒ 다른 데이터베이스를 통해 전자책 버전을 사용한다
    Ⓓ 이번 주 세미나 주제를 바꾼다

[11-12] Listen to an announcement in a computer lab.

Announcer: ⑪ **Here's an update on campus printing. You can now send jobs from your phone or laptop using the Mobile Print uploader on the web.** Attach PDFs only; images should be combined before upload. Each student gets 300 pages per term; double-siding counts as one page per sheet. ⑫ **Large files over twenty-five megabytes won't email correctly, so please use the uploader instead of attachments.** Check the queue at the release station, tap your ID, and confirm cost before printing. If a printer is out of toner, release to another device; your balance carries over automatically.

[11-12] 컴퓨터실 안내방송을 들으세요.

안내원: 교내 인쇄에 대한 최신 안내입니다. 이제 웹의 모바일 프린트 업로더를 사용하여 휴대폰이나 노트북에서 작업을 보낼 수 있습니다. PDF만 첨부할 수 있으며, 이미지는 업로드 전에 합쳐야 합니다. 각 학생은 학기당 300쪽을 사용할 수 있고, 양면 인쇄는 종이 한 장당 한 쪽으로 계산됩니다. 25메가바이트를 초과하는 큰 파일은 이메일이 제대로 전송되지 않으므로, 첨부파일 대신 업로더를 사용해 주시기 바랍니다. 인쇄할 때는 출력소의 대기열을 확인하고, 학생증을 찍은 후 비용을 확인하세요. 프린터에 토너가 없을 경우, 다른 기기로 출력하면 됩니다. 잔액은 자동으로 이월됩니다.

어휘

update n. 최신 정보, 업데이트 | **uploader** n. 업로더, 파일 전송 도구 | **attach** v. 첨부하다 | **double-siding** n. 양면 인쇄 | **sheet** n. 종이 한 장 | **attachment** n. 첨부파일 | **queue** n. 대기열 | **release station** 출력 스테이션 (인쇄 확인/출력 기기) | **toner** n. 토너(프린터 잉크)

11. What is the announcement about?
    Ⓐ A new photo course
    Ⓑ **A mobile printing update**
    Ⓒ A scanner replacement
    Ⓓ A fee increase notice

12. Why does the speaker mention "twenty-five megabytes"?
    Ⓐ He is warning that toner issues can corrupt large documents.

11. 이 안내문의 주제는 무엇인가?
    Ⓐ 새로운 사진 강좌
    Ⓑ 모바일 인쇄 업데이트
    Ⓒ 스캐너 교체
    Ⓓ 요금 인상 공지

12. 화자가 "25메가바이트"를 언급한 이유는 무엇인가?
    Ⓐ 큰 문서는 토너 문제로 손상될 수 있다고 경고하기 위해서

- Ⓑ He is claiming that the uploader cannot accept PDFs.
- Ⓒ He is saying that students must use USB drives for big files.
- **Ⓓ He is explaining that larger attachments may fail to send.**

- Ⓑ 업로더가 PDF를 받을 수 없다고 주장하기 위해서
- Ⓒ 큰 파일은 학생들이 USB 드라이브를 사용해야 한다고 말하기 위해서
- **Ⓓ 큰 첨부파일은 전송이 실패할 수 있다고 설명하기 위해서**

[13-16] Listen to a talk in a psychology class.

Professor: ⑬ **Many students think multitasking saves time, but research points the other way.** When you jump between tasks, your brain needs a moment to reorient. Psychologists call that a switching cost, meaning a small delay each time you shift focus. ⑬ **Those delays pile up, so the total time goes up, not down. Errors rise too, especially when the work involves reasoning rather than simple routines.** Some studies even show reduced activity in brain areas related to sustained attention during rapid task switching. ⑭ **Consider a common example: studying while checking messages. You feel busy and engaged, but memory for the reading typically drops.** In contrast, staying with one activity for a set block, even twenty minutes, produces better recall. ⑮ **I am not saying you must avoid every interruption. A short pause can help if it does not add a second task stream.** Later in the course we will look at ways to train attention. Some students use external cues, like simple timers, to set boundaries. Others practice mindfulness to notice distractions before acting on them. ⑯ **Next class we will compare these approaches side by side and talk about the conditions that make each one effective, such as task difficulty, time of day, and the presence of digital alerts.**

[13-16] 심리학 수업 강의를 들으세요.

교수: 많은 학생들은 멀티태스킹이 시간을 절약한다고 생각하지만, 연구는 반대 방향을 보여줍니다. 작업 사이를 오갈 때마다 뇌는 방향을 다시 잡는 순간이 필요합니다. 심리학자들은 이것을 '전환 비용'이라고 부르는데, 이는 집중을 옮길 때마다 생기는 작은 지연을 의미합니다. 이런 지연이 쌓이면 전체 시간이 줄어드는 것이 아니라 늘어납니다. 오류도 증가하는데, 특히 단순한 루틴이 아닌 추론이 필요한 작업에서 더 심합니다. 일부 연구는 빠른 과제 전환 동안 지속적 주의와 관련된 뇌 영역의 활동이 감소한다는 결과까지 보여줍니다. 흔한 예를 생각해 봅시다: 공부하면서 메시지를 확인하는 경우입니다. 바쁘고 몰입한 것처럼 느껴지지만, 읽은 내용을 기억하는 능력은 보통 떨어집니다. 반대로, 한 활동을 정해진 시간 동안, 20분만이라도, 유지하면 더 나은 회상을 얻을 수 있습니다. 모든 방해를 다 피해야 한다는 뜻은 아닙니다. 짧은 휴식은 두 번째 과제 흐름을 추가하지 않는다면 도움이 될 수 있습니다. 수업 후반에는 주의를 훈련하는 방법을 살펴보겠습니다. 일부 학생들은 단순한 타이머 같은 외부 신호를 사용해 경계를 설정합니다. 다른 학생들은 마음챙김을 실천하여 산만함을 행동으로 옮기기 전에 알아차립니다. 다음 수업에서는 이러한 접근 방식을 나란히 비교하고, 과제 난이도, 하루 중 시간, 디지털 알림의 존재 등 어떤 조건에서 각각 효과적인지를 논의할 것입니다.

어휘

multitasking n 여러 작업을 동시에 하기, 멀티태스킹 | **reorient** v 방향을 다시 잡다, 재적응하다 | **psychologist** n 심리학자 | **switching cost** 전환 비용 | **delay** n 지연 | **pile up** 쌓이다, 누적되다 | **routine** n 일상적인 절차, 규칙적인 일 | **sustained** adj 지속적인 | **attention** n 주의, 집중 | **engaged** adj 몰입한, 바쁘게 관여된 | **recall** n 기억, 회상 | **interruption** n 방해, 중단 | **task stream** 과제 흐름 | **mindfulness** n 마음챙김, 주의집중 명상 | **digital alert** 디지털 알림

13. What is the topic of the talk?
   - **Ⓐ Effects of multitasking on efficiency and accuracy**

13. 이 강의의 주제는 무엇인가?
   - **Ⓐ 멀티태스킹이 효율성과 정확성에 미치는 영향**

Ⓑ The limited impact of study interruptions on performance
  Ⓒ Negative effects of short breaks on long-term recall
  Ⓓ The perceived ease of complex assignments in college courses

14. Why does the professor mention students who check messages while reading?
  Ⓐ To claim that new brain scans are necessary for proof
  Ⓑ To encourage students to text during planned study breaks
  Ⓒ **To exemplify how multitasking harms memory**
  Ⓓ To assert that learners enjoy juggling multiple tasks while studying

15. What does the professor imply about brief pauses?
  Ⓐ **Useful when kept separate from other tasks**
  Ⓑ Always damaging to concentration and recall
  Ⓒ Preferable to single-task study sessions
  Ⓓ Effective only with expensive equipment

16. What does the speaker say about the next class?
  Ⓐ It will examine impacts of multitasking on industrial safety.
  Ⓑ **It will cover methods for strengthening attention control.**
  Ⓒ It will explain how laboratory memory tests are designed.
  Ⓓ It will propose policies to remove digital devices from classrooms.

Writing

[1-10] Make an appropriate sentence.

1. What was most helpful during your research?
   I learned quickly because the librarian guided me.

2. Students need to see the final exam schedule.
   They can check it when they log in.

3. I'm applying for an internship next month.
   Tell me if you need a reference letter.

4. Please find out about the workshop.
   I'll register once the details are posted.

5. Why did the team postpone the presentation?
   They delayed it because the projector broke.

6. I missed the deadline by one day.
   You can still submit it though it's late.

7. We're booking rooms for the conference.
   Choose Cedar Hall since it has more space.

8. How will the lab handle late samples?
   They'll store them until processing begins tomorrow.

9. The coordinator had a question about the form.
   Did she ask because something was unclear?

10. I was unsure about the application steps.
    You'll succeed if you follow the checklist.

---

[11] Write an Email.

This morning, you emailed a report to your client and then discovered the attachment was the wrong version. The file they received does not include revisions discussed with their team, and a review meeting is scheduled soon. You need to correct the mistake quickly and keep the timeline on track.

Write an email to the client. In your email, do the following.

- Apologize for sending the wrong attachment.
- Provide the correct file with key updates.
- Ask for receipt confirmation and next steps.

Write as much as you can and in complete sentences.

Sample Answer
Your Response:
To: client@northbridgeconsulting.com
Subject: Corrected Report Attachment

Dear Northbridge Team,

I am writing to apologize for the incorrect file I sent this morning. Unfortunately, the version you received did not include the revisions we recently discussed during our planning call. I sincerely regret any inconvenience this may have caused.

Please find attached the correct report, which now reflects the updated budget figures, revised timelines, and clarifications on deliverables. I believe this version will provide a more accurate basis for your upcoming review meeting.

Could you kindly confirm that you received this updated file? Also, please let me know if there are any additional adjustments you would like me to make before the scheduled meeting.

Thank you for your patience and understanding.

Sincerely,
Scott Yoon
Project Manager

[12] Write for an Academic Discussion.

Your professor is teaching a class on environmental studies. Write a post responding to the professor's question.

In your response, you should do the following.
- Express and support your opinion.
- Make a contribution to the discussion in your own words.

An effective response will contain at least 100 words.

Professor: Many cities are facing serious air pollution problems caused by traffic, industry, and population growth. Some governments propose stricter regulations on car emissions and factory operations, while others prefer encouraging individuals to change their habits, such as using public transportation or reducing energy use at home. In your opinion, which approach is more effective in improving air quality: government regulation or individual action? Why?

Student A: I believe government regulation is

more effective. Without strong laws, companies and individuals often choose convenience over responsibility. Strict emission standards and enforcement can bring large-scale improvements that personal choices alone cannot achieve.

Student B: I think individual action is more powerful. People can decide to walk, bike, or take buses immediately, while waiting for government rules takes time. If enough people change their habits, the community can see real progress quickly.

Sample Answer

I agree with Student A that government regulation is the most effective way to address air pollution. Individual efforts are valuable, but their impact is often limited without broader coordination. For example, one person taking the bus instead of driving helps a little, but strict rules requiring cleaner car engines and renewable energy use can transform entire industries. At the same time, I also see Student B's point that individuals can act more quickly. Perhaps the best approach combines both: governments set ambitious standards, and individuals support these policies through their daily choices. Together, regulation and personal responsibility can create lasting improvements in air quality.

Speaking

[1-7] Listen and Repeat.

You are training to guide visitors at a city aquarium. Listen to the guide and repeat what she says. Repeat only once.

1. **Guide:** Thank you for visiting the Blue Harbor Aquarium.

2. **Guide:** The coral reef exhibit is located on the first floor.

3. **Guide:** Please handle all touch-tank animals gently.

4. **Guide:** Keep walkways open and stay with your group.

5. **Guide:** The dolphin show begins every half hour and features fun tricks with the trainers.

6. **Guide:** Hand-washing stations are near the exits for visitors to clean their hands after touching animals.

7. **Guide:** Visit the information desk for tickets and schedules, where staff members will gladly assist you.

4. 안내원: 통로는 항상 비워 두시고 그룹과 함께 이동해 주세요.

5. 안내원: 돌고래 쇼는 30분마다 열리며, 조련사와 함께하는 재미있는 묘기를 볼 수 있습니다.

6. 안내원: 출구 근처에는 해양 동물을 만진 뒤 손을 씻을 수 있는 세정대가 있습니다.

7. 안내원: 입장권과 일정 안내는 안내 데스크에서 받을 수 있으며, 직원이 친절히 도와드릴 것입니다.

[8-11] Take an Interview.

You have volunteered for a research study about online learning. You will have a short online interview with a researcher. The researcher will ask you some questions.

[8-11] 인터뷰에 응하세요.

당신은 온라인 학습에 관한 연구에 자원했습니다. 연구원과 짧은 온라인 인터뷰를 하게 됩니다. 연구원이 몇 가지 질문을 할 것입니다.

8. Interviewer: Thank you for joining our study on online learning. Today, I want to ask you about your personal experiences. First, do you prefer studying through online classes or attending classes in person? Why? Please give one main reason for your preference.

8. 면접관: 온라인 학습 연구에 참여해 주셔서 감사합니다. 오늘은 귀하의 개인적인 경험에 대해 여쭙고자 합니다. 먼저, 온라인 수업을 통해 공부하는 것과 대면 수업에 참석하는 것 중 어느 쪽을 더 선호하십니까? 그 이유는 무엇입니까? 본인이 선호하는 것에 대해 한 가지 주된 이유를 말씀해 주세요.

Sample Answer

I prefer in-person classes. When I am physically in a classroom, I can concentrate better and feel more connected to the teacher. For example, if I don't understand something, I can raise my hand and ask immediately. Online classes are convenient, but it's easy to get distracted by my phone or other things at home.

예시 답변

저는 대면 수업을 선호합니다. 교실에 직접 앉아 있으면 더 집중할 수 있고 교사와의 연결도 더 잘 느껴집니다. 예를 들어, 무언가 이해가 되지 않을 때는 손을 들고 바로 질문할 수 있습니다. 온라인 수업은 편리하지만 집에서는 휴대폰이나 집에 있는 다른 것들 때문에 쉽게 산만해집니다.

9. Interviewer: I see. Now imagine you had two choices: one online course with a flexible schedule but limited interaction, or another online course with live sessions and more discussion. Which would you choose, and why would you make that choice?

9. 면접관: 알겠습니다. 이제 두 가지 선택지가 있다고 상상해 보세요. 하나는 일정이 유연하지만 상호작용이 제한적인 온라인 강의이고, 다른 하나는 실시간 수업과 토론이 많은 온라인 강의입니다. 어느 쪽을 선택하시겠습니까? 그리고 왜 그렇게 선택하시겠습니까?

Sample Answer

I would choose the live course with discussion. I learn better when I can exchange ideas with classmates and hear different perspectives. For example, in a business course, listening to other students' examples gave me a deeper understanding of the topic. Even if the schedule is less flexible, the interaction makes the class more valuable.

예시 답변

저는 토론이 있는 실시간 강의를 선택하겠습니다. 저는 반 친구들과 생각을 나누고 다양한 관점을 들을 수 있을 때 더 잘 배웁니다. 예를 들어, 경영학 수업에서 다른 학생들의 사례를 들었을 때 주제에 대해 더 깊이 이해할 수 있었습니다. 일정이 덜 유연하더라도, 상호작용이 수업을 더 가치 있게 만듭니다.

10. Interviewer: Interesting. Some people think online learning can feel lonely and unmotivating. Others believe it offers independence and freedom. What do you think are one or two effective ways to make online classes more engaging for students? Give reasons.

10. 면접관: 흥미롭네요. 어떤 사람들은 온라인 학습이 외롭고 동기부여가 잘 되지 않는다고 생각합니다. 반대로 어떤 사람들은 온라인 학습이 독립성과 자유를 제공한다고 믿습니다. 학생들에게 온라인 수업을 더 흥미롭게 만들 수 있는 효과적인 방법 한두 가지는 무엇이라고 생각합니까? 이유를 말씀해 주세요.

Sample Answer

One way is to include group projects, so students feel connected to each other. Another way is to add interactive tools, like quick quizzes or polls during the lecture. For example, when my teacher used a quiz app, I paid more attention because I wanted to answer correctly. These activities keep students active, not just logged in but passive.

예시 답변

한 가지 방법은 조별 과제를 포함시키는 것입니다. 그러면 학생들이 서로 연결되어 있다고 느낄 수 있습니다. 또 다른 방법은 강의 중에 짧은 퀴즈나 투표 같은 상호작용 도구를 추가하는 것입니다. 예를 들어, 제 선생님이 퀴즈 앱을 사용했을 때 저는 정답을 맞히고 싶어서 더 집중하게 되었습니다. 이러한 활동은 학생들이 로그인만 해 놓고 수동적으로 있는 것이 아니라 능동적으로 참여하도록 합니다.

11. Interviewer: Good points. Lastly, some researchers believe that rapid growth of online learning will change traditional schools and universities. How do you think this shift might positively and negatively affect students? Please give one example of each effect.

11. 면접관: 좋은 지적입니다. 마지막으로, 일부 연구자들은 온라인 학습의 급격한 성장이 전통적인 학교와 대학을 바꿀 것이라고 믿습니다. 이러한 변화가 학생들에게 긍정적, 부정적으로 어떤 영향을 줄 것이라고 생각합니까? 각각의 효과에 대한 예를 하나씩 말씀해 주세요.

Sample Answer

A positive effect is that students can access classes anywhere, even if they live far from good schools. For instance, rural students can learn advanced subjects online. A negative effect is that some students may feel isolated and lose motivation without face-to-face support. This combination of effects shows that online learning brings both opportunities and risks.

예시 답변

긍정적인 효과는 학생들이 좋은 학교에서 멀리 떨어져 살아도 어디서든 수업에 참여할 수 있다는 점입니다. 예를 들어, 농촌 지역 학생들도 온라인으로 고급 과목을 배울 수 있습니다. 부정적인 효과는 일부 학생들이 대면 지원이 없어서 고립감을 느끼고 동기를 잃을 수 있다는 것입니다. 이런 영향의 조합은 온라인 학습이 기회와 위험을 동시에 가져온다는 것을 보여 줍니다.

Actual Test 3

Reading Module 1

01. arg<u>ued</u>   02. free   03. would   04. citi<u>zens</u>   05. opport<u>unities</u>
06. self-imp<u>rovement</u>   07. ci<u>vic</u>   08. Many   09. cons<u>tructed</u>   10. buil<u>dings</u>
11. Ⓒ   12. Ⓐ   13. Ⓑ   14. Ⓓ   15. Ⓐ
16. Ⓓ   17. Ⓑ   18. Ⓐ   19. Ⓑ   20. Ⓒ

[1-10] Fill in the missing letters in the paragraph.

In the nineteenth century, public libraries became important institutions, providing access to knowledge for people who otherwise lacked educational resources. Reformers arg<u>ued</u> that free libraries wo<u>uld</u> provide citi<u>zens</u> with opport<u>unities</u> for self-imp<u>rovement</u> and ci<u>vic</u> engagement. Many cities cons<u>tructed</u> library buil<u>dings</u> where residents could read newspapers, borrow books, and attend lectures. These institutions promoted literacy, encouraged lifelong learning, and strengthened democratic values in rapidly expanding industrial societies. Over time, libraries championed equality of opportunity, reinforcing the idea that knowledge should be universally available.

[1-10] 문단에서 빠진 글자들을 채워 넣으세요.

19세기에 공공 도서관은 중요한 기관으로 자리 잡아, 교육 자원이 부족했던 사람들에게 지식에 접근할 수 있는 기회를 제공했다. 개혁가들은 무료 도서관이 시민들에게 자기 계발과 시민 참여의 기회를 줄 것이라고 주장했다. 많은 도시들은 주민들이 신문을 읽고, 책을 빌리며, 강연에 참석할 수 있는 도서관 건물을 지었다. 이러한 기관들은 문해력을 증진시키고, 평생 학습을 장려하며, 급격히 팽창하는 산업 사회에서 민주적 가치를 강화했다. 시간이 지나면서, 도서관은 기회의 평등을 옹호하며 지식이 보편적으로 제공되어야 한다는 생각을 뒷받침했다.

어휘

institution n 기관 | **resource** n 자원 | **reformer** n 개혁가 | **civic** adj 시민의 | **engagement** n 참여 | **resident** n 주민 | **lecture** n 강연 | **literacy** n 문해력 | **democratic** adj 민주적인 | **equality** n 평등

[11-12] Read a text message.

Riverside College Library

Effective immediately, we have revised our lending regulations. ⑫ Overdue materials will now accrue a daily fine of $1, which will be charged directly to each borrower's account until the item is returned. In cases where an item is declared lost, both the replacement cost and an administrative fee will be imposed. ⑫ Library access rights will be suspended automatically once unpaid fines exceed $10. ⑪ Those with outstanding accounts are urged to monitor them closely to prevent service interruptions.

[11-12] 문자 메시지를 보세요.

리버사이드 대학 도서관

즉시 발효되는 규정에 따라 대출 규정이 개정되었습니다. 연체 자료에는 이제 하루 1달러의 벌금이 부과되며, 해당 물품이 반납될 때까지 각 대출자의 계정에 직접 청구됩니다. 자료가 분실된 것으로 처리될 경우, 교체 비용과 행정 수수료가 모두 부과됩니다. 미납 벌금이 10달러를 초과하면 도서관 이용 권한은 자동으로 정지됩니다. 연체 계정이 있는 분들은 서비스 중단을 막기 위해 계정을 주의 깊게 관리할 것을 권장 드립니다.

어휘

effective adj 발효되는 | revise v 개정하다 | lending n 대출 | regulation n 규정 | overdue adj 연체된 | accrue v 누적되다, 쌓이다 | borrower n 대출자 | replacement n 교체 | impose v 부과하다 | suspend v 정지시키다

11. Who is the message primarily intended for?
    (A) Alumni with limited library access
    (B) Library staff responsible for enforcing fines
    (C) **Students who borrow library materials**
    (D) Community residents with guest borrowing cards

12. What will happen when fines remain unpaid beyond a certain amount?
    (A) **Borrowing privileges will be revoked.**
    (B) Fines will be automatically deducted from the account.
    (C) A final return deadline will be imposed on the account.
    (D) A decrease in borrowing limits will be recorded.

11. 이 메시지는 주로 누구를 대상으로 하는가?
    (A) 제한된 도서관 이용 권한을 가진 졸업생
    (B) 벌금 집행을 담당하는 도서관 직원
    (C) 도서 자료를 대출하는 학생들
    (D) 게스트 대출 카드를 가진 지역 주민

12. 벌금이 일정 금액 이상 미납될 경우 어떻게 되는가?
    (A) 대출 권한이 취소된다.
    (B) 벌금이 계정에서 자동으로 인출된다.
    (C) 계정에 최종 반납 기한이 강제로 설정된다.
    (D) 대출 한도 감소가 기록된다.

[13-15] Read a social media post.

👤 Campus Sustainability Council

Did you know that over 40 percent of our campus waste could be recycled but often ends up in landfills? To address this, the Sustainability Council is launching a "Sort It Right" campaign. **14 Specially marked bins for paper, plastics, and metals are now placed across the main academic buildings.** Clear signage explains which items belong where, and volunteers are available during peak hours to guide proper disposal.

This effort reduces waste and fosters shared responsibility. **15 Improper sorting increases costs for the university and undermines local recycling initiatives.** **13 By participating, students help conserve resources and demonstrate commitment to environmental stewardship.** Join us in making small actions count toward a more sustainable campus community.

👍 Like   💬 Comment

[13-15] 소셜미디어 게시물을 보세요.

👤 캠퍼스 지속 가능성 위원회

우리 캠퍼스 폐기물의 40% 이상이 재활용될 수 있지만, 종종 매립지로 들어간다는 사실을 알고 계셨나요? 이를 해결하기 위해, 지속 가능성 위원회는 "올바르게 분리하기" 캠페인을 시작합니다. 종이, 플라스틱, 금속을 위한 특별하게 표시된 통이 주요 교사 건물에 배치되었습니다. 명확한 안내판이 어떤 품목이 어디에 들어가야 하는지를 설명하며, 봉사자들이 혼잡 시간대에 올바른 배출을 안내할 예정입니다.

이 노력은 폐기물을 줄이고 공동의 책임감을 키웁니다 잘못된 분리 배출은 대학의 비용을 증가시키고 지역 재활용 이니셔티브를 약화시킵니다. 참여함으로써 학생들은 자원을 절약하고 환경 보호에 대한 헌신을 보여줄 수 있습니다. 작은 행동이 모여 더욱 지속 가능한 캠퍼스 공동체를 만드는 데 함께해 주세요.

👍 좋아요   💬 댓글

 어휘

recycle v 재활용하다 | landfill n 매립지 | campaign n 캠페인 | bin n 통, 쓰레기통 | signage n 안내판, 표지 | disposal n 처리, 처분 | foster v 조성하다, 촉진하다 | responsibility n 책임 | undermine v 약화시키다 | stewardship n 관리, 책임 (특히 환경 관리)

13. What is the main purpose of the post?
    A To describe the university's budget for waste disposal
    B **To encourage students to follow new recycling guidelines**
    C To advertise volunteer opportunities in the student council
    D To compare landfill usage at different universities

14. What feature has been added to support the recycling campaign?
    A Additional storage rooms for discarded items
    B Trucks that collect waste every evening
    C A new office within the Sustainability Council
    D **Clearly labeled bins located in campus buildings**

15. What can be inferred about improper waste sorting?
    A **It raises expenses for the institution.**
    B It provides more jobs for student volunteers.
    C It eliminates the need for landfill space.
    D It strengthens recycling programs in the region.

13. 이 게시물의 주요 목적은 무엇인가?
    A 대학의 폐기물 처리 예산을 설명하기 위해
    B 학생들이 새로운 재활용 지침을 따르도록 장려하기 위해
    C 학생회에서 자원봉사 기회를 홍보하기 위해
    D 다른 대학의 매립지 사용량을 비교하기 위해

14. 재활용 캠페인을 지원하기 위해 추가된 특징은 무엇인가?
    A 버려진 물품을 위한 추가 보관실
    B 매일 저녁 쓰레기를 수거하는 트럭
    C 지속 가능성 위원회 내의 새 사무실
    D 캠퍼스 건물에 배치된 명확히 표시된 통

15. 잘못된 폐기물 분리 배출에 대해 추론할 수 있는 것은?
    A 기관의 비용을 증가시킨다.
    B 학생 자원봉사자들을 위한 더 많은 일자리를 제공한다.
    C 매립지 공간의 필요를 없앤다.
    D 지역 재활용 프로그램을 강화한다.

[16-20] The Invention of the Telegraph

Before the nineteenth century, long-distance communication was limited to the speed of messengers, ships, or postal services. This changed dramatically with the invention of the telegraph, a device that used electrical signals transmitted along wires to convey information almost instantly. In 1837, Samuel Morse developed a system that converted messages into a series of dots and dashes, later known as Morse code. **16** **The telegraph transformed communication from a slow, uncertain process into a rapid and reliable exchange of information.**

The telegraph quickly found applications in commerce, journalism, and government. Businesses used it to coordinate shipments and prices across great distances. **16** **Newspapers could receive reports from distant locations within hours rather than weeks, 17 and governments relied on it to send urgent military commands. 16 In this way, the telegraph not only accelerated

[16-20] 전신의 발명

19세기 이전에는 장거리 통신이 전령, 선박, 혹은 우편 서비스의 속도에 제한되어 있었습니다. 그러나 전신의 발명으로 상황은 극적으로 바뀌었습니다. 전신은 전선을 따라 전송되는 전기 신호를 이용해 정보를 거의 즉각적으로 전달하는 장치였습니다. 1837년에 새뮤얼 모스는 메시지를 점과 선의 연속으로 바꾸는 체계를 개발했고, 이는 나중에 모스 부호로 알려지게 되었습니다. 전신은 느리고 불확실했던 통신 과정을 빠르고 신뢰할 수 있는 정보 교환으로 변화시켰습니다.

전신은 곧 상업, 언론, 정부에서 활용되었습니다. 기업들은 이를 이용해 장거리에서 화물과 가격을 조율했습니다. 신문은 몇 주가 아니라 몇 시간 안에 먼 곳의 보도를 받을 수 있었고, 정부는 긴급한 군사 명령을 보내는 데 전신에 의존했습니다. 이런 방식으로 전신은 단순히 통신을 가속화했을 뿐만 아니라 정보의 흐름을 재편해, 멀리 떨어진 지역들을 전례 없는 방식으로 묶어 주었습니다.

communication but also reshaped the flow of information, binding distant regions together in unprecedented ways.

18 Although the telegraph was eventually replaced by the telephone and later by wireless technologies, its influence remained profound. **19** It established the first global communication networks, laying the foundation for later innovations. Historians argue that the telegraph's true legacy lies less in the device itself than in the idea it introduced: **19 20** that information could travel faster than physical movement, forever altering human expectations about speed and connectivity.

비록 전신은 결국 전화와 이후 무선 기술로 대체되었지만, 그 영향력은 깊었습니다. 전신은 최초의 글로벌 통신망을 구축하며 이후 혁신의 토대를 마련했습니다. 역사가들은 전신의 진정한 유산은 기계 자체보다도 그것이 도입한 개념에 있다고 주장합니다. 즉, 정보가 물리적 이동보다 더 빨리 전달될 수 있다는 생각으로, 인간이 속도와 연결성에 대해 가지는 기대를 영원히 바꿔 놓았다는 점입니다.

어휘

century n 세기 | communication n 의사소통, 통신 | messenger n 전령 | dramatically adv 극적으로 | telegraph n 전신 | signal n 신호 | transmit v 전송하다 | convey v 전달하다 | instantly adv 즉각적으로 | system n 체계 | convert v 변환하다 | transform v 변혁하다 | commerce n 상업 | coordinate v 조정하다 | rely v 의존하다 | urgent adj 긴급한 | accelerate v 가속하다 | reshape v 재편하다 | unprecedented adj 전례 없는 | profound adj 깊은

---

16. Why does the author mention newspapers in the passage?
    - (A) To compare the telegraph with the telephone and radio
    - (B) To explain why military commands were often delayed
    - (C) To emphasize the decline of postal services in the nineteenth century
    - (D) **To show how journalism was transformed by rapid communication**

16. 저자는 왜 본문에서 신문을 언급하는가?
    - (A) 전신을 전화와 라디오와 비교하기 위해
    - (B) 군사 명령이 종종 지연된 이유를 설명하기 위해
    - (C) 19세기 우편 서비스의 쇠퇴를 강조하기 위해
    - (D) 신속한 통신으로 언론이 어떻게 변화했는지 보여주기 위해

17. According to the passage, in which area was the telegraph especially important?
    - (A) Religious rituals and ceremonies
    - (B) **Military coordination and decision-making**
    - (C) Agricultural techniques and farming tools
    - (D) Artistic movements and cultural traditions

17. 본문에 따르면, 전신이 특히 중요한 분야는 어디입니까?
    - (A) 종교 의식과 의례
    - (B) 군사 조율과 의사 결정
    - (C) 농업 기술과 농기구
    - (D) 예술 운동과 문화 전통

18. The word "profound" in the passage is closest in meaning to
    - (A) **deep**
    - (B) rare
    - (C) careful
    - (D) unusual

18. 본문에서 "profound"라는 단어의 의미와 가장 가까운 것은?
    - (A) 깊은
    - (B) 드문
    - (C) 신중한
    - (D) 특이한

19. What is the relationship between paragraphs 2 and 3?
- Ⓐ Paragraph 3 raises limitations of the uses described in paragraph 2.
- **Ⓑ Paragraph 3 discusses the long-term impact of the developments described in paragraph 2.**
- Ⓒ Paragraph 3 shifts the focus from practical uses to historical significance, extending ideas in paragraph 2.
- Ⓓ Paragraph 3 presents additional areas of application beyond those mentioned in paragraph 2.

20. What does the passage suggest about the legacy of the telegraph?
- Ⓐ It lies in creating faster physical transport routes for messages.
- Ⓑ It was important mainly for its decorative and mechanical design.
- **Ⓒ It introduced the concept of instantaneous information transfer.**
- Ⓓ It ended the need for later communication technologies.

19. 2단락과 3단락의 관계는 무엇인가?
- Ⓐ 3단락은 2단락에서 설명된 활용의 한계를 제시한다.
- Ⓑ 3단락은 2단락에서 설명된 발전의 장기적 영향을 논의한다.
- Ⓒ 3단락은 실용적 활용에서 역사적 의미로 초점을 옮겨 2단락의 아이디어를 확장한다.
- Ⓓ 3단락은 2단락에서 언급되지 않은 추가적인 활용 영역을 제시한다.

20. 본문에서 전신의 유산에 대해 시사하는 것은?
- Ⓐ 메시지를 위한 더 빠른 물리적 운송 경로 창출에 있다.
- Ⓑ 주로 장식적이고 기계적인 설계를 위해 중요했다.
- Ⓒ 즉각적인 정보 전달 개념을 도입했다.
- Ⓓ 이후 통신 기술의 필요성을 끝냈다.

Reading Module 2

01. arran**ged**	02. of	03. s**ea**ts	04. semic**ir**cular	05. **that**
06. acous**tics**	07. st**age**	08. **the**	09. wh**ere**	10. ch**orus**
11. Ⓑ	12. Ⓑ	13. Ⓒ	14. Ⓐ	15. Ⓐ
16. Ⓑ	17. Ⓐ	18. Ⓒ	19. Ⓓ	20. Ⓐ

[1–10] Fill in the missing letters in the paragraph.

[1–10] 문단에서 빠진 글자들을 채워 넣으세요.

Ancient Greek theaters were architectural masterpieces, designed to amplify sound and provide large audiences with clear views of performances. Builders arran**ged** rows o**f** stone s**ea**ts in a semic**ir**cular plan th**at** enhanced acous**tics** effectively. The st**age** featured **the** orchestra, wh**ere** the ch**orus** performed rituals, dances, and songs. These theaters reflected cultural values of communal gathering, aesthetic harmony, and civic pride and identity in the classical world. Furthermore, their enduring design later influenced Roman architecture and inspired principles of theater construction in many eras.

고대 그리스 극장은 건축학적 걸작으로, 소리를 증폭시키고 대규모 관객에게 공연을 명확하게 볼 수 있도록 설계되었다. 건축가들은 돌 좌석을 반원형 구조로 배치하여 음향을 효과적으로 향상시켰다. 무대에는 합창단이 의식, 춤, 노래를 공연하던 오케스트라 공간이 있었다. 이러한 극장은 공동체 모임, 미적 조화, 시민의 자부심과 정체성이라는 문화적 가치를 반영했다. 또한, 그들의 지속적인 설계는 이후 로마 건축에 영향을 주었고, 여러 시대의 극장 건축 원리에 영감을 주었다.

어휘

architectural [adj] 건축학의 | masterpiece [n] 걸작 | amplify [v] 증폭하다 | semicircular [adj] 반원형의 | acoustics [n] 음향 | orchestra [n] 오케스트라(고대 그리스 극장의 합창 공간) | ritual [n] 의식 | aesthetic [adj] 미학적인, 미적인 | civic [adj] 시민의 | enduring [adj] 지속적인 | era [n] 시대

[11-12] Read a flyer.

Student Art Exhibition

Discover creativity on campus! The Fine Arts Department invites you to view the annual Student Art Exhibition, now open in the Horizon Gallery on the second floor of the Arts Building. Works range from traditional oil paintings to experimental digital media, **11 all produced by current undergraduates**. Admission is free, and **12 exhibition guides provide brief commentaries on selected pieces**. This showcase highlights the diversity of student talent and celebrates the role of the arts in academic life.

[11-12] 전단을 보세요.

학생 미술 전시회

캠퍼스에서 펼쳐지는 창의성을 발견하세요! 미술학부는 여러분을 매년 열리는 학생 미술 전시회에 초대합니다. 이 전시회는 예술관 2층 호라이즌 갤러리에서 현재 열리고 있습니다. 작품은 전통적인 유화부터 실험적인 디지털 미디어까지 다양하며, **모두 현재 재학 중인 학부생들의 작품입니다**. 입장은 무료이며, **전시 안내원들이 선택된 작품에 대해 간단한 해설을 제공합니다**. 이번 전시는 학생들의 다양한 재능을 조명하고, 학문 생활에서 예술의 역할을 기념합니다.

어휘

exhibition [n] 전시회 | creativity [n] 창의성 | department [n] 학부 | annual [adj] 매년의 | gallery [n] 전시실 | experimental [adj] 실험적인 | undergraduate [n] 학부생 | admission [n] 입장 | commentary [n] 해설 | diversity [n] 다양성

11. Who is most likely to have created the works in the exhibition?
- Ⓐ Traditional artists trained on campus
- **Ⓑ Students currently enrolled at the university**
- Ⓒ Faculty members in the Fine Arts Department
- Ⓓ Amateur painters from the community

12. What is offered to visitors at the exhibition?
- Ⓐ Instructions on traditional painting methods
- **Ⓑ Commentaries on artworks**
- Ⓒ Discounts on digital media supplies
- Ⓓ Demonstrations of studio techniques

11. 전시회에 출품된 작품을 제작한 사람은 누구이겠는가?
- Ⓐ 캠퍼스에서 훈련받은 전통 화가들
- **Ⓑ 현재 대학에 재학 중인 학생들**
- Ⓒ 미술학부의 교수진
- Ⓓ 지역 사회의 아마추어 화가들

12. 전시회에서 방문객들에게 제공되는 것은 무엇인가?
- Ⓐ 전통 회화 기법에 대한 설명서
- **Ⓑ 작품에 대한 해설**
- Ⓒ 디지털 미디어 용품 할인
- Ⓓ 작업실 기법 시연

[13-15] Read an e-mail.

To: All Registered Undergraduates
From: Campus IT Services
Subject: Printing Quota Policy Update

[13-15] 이메일을 보세요.

수신: 모든 학부 재학생
발신: 캠퍼스 IT 서비스
제목: 인쇄 할당량 정책 업데이트

13 As part of the university's cost-containment efforts and commitment to sustainability, IT Services has instituted a revised quota framework for student printing. Beginning this semester, each undergraduate is allocated 200 nontransferable credits, **15** valid only for the current term and redeemable at any campus printer. Once these credits are exhausted, additional pages must be purchased at a rate of 5 cents per sheet, payable directly to the bursar's account.

Students with outstanding balances will be unable to release new print jobs until the debt is cleared. **14** Instructions for tracking account activity and making electronic payments are available on the IT Services portal.

This measure is intended not merely to reduce waste but also to foster a more deliberate and responsible use of shared campus resources.

대학의 비용 절감 노력과 지속 가능성에 대한 약속의 일환으로, IT 서비스는 학생 인쇄에 대한 개정된 할당량 체계를 도입했습니다. 이번 학기부터 각 학부 재학생은 양도 불가한 크레딧 200장을 배정받으며, **이는 해당 학기에만 유효하고 캠퍼스 내 모든 프린터에서 사용 가능합니다.** 이 크레딧이 소진되면 추가 인쇄는 장당 5센트가 부과되며, 금액은 바로 재무 계정에 청구됩니다.

미납 잔액이 있는 학생은 부채가 정리될 때까지 새로운 인쇄 작업을 출력할 수 없습니다. **계정 활동을 추적하고 전자 결제를 하는 방법은 IT 서비스 포털에서 확인할 수 있습니다.**

이번 조치는 단순히 폐기물을 줄이려는 것이 아니라, 공유 캠퍼스 자원을 보다 신중하고 책임감 있게 사용하도록 장려하기 위한 것입니다.

어휘

containment n 억제, 통제 | commitment n 약속, 헌신 | institute v 도입하다, 시행하다 | revised adj 개정된 | quota n 할당량 | allocate v 배정하다 | nontransferable adj 양도 불가의 | redeemable adj 교환 가능한, 사용할 수 있는 | exhaust v 다 써버리다, 고갈시키다 | deliberate adj 신중한

---

13. What is the main purpose of the message?
    A) To notify students of mandatory sustainability workshops
    B) To highlight electronic submission procedures for coursework
    C) **To introduce a revised policy on student printing quotas**
    D) To outline equipment upgrades in the computer labs

14. How can students clear their overdue printing balances?
    A) **By settling the charge online using a payment platform**
    B) By requesting additional print credits from their academic department
    C) By submitting previously used printouts to the library for review
    D) By arranging an in-person consultation with the bursar's office

13. 이 메시지의 주요 목적은 무엇인가?
    A) 학생들에게 의무적인 지속 가능성 워크숍을 공지하기 위해
    B) 과제 전자 제출 절차를 강조하기 위해
    C) 학생 인쇄 할당량에 대한 개정된 정책을 소개하기 위해
    D) 컴퓨터실 장비 업그레이드를 설명하기 위해

14. 학생들이 연체된 인쇄 잔액을 어떻게 정리할 수 있는가?
    A) 결제 플랫폼을 사용해 온라인으로 요금을 결제함으로써
    B) 소속 학부에 추가 인쇄 크레딧을 요청함으로써
    C) 이미 사용한 출력물을 검토를 위해 도서관에 제출함으로써
    D) 재무과 사무실에 직접 방문 상담을 예약함으로써

15. What is indicated about the printing credits?
    Ⓐ They cannot be carried over into the following term.
    Ⓑ They may be exchanged for other campus services.
    Ⓒ They increase automatically if students take more courses.
    Ⓓ They apply only to graduate-level research printing.

15. 인쇄 크레딧에 대해 알 수 있는 것은?
    Ⓐ 다음 학기로 이월될 수 없다.
    Ⓑ 다른 캠퍼스 서비스로 교환될 수 있다.
    Ⓒ 학생이 더 많은 과목을 수강하면 자동으로 증가한다.
    Ⓓ 대학원 연구 인쇄에만 적용된다.

[16-20] Streaming's Impact on the Film Industry

16 In recent years, streaming platforms such as Netflix, Disney+, and Amazon Prime have transformed the way audiences consume films. Instead of traveling to theaters, viewers can now access a vast library of movies and television shows at home, often for a modest monthly fee. This convenience has reshaped viewing habits, allowing people to watch content on demand and across multiple devices.

For filmmakers, streaming platforms present both opportunities and challenges. **16** On one hand, independent directors have gained new outlets for distributing their work to international audiences without relying on traditional studios. **17 18** On the other hand, some critics argue that the prevalence of streaming services reduces the visibility of smaller films, since recommendation algorithms often promote popular titles. This tension illustrates how digital platforms can both democratize and limit artistic expression.

The rise of streaming has also raised questions about the future of theaters. While blockbusters may still draw crowds, many viewers prefer the comfort and affordability of home viewing. **20** Industry analysts suggest that theaters may increasingly focus on large-scale releases and special events, while streaming platforms dominate everyday entertainment. **19** This shift reflects a broader cultural change in how audiences value convenience, choice, and accessibility in the arts.

[16-20] 스트리밍이 영화 산업에 미친 영향

최근 몇 년 동안 넷플릭스, 디즈니플러스, 아마존 프라임과 같은 스트리밍 플랫폼은 관객들이 영화를 소비하는 방식을 변화시켰다. 극장에 가지 않고도, 시청자들은 이제 집에서 소정의 월정액만 내고 방대한 영화와 TV 프로그램을 볼 수 있다. 이러한 편리함은 시청 습관을 재편하여, 사람들이 여러 기기에서 원하는 때에 콘텐츠를 시청할 수 있게 했다.

영화 제작자들에게 스트리밍 플랫폼은 기회와 도전을 동시에 제공한다. 한편으로는 독립 감독들이 전통적인 스튜디오에 의존하지 않고 국제적인 관객에게 작품을 배급할 수 있는 새로운 통로를 얻었다. 다른 한편으로는, 일부 비평가들은 스트리밍 서비스의 만연함이 소규모 영화의 가시성을 줄인다고 주장한다. 왜냐하면 추천 알고리즘이 종종 인기 있는 작품을 우선적으로 홍보하기 때문이다. 이러한 긴장은 디지털 플랫폼이 예술적 표현을 민주화하면서 동시에 제한할 수 있음을 보여준다.

스트리밍의 부상은 또한 극장의 미래에 대한 의문을 제기했다. 블록버스터 영화는 여전히 관객을 끌어모을 수 있지만, 많은 시청자들은 집에서 관람하는 편안함과 경제성을 선호한다. 업계 분석가들은 극장이 점점 대규모 개봉작이나 특별 행사에 집중하고, 스트리밍 플랫폼이 일상적인 오락을 지배하게 될 것이라고 시사한다. 이러한 변화는 관객들이 예술에서 편의성, 선택, 접근성을 얼마나 중요하게 여기는지를 보여주는 더 넓은 문화적 변화를 반영한다.

어휘
streaming ⓝ 스트리밍 | platform ⓝ 플랫폼 | consume ⓥ 소비하다 | modest adj 소정의, 많지 않은 | convenience ⓝ 편의 | reshape ⓥ 재편하다 | content ⓝ 콘텐츠 | opportunity ⓝ 기회 | challenge ⓝ 도전 | independent adj 독립적인 | distribute ⓥ 배급하다 | audience ⓝ 관객 | rely ⓥ 의존하다 | prevalence ⓝ 만연, 널리 퍼짐 | visibility ⓝ 가시성 | algorithm ⓝ 알고리즘 | democratize ⓥ 민주화하다 | expression ⓝ 표현 | blockbuster ⓝ 블록버스터 영화 | accessibility ⓝ 접근성

16. Which of the following best states a main idea of the passage?
    Ⓐ Streaming platforms have reshaped viewing habits while also challenging traditional theaters.
    Ⓑ **Streaming platforms have changed how films are distributed and viewed.**
    Ⓒ Streaming platforms have provided new opportunities but also limitations for filmmakers.
    Ⓓ Streaming platforms have made convenience and accessibility central to cultural consumption.

17. The word "prevalence" in paragraph 2 is closest in meaning to
    Ⓐ **frequency**
    Ⓑ limitation
    Ⓒ strength
    Ⓓ occurrence

18. According to the passage, all of the following are true about streaming platforms EXCEPT:
    Ⓐ They allow people to watch films without leaving home.
    Ⓑ They help independent directors reach international audiences.
    Ⓒ **They guarantee equal visibility for smaller films.**
    Ⓓ They often use algorithms to promote popular titles.

19. What is the relationship between paragraphs 2 and 3?
    Ⓐ Paragraph 3 emphasizes limitations that contrast with the opportunities noted in paragraph 2.
    Ⓑ Paragraph 3 introduces examples that appear to challenge the arguments in paragraph 2.
    Ⓒ Paragraph 3 shifts from specific applications to the cultural implications introduced in paragraph 2.
    Ⓓ **Paragraph 3 discusses broader industry effects following the issues described in paragraph 2.**

20. What does the passage suggest about the future of theaters?
    Ⓐ **They will specialize in blockbuster films and limited-run showings.**
    Ⓑ They will dominate everyday entertainment instead of streaming platforms.
    Ⓒ They will disappear entirely within the next decade.
    Ⓓ They will replace streaming services as the most affordable option.

---

16. 다음 중 글의 주제를 가장 잘 나타낸 것은 무엇인가?
    Ⓐ 스트리밍 플랫폼은 시청 습관을 재편하면서 전통적인 극장에 도전하고 있다.
    Ⓑ **스트리밍 플랫폼은 영화가 배급되고 시청되는 방식을 바꾸어 놓았다.**
    Ⓒ 스트리밍 플랫폼은 영화 제작자들에게 새로운 기회와 동시에 한계를 제공했다.
    Ⓓ 스트리밍 플랫폼은 편의성과 접근성을 문화적 소비의 중심으로 만들었다.

17. 두 번째 단락의 "prevalence"라는 단어와 의미상 가장 가까운 것은?
    Ⓐ **빈도**
    Ⓑ 한계
    Ⓒ 강도
    Ⓓ 발생

18. 본문에 따르면, 스트리밍 플랫폼에 대한 설명 중 사실이 아닌 것은 무엇인가?
    Ⓐ 사람들은 집을 나서지 않고도 영화를 볼 수 있다.
    Ⓑ 독립 감독들은 국제적인 관객에게 다가갈 수 있다.
    Ⓒ **소규모 영화에 동등한 가시성이 보장된다.**
    Ⓓ 인기 있는 작품을 홍보하기 위해 종종 알고리즘을 사용한다.

19. 2단락과 3단락의 관계는 무엇인가?
    Ⓐ 3단락은 2단락의 기회와 대조되는 한계를 강조한다.
    Ⓑ 3단락은 2단락의 주장을 반박하는 사례를 제시한다.
    Ⓒ 3단락은 구체적 활용에서 2단락에 소개된 문화적 함의로 초점을 옮긴다.
    Ⓓ **3단락은 2단락에서 설명된 문제에 뒤이은 산업적 영향을 논의한다.**

20. 본문에서 극장의 미래에 대해 시사하는 것은?
    Ⓐ **블록버스터 영화와 제한된 기간 상영에 특화할 것이다.**
    Ⓑ 스트리밍 플랫폼 대신 일상적인 오락을 지배할 것이다.
    Ⓒ 앞으로 10년 내에 완전히 사라질 것이다.
    Ⓓ 가장 경제적인 선택으로 스트리밍을 대체할 것이다.

Listening Module 1

01. Ⓑ	02. Ⓓ	03. Ⓐ	04. Ⓒ	05. Ⓓ
06. Ⓑ	07. Ⓐ	08. Ⓒ	09. Ⓒ	10. Ⓓ
11. Ⓒ	12. Ⓑ	13. Ⓓ	14. Ⓒ	15. Ⓓ
16. Ⓑ	17. Ⓒ	18. Ⓐ		

[1-8] Choose the best response.

[1-8] 가장 적절한 응답을 고르세요.

1. M: The career fair is scheduled for the gym.
   Ⓐ Yes, it does.
   Ⓑ **That's where it was last year.**
   Ⓒ It's on Friday afternoon.
   Ⓓ Great, parking's tight near there.

1. 남: 취업 박람회가 체육관으로 예정되어 있어요.
   Ⓐ 네, 그렇습니다.
   Ⓑ 작년에도 거기였죠.
   Ⓒ 금요일 오후에 있어요.
   Ⓓ 잘됐네요, 그 근처는 주차가 빠듯해요.

2. W: Would you happen to know how often the downtown bus runs?
   Ⓐ They raised the fare last month.
   Ⓑ At the stop by the library.
   Ⓒ The transit desk opens at nine.
   Ⓓ **About every twenty minutes or so.**

2. 여: 시내로 가는 버스가 얼마나 자주 오는지 아시나요?
   Ⓐ 지난달에 요금을 올렸어요.
   Ⓑ 도서관 옆 정류장에서요.
   Ⓒ 교통 안내 데스크는 아홉 시에 열어요.
   Ⓓ 대략 20분마다 한 번 정도요.

3. M: The parking pay station won't take cash?
   Ⓐ **It's card-only now.**
   Ⓑ Try the south garage.
   Ⓒ Yes, it won't.
   Ⓓ After peak hours.

3. 남: 주차 요금 기계가 현금을 받지 않네요.
   Ⓐ 이제 카드만 받아요.
   Ⓑ 남쪽 주차장을 이용해 보세요.
   Ⓒ 네, 아닐 거예요.
   Ⓓ 혼잡 시간대 이후에요.

4. M: Isn't safety training required before booking equipment?
   Ⓐ The gear is in Room 110.
   Ⓑ Yes, all of this equipment is needed for the training.
   Ⓒ **A quiz replaced training this term.**
   Ⓓ Ask the cashier about equipment rentals.

4. 남: 장비 예약 전에 안전 교육이 필수 아닌가요?
   Ⓐ 장비는 110호실에 있어요.
   Ⓑ 네, 이 모든 장비가 훈련에 필요해요.
   Ⓒ 이번 학기에는 교육이 퀴즈로 대체됐어요.
   Ⓓ 장비 대여는 계산원에게 물어보세요.

5. W: I wasn't able to finish the group project.
   Ⓐ Deadline's posted.
   Ⓑ On the course site.
   Ⓒ That's not a bad idea.
   Ⓓ **That's unfortunate.**

5. 여: 조별 과제를 끝내지 못했어요.
   Ⓐ 마감일이 공지돼 있어요.
   Ⓑ 강의 사이트에요.
   Ⓒ 그건 나쁜 생각이 아니네요.
   Ⓓ 유감이네요.

6. M: Isn't the music club performing tonight?
   Ⓐ Doors open at seven tomorrow.
   Ⓑ **Just a rehearsal tonight.**
   Ⓒ At the Black Box.
   Ⓓ Auditions were this morning.

6. 남: 음악 동아리가 오늘 밤 공연하지 않나요?
   Ⓐ 내일은 일곱 시에 개장해요.
   Ⓑ 오늘밤엔 리허설만 있어요.
   Ⓒ 블랙박스에요.
   Ⓓ 오디션은 오늘 아침이었어요.

Actual Test 3

7. W: How long does the campus tour usually take?
   - Ⓐ **It wraps up just before noon.**
   - Ⓑ By the main gate entrance.
   - Ⓒ Ten dollars with student ID.
   - Ⓓ The tour guide wouldn't know.

8. M: Would it be okay to list your personal email on the department website?
   - Ⓐ Where can I edit the page?
   - Ⓑ The website went live today.
   - Ⓒ **I'd rather not.**
   - Ⓓ No, it's up to you.

7. 여: 캠퍼스 투어는 보통 얼마나 걸리나요?
   - Ⓐ **정오 직전에 마무리됩니다.**
   - Ⓑ 본관 입구 쪽에서요.
   - Ⓒ 학생증 있으면 10달러예요.
   - Ⓓ 안내원도 모를 거예요.

8. 남: 학과 웹사이트에 당신 개인 이메일을 올려도 될까요?
   - Ⓐ 그 페이지는 어디서 수정하죠?
   - Ⓑ 웹사이트가 오늘 공개됐어요.
   - Ⓒ **그러고 싶지 않습니다.**
   - Ⓓ 아니요, 당신 마음대로 하세요.

어휘

1 **career** n 직업, 진로 | **fair** n 박람회 | **schedule** v 예정하다
2 **happen to** 우연히 ~하다 | **downtown** adj 시내의 adv 시내로 | **run** v (버스가) 운행하다
3 **pay station** 요금 지불기[결제기] | **take** v 받다, 수납하다 | **cash** n 현금
4 **safety** n 안전 | **require** v 요구하다, 필요로 하다 | **booking** n 예약
5 **be able to** ~할 수 있다 | **finish** v 끝내다 | **project** n 과제, 프로젝트
6 **club** n 동아리 | **perform** v 공연하다 | **tonight** adv 오늘 밤에
7 **campus** n 캠퍼스 | **tour** n 견학, 투어 | **usually** adv 보통, 대개
8 **list** v 기재하다, 등재하다 | **personal** adj 개인의 | **department** n 학과, 부서

[9-10] Listen to a conversation.

- W: ⑨ **I'm calling because my card was declined at the market, but my balance is fine.**
- M: A fraud hold was triggered after an overseas attempt. ⑩ **I can clear it if you verify a text code.**
- W: Please send it—my groceries are still at the register.
- M: Once verified, insert the chip again. It should be approved.
- W: Great. I'll retry after the code.

[9-10] 대화를 들으세요.

- 여: 제 카드가 마트에서 결제 거절당해서 전화드렸어요. 그런데 제 잔액은 충분하거든요.
- 남: 해외 결제 시도가 있어서 사기 방지 보류가 걸렸습니다. 문자 인증 코드를 확인해 주시면 제가 해제해드릴 수 있습니다.
- 여: 코드를 보내 주세요—제 장바구니가 아직 계산대에 있어요.
- 남: 인증이 끝나면 다시 칩을 꽂으세요. 승인될 겁니다.
- 여: 좋아요. 코드 받은 뒤에 다시 해볼게요.

어휘

decline v 거절하다, 승인되지 않다 | **balance** n 잔액 | **fraud** n 사기 | **trigger** v 유발하다, 촉발하다 | **verify** v 확인하다, 인증하다

9. Why did the woman call the bank?
   - Ⓐ To dispute a late fee
   - Ⓑ To open a new account
   - Ⓒ **To resolve a payment rejection**
   - Ⓓ To raise her limit

9. 여자가 은행에 전화한 이유는 무엇인가?
   - Ⓐ 연체료에 이의를 제기하려고
   - Ⓑ 새 계좌를 개설하려고
   - Ⓒ **결제 거절 문제를 해결하려고**
   - Ⓓ 한도를 올리려고

10. What does the man imply that she should do?
  (A) Pay with cash
  (B) Switch to contactless
  (C) Call the store manager
  (D) **Verify with a text code**

10. 남자는 여자가 무엇을 해야 한다고 암시하는가?
  (A) 현금으로 결제하기
  (B) 비접촉 결제로 전환하기
  (C) 가게 매니저에게 전화하기
  (D) 문자 코드로 인증하기

[11-12] Listen to a conversation.

W: Hi, this is Mia from Community Programs. **11** **Tonight's "Intro to Python" session is called off—our instructor's sick.**
M: Oh no. Is the whole course off?
W: Not at all. **12** **We'll post a recorded micro-lesson** and hold a live make-up next Tuesday.
M: Same time, 7 p.m.?
W: Yes, and we'll add office hours on Thursday for questions.
M: **12** How will we know when the video's up?
W: **I'll push a notification tonight** and e-mail a link to the class portal.
M: Thanks—I'll check the portal after dinner.

[11-12] 대화를 들으세요.

여: 안녕하세요, 커뮤니티 프로그램의 미아입니다. 오늘 밤 "파이썬 입문" 수업은 취소되었습니다—강사님이 아프세요.
남: 이런, 그럼 강좌 전체가 취소된 건가요?
여: 아뇨, **녹화된 짧은 강의를 올리고**, 다음 주 화요일에 보강 수업을 진행할 예정입니다.
남: 같은 시간인 오후 7시인가요?
여: 네, 그리고 목요일에는 질문을 위한 면담 시간도 추가될 겁니다.
남: 비디오가 올라오면 어떻게 알 수 있나요?
여: 오늘 밤에 알림을 보내고, 수업 포털에 접속할 수 있는 링크를 이메일로 보내드릴게요.
남: 감사합니다—저녁 먹고 포털을 확인하겠습니다.

어휘
session n 수업, 회기 | micro-lesson n 짧은 강의, 마이크로 강의 | notification n 알림 | portal n 포털, 접속 창구

11. What is the main purpose of the call?
  (A) To confirm the man's course enrollment
  (B) To collect payment for a workshop
  (C) **To inform a participant about a session cancellation**
  (D) To advertise an advanced certificate track

11. 이 전화의 주요 목적은 무엇인가?
  (A) 남자의 수강 등록을 확인하기 위해
  (B) 워크숍 결제를 받기 위해
  (C) 참가자에게 수업 취소를 알리기 위해
  (D) 고급 자격증 과정을 홍보하기 위해

12. What does the woman mean when she says, "I'll push a notification tonight"?
  (A) She will send a paper notice by mail.
  (B) **She will deliver an app alert to participants.**
  (C) She will update the course syllabus automatically.
  (D) She will postpone the make-up until next week.

12. 여자가 "오늘 밤 알림을 보내겠다"고 말할 때 의미하는 것은?
  (A) 종이 안내문을 우편으로 보낼 것이다.
  (B) 참가자들에게 앱 알림을 보낼 것이다.
  (C) 강의계획서를 자동으로 업데이트할 것이다.
  (D) 보강 수업을 다음 주까지 연기할 것이다.

[13-14] Listen to an announcement from Dining Services.

Dining Manager: ⑬ **To improve safety, we've added clear allergen labels at every station**—peanuts, tree nuts, dairy, eggs, wheat, soy, fish, and shellfish. Ingredient lists are posted above the menu cards, and staff can check recipes on request. ⑭ **Fryer oil at Grill Three contains peanut oil; please choose another station if needed.** Feedback cards are available near the exits.

어휘

allergen ⓝ 알레르기 유발 물질 | label ⓝ 라벨, 표시 | ingredient ⓝ 재료, 성분 | recipe ⓝ 조리법 | fryer ⓝ 튀김기, 튀김용 기계

13. What is the main topic of the announcement?
- Ⓐ A change to dining hours
- Ⓑ A meal-plan upgrade program
- Ⓒ A campus chef competition
- Ⓓ **A new allergen labeling policy**

14. Why does the speaker mention "Grill Three"?
- Ⓐ To praise a recipe
- Ⓑ To promote new sauces
- Ⓒ **To warn about peanut oil**
- Ⓓ To close the grill

[15-18] Listen to a talk in a history class.

Professor: ⑮ **The printing press reshaped European society in the fifteenth century.** Before printing, books were copied by hand, which was slow and expensive. That kept access mostly in the hands of a small elite. With Gutenberg's movable type, books could be produced much faster and in larger numbers. Prices fell, and more people learned to read because books were finally reachable. Printing changed religion as well. ⑯ **Martin Luther's ideas spread quickly because pamphlets could be printed and carried across regions.** Authorities sometimes tried to restrict presses, fearing the fast spread of dissent, but once the technology took hold, ideas became much harder to control. Beyond religion, printing accelerated science. ⑰ **Scholars could share results more reliably, compare**

diagrams, and correct errors across distances. **That kind of standardization helped communities of researchers grow and coordinate their work.** So the press was not just a clever machine. It was a catalyst for social change. **18 In the next class we will follow the line forward. We will see how newspapers and scholarly journals built on the same basic technology to create new forms of public communication, from daily reports of events to peer review.** We will also note how faster circulation changed the pace of debate in politics and science.

는 데 도움을 주었습니다. 그러니 인쇄기는 단지 영리한 기계가 아니었습니다. 사회 변화를 일으킨 촉매였습니다. 다음 시간에는 그 흐름을 이어가 보겠습니다. 신문과 학술지가 어떻게 같은 기본 기술을 바탕으로 일간 사건 보도부터 동료 평가까지 새로운 대중 소통 형태를 만들어 냈는지 살펴볼 것입니다. 또한 더 빠른 순환이 정치와 과학에서 논쟁의 속도를 어떻게 바꾸었는지도 주목할 것입니다.

어휘

reshape ⓥ 재편하다 | fifteenth adj 열다섯 번째의, 15세기의 | elite ⓝ 엘리트, 지배층 | movable adj 가동식의, 이동 가능한 | pamphlet ⓝ 팸플릿, 소책자 | authority ⓝ 당국 | restrict ⓥ 제한하다 | dissent ⓝ 반대, 이견 | technology ⓝ 기술 | accelerate ⓥ 가속화하다 | reliably adv 신뢰할 수 있게 | standardization ⓝ 표준화 | coordinate ⓥ 조정하다 | catalyst ⓝ 촉매 | circulation ⓝ 유통, 순환

---

15. What point does the professor mainly make?
    Ⓐ Movable type disappeared soon after invention.
    Ⓑ Hand copying was more accurate than machine typesetting.
    Ⓒ Authorities largely prevented the spread of books.
    Ⓓ **The press transformed European society.**

16. Why does the professor mention Martin Luther?
    Ⓐ To prove that rulers opposed new media equally
    Ⓑ **To show how pamphlets carried religious ideas widely**
    Ⓒ To argue pamphlets were superior to bound volumes
    Ⓓ To suggest Luther invented movable type

17. What does the professor imply about science in this period?
    Ⓐ Data exchange stayed confined to monasteries.
    Ⓑ Standardization declined after books spread.
    Ⓒ **Shared texts helped research communities grow.**
    Ⓓ Printed diagrams lost precision.

18. According to the professor, what will be discussed next?
    Ⓐ **Development of newspapers, then journals**
    Ⓑ Monastic methods for preserving manuscripts
    Ⓒ Storage of ancient scrolls in libraries
    Ⓓ Oral traditions replacing written media

---

15. 교수의 핵심 주장은 무엇인가?
    Ⓐ 가동식 활자는 발명 직후 곧 사라졌다.
    Ⓑ 손 필사본이 기계 식자보다 더 정확했다.
    Ⓒ 당국은 대체로 책의 확산을 막았다.
    Ⓓ 인쇄기는 유럽 사회를 변화시켰다.

16. 교수가 마틴 루터를 언급한 이유는 무엇인가?
    Ⓐ 통치자들이 새로운 매체에 똑같이 반대했음을 입증하려고
    Ⓑ 팸플릿이 종교 사상을 널리 전파했음을 보여 주려고
    Ⓒ 팸플릿이 제본된 책보다 우월하다고 주장하려고
    Ⓓ 루터가 가동식 활자를 발명했음을 제시하려고

17. 이 시기의 과학에 대해 교수가 암시하는 바는 무엇인가?
    Ⓐ 데이터 교류는 수도원에 국한되었다.
    Ⓑ 책이 퍼진 뒤 표준화가 쇠퇴했다.
    Ⓒ 공유된 텍스트가 연구 공동체의 성장을 도왔다.
    Ⓓ 인쇄된 도표는 정밀성을 잃었다.

18. 교수에 따르면 다음 시간에 무엇을 다룰 예정인가?
    Ⓐ 신문과 학술지의 발전
    Ⓑ 필사본 보존을 위한 수도원의 방식
    Ⓒ 고대 두루마리의 도서관 보관
    Ⓓ 구전 전통이 문자 매체를 대체함

Listening Module 2

01. Ⓑ	02. Ⓐ	03. Ⓐ	04. Ⓒ	05. Ⓒ
06. Ⓐ	07. Ⓓ	08. Ⓓ	09. Ⓓ	10. Ⓐ
11. Ⓐ	12. Ⓒ	13. Ⓑ	14. Ⓐ	15. Ⓐ
16. Ⓓ				

[1-8] Choose the best response.

1. M: Which department won the award?
   - Ⓐ By a narrow margin.
   - **Ⓑ Engineering did.**
   - Ⓒ The judges announced it.
   - Ⓓ Today's winner.

2. W: The Wi-Fi here keeps timing out—any idea what to try?
   - **Ⓐ Toggle airplane mode and reconnect.**
   - Ⓑ Building Services handles cleaning.
   - Ⓒ Floor maps are posted by the elevator.
   - Ⓓ Fire-drill notices go up on Mondays.

3. M: Can you remind me what chapters the quiz covers?
   - **Ⓐ Four through six.**
   - Ⓑ Yes, but only chapter four.
   - Ⓒ In the syllabus.
   - Ⓓ The professor said it skips five.

4. W: With the weather advisory still in effect, wasn't the hiking trip called off?
   - Ⓐ That update was about the campus concert.
   - Ⓑ The shuttle roster's posted at the union.
   - **Ⓒ It's been moved to Saturday instead.**
   - Ⓓ Registration remains open through tomorrow.

5. W: We should register for the language workshop soon.
   - Ⓐ The room fits fifty.
   - Ⓑ Advising does placement, not registration.
   - **Ⓒ The deadline is this Friday.**
   - Ⓓ The atrium kiosk shows maps.

6. M: When does the keynote begin?
   - **Ⓐ The doors close at six—don't be late.**
   - Ⓑ Check-in opens at five-thirty, though.
   - Ⓒ It's in the Grand Hall upstairs.
   - Ⓓ They emailed the schedule this morning.

[1-8] 가장 적절한 응답을 고르세요.

1. 남: 어떤 학과가 우승했나요?
   - Ⓐ 근소한 차이로요.
   - **Ⓑ 공대가 우승했어요.**
   - Ⓒ 심사위원들이 발표했어요.
   - Ⓓ 오늘의 우승자예요.

2. 여: 여기 와이파이가 자꾸 끊기는데—시도해 볼 만한 게 있을까요?
   - **Ⓐ 비행기 모드를 켰다가 끈 후 다시 연결하세요.**
   - Ⓑ 청소는 건물 관리팀이 담당합니다.
   - Ⓒ 층별 안내도는 엘리베이터 옆에 붙어 있습니다.
   - Ⓓ 화재 대피 훈련 안내는 월요일에 게시됩니다.

3. 남: 퀴즈가 어느 장을 다루는지 다시 알려줄래요?
   - **Ⓐ 4장에서 6장까지요.**
   - Ⓑ 네, 하지만 4장만요.
   - Ⓒ 강의계획서에요.
   - Ⓓ 교수님이 5장은 건너뛴다고 했어요.

4. 여: 기상 주의보가 여전히 유효한데, 하이킹 여행이 취소되지 않았나요?
   - Ⓐ 그 공지는 캠퍼스 콘서트에 관한 거였어요.
   - Ⓑ 셔틀버스 명단은 학생회관에 게시되어 있어요.
   - **Ⓒ 토요일로 옮겨졌어요.**
   - Ⓓ 등록은 내일까지 여전히 열려 있어요.

5. 여: 곧 언어 워크숍 등록을 해야겠어요.
   - Ⓐ 그 방은 50명을 수용할 수 있어요.
   - Ⓑ 상담 부서는 배정을 하지, 등록은 안 해요.
   - **Ⓒ 마감일은 이번 주 금요일이에요.**
   - Ⓓ 아트리움 키오스크에 지도가 나와요.

6. 남: 기조연설은 언제 시작하나요?
   - **Ⓐ 늦지 마세요—문은 6시에 닫힙니다.**
   - Ⓑ 체크인이 5시 30분에 시작하긴 합니다.
   - Ⓒ 위층 대강당에서 열려요.
   - Ⓓ 그들이 오늘 아침에 일정을 이메일로 보냈어요.

7. W: Isn't the shuttle route changing next month?
   (A) On weekdays only.
   (B) Service still runs every ten minutes.
   (C) Parking permit renewals.
   (D) They're adding two new stops.

8. M: I didn't get the announcement about the volunteer program.
   (A) The bulletin covered last year's program.
   (B) The sign-up link opens next month.
   (C) That was for the orientation session.
   (D) It was emailed to all students.

7. 여: 셔틀 노선이 다음 달에 바뀌지 않나요?
   (A) 평일에만요.
   (B) 여전히 10분마다 운행합니다.
   (C) 주차 허가증 갱신입니다.
   (D) 정류장이 두 곳 더 추가돼요.

8. 남: 자원봉사 프로그램에 대한 공지를 못 받았어요.
   (A) 그 게시물은 작년 프로그램을 다뤘어요.
   (B) 신청 링크는 다음 달에 열립니다.
   (C) 그건 오리엔테이션에 관한 거였어요.
   (D) 모든 학생들에게 이메일로 발송되었어요.

📘 어휘

1. **department** n 학과, 부서 | **margin** n 차이, 여유
2. **Wi-Fi** n 와이파이 | **time out** ((연결 등이) 끊기다 | **reconnect** v 다시 연결하다
3. **remind** v 상기시키다 | **chapter** n 장, 단원 | **syllabus** n 강의계획서
4. **advisory** n 주의보, 알림 | **in effect** 효력이 있는 | **call off** 취소하다
5. **register** v 등록하다 | **workshop** n 워크숍, 연수 | **deadline** n 마감일
6. **keynote** n 기조연설 | **begin** v 시작하다 | **schedule** n 일정
7. **shuttle** n 셔틀버스 | **route** n 노선, 경로 | **add** v 추가하다
8. **announcement** n 공지, 발표 | **volunteer** n 자원봉사자 | **bulletin** n 공고, 게시물

[9-10] Listen to a conversation.

- M: We booked Studio 204 from 4 to 6 for a trio rehearsal.
- W: Funny—my quartet got a confirmation for the same room and time.
- M: Our e-mail has a code ending in 7F2.
- W: Mine shows 7F2 as well. That can't be right.
- M: Could there be two calendars? **9 I reserved via the department site; you?**
- W: **9 Through the building kiosk. Maybe they aren't synced.**
- M: The hall manager is walking by—let's ask.
- W: **10 He says Studio 206 just opened up. Want to take it?**
- M: **10 Works for us—we'll move now.**

[9-10] 대화를 들으세요.

- 남: 우리는 4시부터 6시까지 트리오 리허설을 위해 204호 스튜디오를 예약했어요.
- 여: 황당하네요—제 쿼텟도 같은 방과 시간에 대한 확인 메일을 받았거든요.
- 남: 우리 이메일에는 끝자리가 7F2인 코드가 있어요.
- 여: 제 것도 7F2로 되어 있네요. 이건 말이 안 돼요.
- 남: 일정표가 두 개가 있는 걸까요? **저는 학과 사이트로 예약했는데, 당신은요?**
- 여: 건물에 비치된 키오스크로 했어요. 아마 동기화가 안 됐나 봐요.
- 남: 홀 매니저가 지나가네요—가서 물어봅시다.
- 여: 206호 스튜디오가 방금 비었다고 하네요. 그 방 쓸래요?
- 남: 좋아요—우리가 바로 옮길게요.

📘 어휘

trio n 트리오(삼중주단, 3인조 그룹) | **quartet** n 쿼텟(사중주단, 4인조 그룹) | **confirmation** n 확인, 승인 | **sync** v 동기화하다, 맞추다 | **relocate** v 다른 곳으로 옮기다, 이전하다

9. What caused the scheduling conflict?
   Ⓐ The man arrived on the wrong day.
   Ⓑ The door code expired after check-in.
   Ⓒ The building closed early for a recital.
   Ⓓ The system made double bookings.

10. What will the man most likely do next?
    Ⓐ Relocate to another room
    Ⓑ Cancel the rehearsal entirely
    Ⓒ Postpone until next weekend
    Ⓓ Request a fee refund from the cashier

9. 일정 충돌의 원인은 무엇인가?
   Ⓐ 남자가 잘못된 날짜에 도착했다.
   Ⓑ 출입 코드가 체크인 후 만료되었다.
   Ⓒ 건물이 리사이틀 때문에 일찍 닫혔다.
   Ⓓ 시스템이 이중 예약을 했다.

10. 남자는 다음에 무엇을 할 가능성이 가장 높은가?
    Ⓐ 다른 방으로 옮긴다
    Ⓑ 리허설을 완전히 취소한다
    Ⓒ 다음 주말로 연기한다
    Ⓓ 계산대에서 요금 환불을 요청한다

[11-12] Listen to an announcement from Campus Safety.

Announcer: 🔢 **We're updating e-scooter rules to reduce accidents.** Riders must slow to walking speed near entrances and yield to pedestrians at all times. Helmets are strongly recommended, and lighting is required after dusk. Scooters may not be ridden inside, on ramps, or in elevators; park in bike racks, not by doorways. 🔢 **At busy crosswalks, dismount and walk the scooter across.** Using phones or earbuds while riding is unsafe and prohibited during patrol hours. Fines begin next week; 🔢 **repeat violations may lead to impound and a temporary access ban.**

[11-12] 캠퍼스 안전팀의 안내방송을 들으세요.

안내원: 사고를 줄이기 위해 전동스쿠터 규정을 개정합니다. 탑승자는 출입구 근처에서는 보행 속도로 줄이고, 항상 보행자에게 양보해야 합니다. 헬멧 착용은 강력히 권장되며, 해가 진 뒤에는 조명이 필수입니다. 스쿠터는 실내나 경사로, 엘리베이터 안에서는 탈 수 없으며, 문 앞이 아니라 자전거 거치대에 주차해야 합니다. 혼잡한 횡단보도에서는 스쿠터에서 내려 끌고 건너야 합니다. 주행 중 휴대폰이나 이어폰 사용은 위험하므로 순찰 시간에는 금지됩니다. 벌금은 다음 주부터 시작되며, 반복 위반 시 압류와 일시적인 출입 금지로 이어질 수 있습니다.

어휘

update ⓥ 개정하다, 새로 고치다 | **e-scooter** ⓝ 전동스쿠터 | **yield** ⓥ 양보하다 | **pedestrian** ⓝ 보행자 | **helmet** ⓝ 헬멧 | **dusk** ⓝ 황혼, 해질녘 | **ramp** ⓝ 경사로 | **dismount** ⓥ (말·자전거 등에서) 내리다 | **earbuds** ⓝ 이어폰 | **impound** ⓥ 압류하다, 몰수하다

---

11. What should riders do at busy crosswalks?
    Ⓐ Get off and walk the scooter across
    Ⓑ Wait until a security guard signals them to cross
    Ⓒ Stay on the scooter but reduce speed to walking pace
    Ⓓ Use the pedestrian lane next to the bicycle racks

12. Why does the speaker mention "fines begin next week"?
    Ⓐ It promises no first-offense fines.
    Ⓑ It announces a campus-wide scooter ban.
    Ⓒ It signals imminent enforcement.
    Ⓓ It limits lighting rules to week one.

11. 혼잡한 횡단보도에서 탑승자는 무엇을 해야 하는가?
    Ⓐ 스쿠터에서 내려 끌면서 건넌다
    Ⓑ 보안 요원이 건너라고 신호할 때까지 기다린다
    Ⓒ 스쿠터에 탄 채 보행 속도로 줄인다
    Ⓓ 자전거 거치대 옆 보행자 통로를 이용한다

12. 화자가 "벌금은 다음 주부터 시작된다"고 언급한 이유는 무엇인가?
    Ⓐ 첫 위반에는 벌금을 부과하지 않겠다고 약속한다.
    Ⓑ 캠퍼스 전체의 스쿠터 금지를 발표한다.
    Ⓒ 곧 단속이 시작됨을 알린다.
    Ⓓ 조명 규정을 첫 주에만 한정한다.

[13-16] Listen to a talk on a podcast about learning and study skills.

Podcast Host: **13** If lecture notes are just storage, any method seems fine. But understanding depends on how you take them. Typing captures material quickly, yet speed can encourage transcription rather than thinking. **14** People often end up with pages of sentences, but make few decisions about what matters. **13** Handwriting slows the pace, which pushes selection, paraphrasing, and small drawings that connect ideas. That extra effort feels inconvenient in the moment, yet it tends to deepen comprehension later. Consider highlighting. **15** Many students swipe a neon marker across entire paragraphs and feel productive. The problem is low yield. **15** Broad highlighting marks everything which means nothing stands out. A better move is to pause for ten seconds, then write a six-word cue in the margin. That cue forces you to name the idea in your own words. **16** I am not anti-laptop. In some courses, digital tools work well when use is structured—single document, no tabs, timed recap prompts. Under those conditions, keyboards can support attention rather than divide it. If you want to experiment this week, try a split approach: write by hand during explanations, then type a short summary after each section. Next episode we will compare three note formats—Cornell layout, sketchnotes, spaced reviews—and look at simple ways to test which one helps you remember more after two days.

어휘

storage n 저장 | **transcription** n 필사, 받아쓰기 | **paraphrase** n 바꿔쓰기 v 다른 말로 표현하다 | **inconvenient** adj 불편한 | **comprehension** n 이해 | **highlight** v 강조 표시하다 | **neon** adj 형광색의 | **yield** n 결과, 산출 v 산출하다 | **stand out** 눈에 띄다 | **pause** v 짐시 멈추다 n 멈춤, 휴지 | **cue** n 단서, 신호 | **margin** n 여백 | **structured** adj 체계적인, 구조화된 | **recap** n 요약 v 요약하다 | **spaced reviews** 분산 복습

---

13. What is the main topic of the talk?

Ⓐ Benefits of handwritten note-taking during college lectures

Ⓑ **How note-taking methods shape understanding in college lectures**

Ⓒ Whether laptop use influences the way notes are taken

Ⓓ Why students avoid writing by hand during lectures

14. What does the speaker say about typed notes?
   - (A) **Typed notes typically record more words, but prompt less thinking.**
   - (B) Typing reduces distraction for most students during long lectures.
   - (C) Typing slows writing speed compared with paper notebooks.
   - (D) Typed notes eliminate later review for exams in many cases.

15. Why does the speaker mention highlighting entire paragraphs?
   - (A) **To show a passive review habit that only feels productive**
   - (B) To encourage frequent highlighting for dense exam chapters
   - (C) To contrast low-effort review with deeper generative processing
   - (D) To argue that highlighters damage library books over time

16. According to the speaker, what can be inferred about laptop bans?
   - (A) Blanket bans should replace device policies across all departments.
   - (B) Such bans guarantee higher grades in nearly every course.
   - (C) Bans are preferred by most students who take notes.
   - (D) **Blanket bans may be unnecessary with structured digital use.**

14. 화자가 타이핑한 노트에 대해 말한 것은?
   - (A) 타이핑된 노트는 강의에서 보통 더 많은 단어를 기록하지만 생각은 덜 유발한다.
   - (B) 타이핑은 긴 강의 동안 대부분의 학생에게 산만함을 줄여 준다.
   - (C) 타이핑은 종이 노트에 비해 작성 속도를 늦춘다.
   - (D) 타이핑된 노트는 많은 경우 시험을 위한 복습을 불필요하게 만든다.

15. 화자가 전체 단락을 형광펜으로 강조 표시하는 것을 언급한 이유는 무엇인가?
   - (A) 생산적으로 느껴지기만 하는 수동적 복습 습관을 보여주기 위해
   - (B) 시험 범위가 많은 장에서는 빈번한 강조 표시를 권장하기 위해
   - (C) 적은 노력의 복습을 더 깊은 생성적 처리와 대비시키기 위해
   - (D) 형광펜이 시간이 지나면 도서관 책을 손상시킨다고 주장하기 위해

16. 화자에 따르면, 노트북 금지에 대해 추론할 수 있는 것은 무엇인가?
   - (A) 전면 금지가 전 학과의 기기 정책을 대체해야 한다.
   - (B) 그런 금지는 거의 모든 수업에서 높은 성적을 보장한다.
   - (C) 금지는 노트 필기하는 대부분의 학생들이 선호한다.
   - (D) 구조적인 디지털 사용이 가능하다면 전면 금지는 불필요할 수 있다.

Writing

[1-10] Make an appropriate sentence.

1. I missed the orientation yesterday.
   <u>You</u> <u>can</u> <u>watch</u> the <u>recorded</u> <u>session</u>.

2. Could you check the lab schedule?
   <u>Do</u> <u>you</u> <u>need</u> the <u>timetable</u> <u>for</u> <u>this</u> <u>week</u>?

3. The library is closed on Sundays.
   I'll <u>plan</u> the <u>library</u> <u>visit</u> <u>for</u> <u>another</u> <u>day</u>.

[1-10] 알맞은 문장을 만드세요.

1. 어제 오리엔테이션을 놓쳤어요.
   녹화된 세션을 볼 수 있어요.

2. 실험실 일정을 확인해 줄래?
   이번 주 시간표가 필요한 거야?

3. 도서관은 일요일에 문을 닫아요.
   다른 날에 도서관 방문을 계획할게요.

4. I'm applying for the internship.
   Which company are you applying to?

5. I heard there's a guest lecture tomorrow.
   It's scheduled in the Science Museum at 2 p.m.

6. The printer was jammed all morning.
   Did maintenance manage to fix it?

7. I'm choosing courses for next term.
   Have you checked the prerequisites?

8. Can you share the photos from the event?
   I'll upload them to the shared drive this evening.

9. We booked a cabin for the retreat.
   Where is it located, near the lake or in the woods?

10. The team is meeting on Friday.
    Do you know what time the meeting will begin?

[11] Write an Email.

The course you need for your program filled during registration, and the online system lists it as closed with a waitlist. You have completed the prerequisites, the topic fits your plan of study, and the meeting time works. You hope to obtain permission to enroll if a space becomes available.

Write an email to the course instructor. In your email, do the following.

- State your interest and relevant background.
- Request permission to enroll in the course.
- Ask about waitlist process and enrollment steps.

Write as much as you can and in complete sentences.

Sample Answer

Your Response:
To: Professor Chen
Subject: Enrollment Request for Cognitive Psychology

Dear Professor Chen,

I hope this message finds you well. I am very interested in enrolling in your Cognitive Psychology course this semester. I noticed during registration that the course was listed as closed with a waitlist, but I would like to ask for your consideration.

I have already completed the prerequisite courses in General Psychology and Research Methods, and I believe my background has prepared me to succeed in this class. The subject also fits closely with my academic plan, since I am focusing on cognitive science for my program. In addition, the scheduled meeting time works perfectly with my other courses.

Would it be possible to grant me permission to join the course if a seat becomes available? I would also appreciate it if you could explain how the waitlist process works and what steps I should follow to secure enrollment.

Thank you very much for your time and consideration.

Sincerely,
Alex Moon
Psychology Major, Class of 2026

[12] Write for an Academic Discussion.

Your professor is teaching a class on economics and society. Write a post responding to the professor's question.

In your response, you should do the following.

- Express and support your opinion.
- Make a contribution to the discussion in your own words.

An effective response will contain at least 100 words.

Professor: Many countries are debating whether governments should raise the minimum wage to support workers. Supporters argue that a higher wage helps families escape poverty and increases consumer spending. Opponents say it could make businesses cut jobs or raise prices, which may harm the economy. What do you think? Should the minimum wage be increased? Why or why not?

Student A: I believe the minimum wage should definitely be raised. Too many workers struggle to cover basic expenses like rent and groceries, and this creates long-term stress for families. A higher wage would not only improve living conditions but also give people more money to spend, which can support local businesses.

Student B: I disagree with raising the minimum wage at this time. When labor costs increase, small businesses may reduce staff hours or stop hiring new workers, which can harm employees overall. Higher wages could also force companies to raise prices, and consumers may end up paying more for everyday goods and services.

Sample Answer

I agree with Student A that raising the minimum wage is necessary to improve workers' lives. Too many employees cannot afford basic needs, and this creates long-term financial stress that hurts families and communities. A higher wage would give people more security and increase their ability to spend money locally, which supports small businesses. At the same time, Student B makes a valid point about potential costs for employers. To address that concern, governments could offer tax breaks or subsidies to small businesses during the transition. This way, workers would benefit from higher wages while companies would have support to adjust. Overall, raising the minimum wage with protective measures is the most balanced solution.

학생 A: 저는 최저임금이 반드시 인상되어야 한다고 생각합니다. 너무 많은 근로자들이 집세와 식료품 같은 기본적인 생활비를 감당하는 데 어려움을 겪고 있으며, 이는 가정에 장기적인 스트레스를 줍니다. 더 높은 임금은 생활 여건을 개선할 뿐 아니라 사람들이 더 많은 돈을 소비할 수 있게 하여 지역 사업체들을 지원할 수 있습니다.

학생 B: 저는 지금 시점에서 최저임금을 인상하는 것에 반대합니다. 인건비가 증가하면, 소규모 사업체들은 직원들의 근무 시간을 줄이거나 신규 채용을 중단할 수 있으며, 이는 전체적으로 근로자들에게 해를 끼칠 수 있습니다. 또한 더 높은 임금은 기업들이 가격을 인상하도록 만들 수 있고, 결국 소비자들은 일상적인 상품과 서비스에 더 많은 돈을 지불하게 될 수 있습니다.

예시 답변

저는 근로자들의 삶을 개선하기 위해 최저임금을 인상해야 한다는 학생 A의 의견에 동의합니다. 너무 많은 근로자들이 기본적인 생활필수품조차 감당하지 못하고 있으며, 이는 가정과 지역사회에 장기적인 재정적 압박을 주고 있습니다. 더 높은 임금은 사람들에게 더 큰 안정감을 제공하고 지역에서 소비할 수 있는 여력을 늘려 소규모 사업체들을 지원하게 됩니다. 동시에, 고용주에게 발생할 수 있는 비용 문제에 대한 학생 B의 지적 역시 타당합니다. 이러한 우려를 해결하기 위해 정부는 전환 기간 동안 소규모 사업체에 세금 감면이나 보조금을 제공할 수 있을 것입니다. 그렇게 하면 근로자들은 더 높은 임금의 혜택을 얻는 동시에 기업들은 적응할 수 있는 지원을 받게 됩니다. 전반적으로, 보호 장치를 동반한 최저임금 인상이 가장 균형 잡힌 해결책이라고 생각합니다.

Speaking

[1-7] Listen and Repeat.

You are learning to assist visitors at a city train station. Listen to the coordinator and repeat what he says. Repeat only once.

1. **Coordinator:** We're pleased to have you at Central City Station.

2. **Coordinator:** Trains to the airport depart every twenty minutes.

[1-7] 듣고 따라 말하세요.

여러분은 도시 기차역에서 방문객을 돕는 법을 배우고 있습니다. 안내자의 말을 듣고 따라 하십시오. 한 번만 반복하세요.

1. **안내자:** 센트럴시티 기차역에 오신 것을 환영합니다.

2. **안내자:** 공항행 열차는 20분마다 출발합니다.

3. **Coordinator:** Tickets can be purchased at the machines or online.

4. **Coordinator:** For safety, please stand behind the yellow line at all times.

5. **Coordinator:** Recycling bins are located near each platform exit to help keep the station clean.

6. **Coordinator:** The waiting lounge stays open until midnight and offers comfortable seating for travelers.

7. **Coordinator:** Visit the information desk if you need help with lost items, directions, or travel schedules.

3. 안내자: 승차권은 기계나 온라인에서 구매하실 수 있습니다.

4. 안내자: 안전을 위해 항상 노란 선 뒤에 서 주시기 바랍니다.

5. 안내자: 역을 깨끗하게 유지하기 위해 재활용 통이 각 승강장 출구 근처에 설치되어 있습니다.

6. 안내자: 대합실은 자정까지 운영되며, 여행객들을 위한 편안한 좌석이 마련되어 있습니다.

7. 안내자: 분실물, 길 안내, 또는 여행 일정에 대한 도움이 필요하면 안내 데스크를 방문해 주세요.

[8-11] Take an Interview.

You have agreed to take part in a research study about travel and tourism. You will have a short online interview with a researcher. The researcher will ask you some questions.

[8-11] 인터뷰에 응하세요.

당신은 여행과 관광에 관한 연구에 자원했습니다. 연구원과 짧은 온라인 인터뷰를 하게 됩니다. 연구원이 몇 가지 질문을 할 것입니다.

8. Interviewer: Thank you for agreeing to this study on travel and tourism. I'd like to begin with a simple question. Do you prefer traveling to domestic destinations within your own country, or do you enjoy visiting foreign countries more? Why? Please give one reason to support your preference.

8. 면접관: 여행과 관광에 관한 이번 연구에 참여해 주셔서 감사합니다. 간단한 질문으로 시작하고 싶습니다. 본인 나라 안의 국내 여행지를 선호하십니까, 아니면 해외 국가를 방문하는 것을 더 즐기십니까? 그 이유는 무엇입니까? 선호하는 이유를 하나 말씀해 주십시오.

Sample Answer

I prefer traveling abroad. Visiting foreign countries allows me to experience new cultures and languages, which I find very exciting. For example, when I traveled to Japan, I tried different foods and saw traditions I had never experienced before. Domestic travel is nice, but international trips feel more adventurous and memorable for me.

예시 답변

저는 해외여행을 선호합니다. 해외를 방문하면 새로운 문화와 언어를 경험할 수 있는데, 저는 그것이 매우 흥미롭다고 느낍니다. 예를 들어 일본에 여행했을 때, 다양한 음식을 맛보고 이전에 접해 보지 못했던 전통들을 볼 수 있었습니다. 국내 여행도 좋지만, 국제 여행은 저에게 더 모험적이고 기억에 남는 경험이 됩니다.

9. Interviewer: That's helpful. Some people say travel is exciting because it allows them to discover new cultures and experiences. Others feel travel can be stressful, exhausting, and even expensive. What is your personal reaction to traveling, and why do you feel this way when you take trips?

9. 면접관: 도움이 되는 답변이었습니다. 어떤 사람들은 여행이 새로운 문화와 경험을 발견하게 해주기 때문에 흥미롭다고 말합니다. 반면에 어떤 사람들은 여행이 스트레스가 되고, 피곤하며, 심지어 비용이 많이 든다고 느낍니다. 당신은 여행에 대해 개인적으로 어떻게 느끼나요? 그리고 여행할 때 그렇게 느끼는 이유는 무엇인가요?

Sample Answer

I feel very positive about traveling. Although it can be tiring, the excitement of discovering new places is greater. Traveling makes me feel refreshed and gives me stories to share with friends. For instance, even a short trip to another city helps me forget daily stress. So overall, travel energizes me rather than draining me.

10. Interviewer: Interesting. Now, I'd like your opinion on this claim: People who travel often lead richer lives because they see more of the world. They argue travel provides unique perspectives and stories. Do you agree that traveling frequently leads to a more meaningful life? Why or why not?

Sample Answer

Yes, I agree. Travel broadens people's perspectives and helps them understand the world better. For example, when someone visits another country, they learn about different lifestyles and values. These experiences make their lives more meaningful than just reading about cultures in books. Travel also creates strong memories that people keep for a lifetime.

11. Interviewer: Good points. Finally, I'd like to ask about public policy. Some argue that governments should invest more in tourism by building museums, preserving heritage, or improving transportation. Do you think supporting tourism should be a priority for governments? Why or why not? Give one reason.

Sample Answer

Yes, governments should invest in tourism. Tourism brings money to local businesses like hotels, restaurants, and shops. For example, when my city built a new museum, many visitors came and supported the local economy. Also, preserving cultural sites benefits both citizens and tourists. Overall, tourism can strengthen a country's economy and identity at the same time.

예시 답변

저는 여행에 대해 매우 긍정적으로 생각합니다. 피곤할 수는 있지만, 새로운 장소를 발견하는 설렘이 더 큽니다. 여행은 저를 상쾌하게 해주고 친구들과 나눌 이야기도 만들어 줍니다. 예를 들어, 다른 도시로의 짧은 여행조차도 일상의 스트레스를 잊게 도와줍니다. 그래서 전체적으로 볼 때, 여행은 저를 지치게 하기보다 오히려 활력을 줍니다.

10. 면접관: 흥미롭군요. 이제 이런 주장에 대한 당신의 의견을 듣고 싶습니다. 자주 여행하는 사람들은 더 많은 세상을 보기 때문에 더 풍요로운 삶을 산다는 것입니다. 이들은 여행이 독특한 관점과 이야기를 제공한다고 주장합니다. 당신은 자주 여행하는 것이 더 의미 있는 삶으로 이어진다는 데 동의하나요? 그렇다면 왜 그렇고, 아니라면 왜 그렇지 않은지 말씀해 주십시오.

예시 답변

네, 동의합니다. 여행은 사람들의 시야를 넓혀 주고 세상을 더 잘 이해하도록 도와줍니다. 예를 들어, 누군가 다른 나라를 방문하면 서로 다른 생활 방식과 가치관을 배우게 됩니다. 이러한 경험은 단순히 책에서 문화를 읽는 것보다 삶을 더 의미 있게 만듭니다. 또한 여행은 사람들이 평생 간직할 수 있는 강렬한 추억을 만들어 줍니다.

11. 면접관: 좋은 지적이네요. 마지막으로 공공 정책에 대해 묻고 싶습니다. 일부 사람들은 정부가 박물관을 짓고, 유산을 보존하며, 교통을 개선함으로써 관광에 더 많은 투자를 해야 한다고 주장합니다. 당신은 관광 지원이 정부의 우선순위가 되어야 한다고 생각합니까? 그렇다면 왜 그런지, 아니면 왜 그렇지 않은지 이유를 하나 말씀해 주십시오.

예시 답변

네, 정부는 관광에 투자해야 합니다. 관광은 호텔, 식당, 상점 같은 지역 사업체에 수익을 가져다줍니다. 예를 들어, 제 도시에 새 박물관이 세워졌을 때 많은 방문객이 찾아와 지역 경제를 지원했습니다. 또한 문화 유적지를 보존하는 것은 시민과 관광객 모두에게 이익이 됩니다. 전반적으로 관광은 한 나라의 경제와 정체성을 동시에 강화할 수 있습니다.

PAGODA TOEFL
Actual Test

PAGODA
TOEFL
Actual Test | 해설서